PRAISE FOR BACKSTAGE PASS

This book is a triumph in honesty and transparency in the supplier diversity space. It explores the depths of supplier diversity history and educates you on the new frontier of inclusion. A must-read!

—*Daryl Hammett, GM & COO,*
ConnXus

Jamie has accurately captured the complex and ever-changing world of supplier diversity with *Backstage Pass*. As a long-time diverse business owner, I can relate to her findings and definitely share her perceptions. *Backstage Pass* is poignant, funny, educational, and well written. A must-read for all supplier diversity cast members.

—*Avis Yates Rivers, CEO,*
Technology Concepts Group International

Backstage Pass leverages Jamie's depth of knowledge in supply chain with supplier diversity as her sweet spot and provides a grounded perspective on the cast of characters. The book is sprinkled with nuggets of insights and a-ha moments. *Backstage Pass* provides a highly engaging view of the topic. A great read!

—Mary Anderson,
Founder and Retired President
of WBE Canada

An excellent, pragmatic book to help businesses develop a robust supplier diversity *strategy*. It empathetically incorporates a 360-degree perspective to align the interests of all the stakeholders.

—Arvin Chaudhary, Founder,
and President, Nadicent Technologies;
Board Member, Greater New England
Supplier Development Council

BACKSTAGE
PASS

BACKSTAGE PASS

Pulling the Curtain Back on the
Business of Supplier Diversity

JAMIE S. CRUMP

PUBLISH
YOUR
PURPOSE
PRESS

For permission requests, write to the publisher, addressed "Attention: Permissions Coordinator," at the address below.

Publish Your Purpose Press
141 Weston Street, #155
Hartford, CT, 06141

PUBLISH
YOUR
PURPOSE
PRESS

The opinions expressed by the Author are not necessarily those held by Publish Your Purpose Press.

Ordering Information: Quantity sales and special discounts are available on quantity purchases by corporations, associations, and others. For details, contact the publisher at orders@publishyourpurposepress.com.

Edited by: Heather B. Habelka
Cover design by: Alexander Vulchev
Typeset by: Medlar Publishing Solutions Pvt Ltd., India

Printed in the United States of America.
ISBN: 978-1-951591-22-9 (paperback)
ISBN: 978-1-951591-23-6 (hardcover)
ISBN: 978-1-951591-24-3 (ebook)

Library of Congress Control Number: 2020901060

First edition, June 2020

The information contained within this book is strictly for informational purposes. This publication contains the opinions and ideas of its author. It is intended to provide helpful and informative material on the subjects addressed in the publication. It is sold with the understanding that the author and publisher are not engaged in rendering medical, health, financial, legal, or any other kind of personal professional services in the book. The material may include information, products, or services by third parties. As such, the Author and Publisher do not assume responsibility or liability for any third-party material or opinions. The publisher is not responsible for websites (or their content) that are not owned by the publisher. Readers are advised to do their own due diligence when it comes to making decisions.

Publish Your Purpose Press works with authors, and aspiring authors, who have a story to tell and a brand to build. Do you have a book idea you would like us to consider publishing? Please visit PublishYourPurposePress.com for more information.

DEDICATION

This book is dedicated to Jewell Rich and Fannie Colwell Rich, my Papaw and Mamaw, who showed me unconditional love and acceptance and made me believe I could do anything I set my mind to if I was willing to work for it. I believed.

And to my husband, Bill Thebert, whose love, friendship, and support is the bedrock of all things worthwhile in my life. I do love you so. 999

ACKNOWLEDGMENTS

It takes a network of skill and support to make a book happen, regardless of the topic.

To the PYP family, especially Jenn Grace and Mark David Gibson: You took a wisp of an idea and nurtured it until a book grew and I grew along with it. Mark, you refused to accept anything but that I believed in myself as you did, thank you.

To Heather Habelka and Niki Garcia at PYP, you have kept me on task, even when I resisted, and always kept the reader experience front and center. You have made this first experience for me a wonderful education, thank you.

To Melissa Simmons, who refused to let my dream die and checked on me religiously throughout the process. You are a colleague, mentor, sounding board, vent recipient, collaborator, and playmate, and I am proud to call you friend.

To cousins Lee and Lyn, aka the twins: You have welcomed me back home and have been there every step of the way with wide-eyed wonder and unflinching belief. I love having you back in my life on a regular basis.

To Sue Casale, who continues to help me unravel the parts of me that I find the most annoying and the most interesting.

To Dale Asplund, who showed me that I needed to go make this happen. I will be eternally grateful.

And to my granddaughter Claire, who never considers the hurdles might be too high, or the road too rough. You show me the way it should be done.

TABLE OF CONTENTS

ACT III

ACT IV

FOREWORD

I came to know Jamie Crump, in 2007, shortly before I became the non-executive Chairman of the Board of United Rentals (NYSE:URI). Under Jamie's leadership and with strong support from management and the board, URI committed to and embarked on a strategic program of supplier diversity. In the 13 years since then, this philosophy and the practices it informs have been embedded throughout the company. It has become the "ultimate business strategy" the author describes.

Often, businesses invest in diversity programs for social goals. Although such goals are an important part of a company's values and culture, the author believes "executives don't understand how they can tell if business diversity actually helps their business."

Although the primary audience for this book may be the supplier diversity professional (SDP) and the supply chain professional (SCP), I believe the book holds valuable information, strategies, and tactics for three other groups the author identifies and discusses: the C-suite, principally the chief operating officer (COO) and chief financial officer (CFO); diverse business owners (DBOs), who are the suppliers or vendors; and the corporate end users—the consumers—who directly or indirectly purchase the products and services. The better educated they are, the more they appreciate and value a business strategy marked by supplier diversity.

You may ask why these groups need to be involved and eventually demand "supplier diversity" in the staff-managed supply chain function. The answer, which becomes compelling—as well as obvious after one reads this book—is, as the author writes, to enable all business units "to make informed choices about how to select solutions and spend their money."

According to the author, "diversity is the gold standard when it comes to financial success." To prove the point, she references research that provides evidence of a "significant relationship between diversity and innovation," as well as between diversity and profitability. She also notes that diversity, by definition, avoids a sole-source circumstance with all its problems. She is right.

As we learn more about supply chain management, we increasingly recognize its critical strategic role and its contribution to business outcomes. With a strategy that incorporates supplier diversity, a company can increase its flexibility, better explore its options, and stay competitive today and tomorrow. In *Backstage Pass*, Jamie Crump provides a primer for these efforts.

Jenne K. Britell, Ph.D

ACT I

INTRODUCTION

I grew up in Flint, Michigan. It was in the 1960s when people wanted to live in Flint and you could drink the water from a garden hose and not worry about your health.

Although I lived in Flint, Blairsville, Georgia, was "home." Mama and Daddy were both from there. They had left to go north for the good automotive jobs. Daddy worked for General Motors Parts and, as my grandmother liked to tell people, "If they get sick and have to go to the hospital, it is almost completely paid for!" Despite this miracle the north gave us, if we had three consecutive days off, we went "home" to Blairsville. That was where we all wanted to be.

When I was four, Mama and I took a bus from Flint to Blairsville. It was 1964 and we had a layover in Chattanooga, Tennessee. Mama was reading a movie magazine and I was bored. Across the waiting room I saw a little boy about my age. We shyly looked at each other and smiled, the way young children do. I edged away from Mama and toward him. He had a toy in his hand that I couldn't quite make out and I was curious. He walked over to a stool and stood on it and took a drink of water from an old fountain. When he got down, I stepped on it and put my hand on the button and leaned in for a drink. From out of nowhere, a white-gloved hand slapped my hand and shouted in perfect Tennessee twang, "Don't you touch that nasty thaing, that's a Colored fountain!" Mama was there in a millisecond and leaned over and said something to the white-gloved woman that I couldn't hear. It made the woman's face turn very red. She muttered something about how Mama should be happy she stopped me and stomped off.

At the same time Mama had crossed the room to get to me, the little boy's mother had likewise crossed to him. She stood tall in her clean, starched housedress but her bottom lip was trembling. She was clearly afraid, and I didn't understand that. I was the one who had been yelled at. I was the one who was in trouble. Mama asked her if she was okay and she nodded. As I was dragged back across the waiting room, I looked back at the little boy. He wasn't smiling at me anymore and my mama and his kept a tight grip on their children until it was time to board the bus.

This was the first time I realized that not everyone was always treated the same. And it would forevermore change my outlook on almost everything.

FROM THE WAITING ROOM TO THE BOARD ROOM

I have spent almost 30 years as a supply chain professional. Yes, I am first and foremost a procurement professional. There are a lot of terms for what I do: strategic sourcing, supply chain, procurement, purchasing. We won't suffer the intricacies of those terms in this book and will refer to it as supply chain. Suffice to say, while there are differences professionally, at the end of the day, I get paid for helping internal clients (the business units in the company) make informed choices about how to select solutions and spend their money. During most of my career, I was interacting with a supplier diversity program, department, or liaison. The last 11 years of my corporate career, I was in charge of both strategic sourcing and supplier diversity. In what probably amounts to weeks of my life, I have been listening to people commiserate about:

- How supply chain doesn't understand supplier diversity and isn't supportive

- How supplier diversity doesn't understand supply chain and isn't supportive
- How executives don't understand how they can tell if supplier diversity actually helps their business
- How often diverse-owned business owners get no business from all of this talk about helping diverse-owned businesses

Don't get me wrong, it's not all like that. Many companies have fine programs that work in concert with the members of the cast of this production known as supplier diversity and supply chain. However, when I started my own company to work with these different cast members, I found the gap between intent and results was wider than I had imagined. Even the successful programs often leave piles of money on the table. I mean, it's all well and good to be sitting at the Billion Dollar Roundtable, but if you are leaving another billion on the table, how successful is it really?

To help my clients, I began looking for published material on the topic. What I found was there was a gap here as well. Most of what I found was about changing hearts and minds on why diversity was a good idea. That's fine, we need that. Others addressed the economic impact, the number of jobs created when one part of the population begins to earn more. Also fine, but in all of my years of corporate, I had never received funding for a project based upon that. The fact was that none of that would help obtain the support for supplier diversity initiatives or get a dialogue going on supply chain practices. It was too dependent upon the community strategies that companies had. If a company has a strong sense of community and giving back, that's fine. But that doesn't even make the top five in reasons to have the supplier diversity business strategy at your company. If we were going to make real strides, we had to get beyond that. So, what was happening?

At the root, I found a group of people (the cast) who often thought they understood everything about the other players but in most cases did not. In fact, they often did not realize who all of the cast members were. I found the supplier diversity initiative was often supported and funded differently than traditional business practices. This frequently led to support, funding, or both being reduced or removed when the economy or the business took a downturn. I found that it often becomes more about how to find a few pieces of the puzzle that can fit together than developing pieces that could create a new and more profitable picture. In short, supplier diversity often isn't treated as a business strategy. If it's not a business strategy, then even in the most successful of situations, it came, it grew, it plateaued, and it either stayed the same or gradually wasted away. I wanted to provide a way to bridge these gaps.

That pursuit led me here. I want to pull the curtain back on the global discussions and practices taking place in large corporations and small businesses. This look, or backstage pass, will act like any good playbill. It outlines the cast of characters of the production and tells you a bit about them, provides an overview of the play (the script), who helps to make it happen (producers and crew), and information you need to thoroughly enjoy it. We will also call out the occasional elephant in the room that needs to be addressed to move the production along smoothly.

HOW THIS BOOK IS ORGANIZED

This book is intended for any of the five primary cast members who wish to better understand the other cast members and/or how their own role can make a better contribution to the supplier diversity and financial results of their business.

Throughout the book, you will find icons that represent each of the five main cast members and the elephant in the room. This will allow you to peruse chapters from the perspective of different actors in the production.

We will look at each of these cast members in more detail beginning in Chapter 4. For now, just know that they are the main players that comprise a successful supplier diversity business strategy:

 The elephant in the room

 The C-Suite: All worthwhile business strategies begin at the top. The C-suite executives are those at the top of the executive chain in a business. Depending upon the size of the company, this can be one person or dozens. Starting with the CEO and the rest of the "Chief" titles—operations officer (COO), financial officer (CFO), marketing officer (CMO), procurement officer (CPO), and so on.

 The Supplier Diversity Professional (SDP): The SDP works to add qualified diverse-owned businesses to the company supply chain. They attend events to meet prospective suppliers and vet them for introduction to their supply chain group and end users inside their company.

 The Supply Chain Professional (SCP): The SCP works in the group that oversees the bidding, selection, contracting, and otherwise buying of goods and services. In addition to supply chain, the department may also be known as procurement, strategic sourcing, or purchasing.

 The Diverse Business Owner (DBO): The DBO is the owner or owners who own and operate the company. In the U.S. they may be disabled, LGBTQ, minority, veteran, service-disabled veteran, or woman owners.

The End User: This is the person who ultimately uses the goods and services being purchased by supply chain. It is the need of the end user that drives the rest of the activity.

This book is not an indictment of supplier diversity as it exists today. My hope is that by the end of this book, each of the cast members will have a deeper understanding of, and appreciation for, the process their colleagues and customers are engaged in. Through that understanding, they can work to help each other—instead of frustrate each other. The end game is a superior and diverse supply chain that provides value and is competitively priced, a differentiator for those who do it well. Are you ready to engage in a business strategy that is supplier diversity? Break a leg!

CHAPTER 1

SUPPLIER DIVERSITY 101

THE HISTORY OF SUPPLIER DIVERSITY

Where did supplier diversity begin? For some, it seems it recently came out of nowhere. For others, it has been going on far longer than it should have to. As with most things, opinions vary. Diversity, in and of itself, is not limited to a particular ethnicity, country, or flavor of racism. If you look up the term "diversity" on dictionary. com it tells you:

"*noun*
1. the state of being diverse; difference; unlikeness: diversity of opinion.
2. Variety; multiformity.
3. The inclusion of individuals representing more than one national origin, color, religion, socioeconomic stratum, sexual orientation, etc.: diversity in the workplace
4. A point of difference."[1]

Inclusion, another term you hear along with diversity so much these days that it seems to go like peanut butter and jelly, is defined as:

---

[1] Dictionary.com, "diversity."

"*noun*

1. The act of including.
2. The state of being included.
3. Something that is included.
4. *Biology.* A body suspended in the cytoplasm, as a granule.
5. *Mineralogy.* A solid body or a body of gas or liquid enclosed within the mass of a mineral.
6. *Petrography.* Xenolith.
7. *Logic, Mathematics.* The relationship between two sets when the second is a subset of the first."[2]

Supplier diversity has not yet made it to dictionary.com as a term. Wikipedia says:

"A Supplier Diversity program is a proactive business program which encourages the use of minority-owned, women owned, veteran owned, LGBT-owned, service disabled veteran owned, historically underutilized business, and Small Business Administration (SBA)-defined small business concerns as suppliers."[3]

In the United States, it all began with President Richard M. Nixon signing Executive Order (EO) 11458 that directed the Secretary of Commerce to make arrangements for the developing and coordinating of a national program for minority business enterprise. It was signed March 5, 1969. This EO did not create the parameters and nuances of the program we know today. In fact, it didn't even define what the term "minority" meant. Nixon's diary does note that "Approximately 40 individuals of Black, Mexican-American, Puerto Rican or Indian backgrounds involved in various aspects of minority business enterprise ..."[4] were invited to attend the signing of the order. It is also noted that no attempt was made to confirm

[2] Dictionary.com, "inclusion."
[3] Wikipedia, "Supplier diversity."
[4] Nixon Library, "Diary."

the attendance of the invitees. However, it did establish the Office of Minority Business Enterprise (OMBE) and the Advisory Council for Minority Business Enterprise.

In 1971, Nixon signed EO 11625. This superseded EO 11458 and provided "additional arrangements for developing and coordinating a national program for minority business enterprise."[5] It states that "The opportunity for full participation in our free enterprise system by socially and economically disadvantaged persons is essential if we are to obtain social and economic justice for such persons and improve the functioning of our national economy."

It is in this EO that we first see where the Secretary can direct other federal departments to name a representative who is responsible for seeing that this is upheld. It is the first time we see mention of an annual report to the President on progress. It is also where funding is provided for things like outreach, grants, a center for information, and coordination of all federal training. It is also where a definition is provided: "Minority business enterprise means a business enterprise that is owned or controlled by one or more socially or economically disadvantaged persons. Such disadvantage may arise from cultural, racial, chronic economic circumstances or background or other similar cause. Such persons include, but are not limited to, Negroes, Puerto Ricans, Spanish-speaking Americans, American Indians, Eskimos, and Aleuts."

This EO established the Minority Business Development Agency (MBDA). It also provided seed funding for organizations such as the National Minority Purchasing Council (which became the National Minority Supplier Development Council (NMSDC)), the Hispanic Chamber of Commerce, and others.

In 1976, Senator Parren Mitchell included language in a Public Works Bill to set aside 10% of the funds to retain minority firms as contractors and subcontractors. If you are not familiar with Senator

---

[5] MBDA, "History."

Mitchell, you are not familiar with the history of supplier diversity. His fingerprints appear on stacks of legislation around the spirit of diversity, inclusion, and supplier diversity.

By the late 1970s, it wasn't just government that had an interest in supplier diversity. Corporations across the United States were taking an interest in how to best develop their own supplier diversity initiatives and meet the new set asides and goals that the U.S. government had given them. The automotive industry was one of the first to sit down with their competition and discuss not just how to find businesses but how to develop them to meet the capacity that the automotive industry demanded. Ford, General Motors (GM), and Chrysler began to discuss how to do this. Ford's program was created in 1978. It wasn't long before they were taking their program to their suppliers.

I was working in supply chain at a bank in Detroit in 1987 when Ford and GM came in and did a presentation to the executive staff about supplier diversity. My Chief Procurement Officer (CPO) came back from the meeting and brought me into his office to discuss how we could support two of the banks' biggest clients. With their advisement we did our first supplier diversity fair at our headquarters building and brought in over 50 companies to meet with supply chain, real estate, facilities, transport, and other groups that hired outside companies for the bank. It was my first exposure to the concept.

After the Carter administration, supplier diversity didn't receive the same priority from subsequent administrations. The requirements were still present and SBA initiatives continued to grow, but you didn't see as much attention and support from the Executive Office. Where it did begin to take root more strongly during the 1980s and 1990s was in corporate America. Part of that was the support from the large automotive companies and companies that did major portions of their business with the government, such as Raytheon. It was during this time that woman-owned businesses became part of the diversity community. Women Business Enterprise National Council (WBENC, pronounced WEE-bank) was founded in 1997 and took up the mission for woman-owned business and certification that NMSDC had done for minority-owned businesses.

As we entered the new millennium, the advent of social media and social conscience began to inform consumers about how companies did business and treated employees, suppliers, and the planet. We hear a lot about the demands of millennials for diversity and inclusion, but studies show that more than just that generation now want to do business with companies that honor and support the tenets of their customers. This has put companies in a place they usually tried to stay out of, or at least keep under wraps—politics. It now takes milliseconds to find out where a company has donated money, how they support (or do not support) diversity and inclusion in their own business, and how their supply chains are structured. In addition, sins committed are global news. Twenty years ago, if a Starbucks employee had called the police to have two Black businessmen removed from their store it might have garnered a couple of lines in a local paper. Today, it is on camera for the world to see. Just as television cameras brought racism in the South into everyone's living room, smartphones bring diversity or the lack thereof to everyone in the world with internet access.

If you want to know more about the history of supplier diversity in the United States, take a look at this video from NMSDC at: https://nmsdc.org/history-supplier-diversity-minority-business-development/.

THE VOCABULARY OF SUPPLIER DIVERSITY

For the purposes of our discussion here, we will stick with the terms and best practices used in North America. While the glossary at the end of the book provides definitions and references for many of the terms used in the book, here is a quick guide on who makes up the categories of diversity, listed in alphabetical order:

8a—The U.S. Small Business Administration has a program to "help provide a level playing field for small businesses owned by socially and economically disadvantaged peoples or entities, the government limits the competition for certain contracts to businesses that participate in the 8(a) Business Development program.

Disadvantaged businesses in the 8(a) program can:

- Compete for set-aside and sole-source contracts in the program
- Get a Business Opportunity Specialist to help navigate federal contracting
- Form joint ventures with established businesses through the SBA's mentor-protege program
- Receive management and technical assistance, including business training, counseling, marketing assistance, and high-level executive development"[6]

The U.S. federal government has a goal to award at least 5% of all federal contracting dollars to small disadvantaged businesses each year.

Asian-Indian—A U.S. citizen whose origins are from India, Pakistan, or Bangladesh.

Asian-Pacific—A U.S. citizen whose origins are from Japan, China, Indonesia, Malaysia, Taiwan, Korea, Vietnam, Laos, Cambodia, the Philippines, Thailand, Samoa, Guam, the U.S. Trust Territories of the Pacific, or the Northern Marianas.

Black—A U.S. citizen who is of African descent.

---

[6] U.S. Small Business Administration, "8(a)."

Disabled—A disability-owned business enterprise (DOBE) is a for-profit business that is at least 51% owned, managed, and controlled by a person with a disability. Disability is defined as a physical and/or mental impairment that substantially limits one or more major life activities.

Hispanic—A U.S. citizen of true-born Hispanic heritage, from any of the Spanish-speaking areas of the following regions: Mexico, Central America, South America, and the Caribbean Basin only. Brazilians (Afro-Brazilian, indigenous/Indian only) shall be listed under Hispanic designation for review and certification purposes.[7]

HUBZone—The SBA administers this program. "The Historically Underutilized Business Zones (HUBZone) program helps small businesses in urban and rural communities gain preferential access to federal procurement opportunities."[8] A small business whose primary office and 35% of its employees reside in a HUBZone area. The U.S. federal government has a goal to award at least 3% of all federal contracting dollars to HUBZone-certified small businesses each year.

Indigenous—By definition, this means "originating or occurring naturally in a particular place; native."[9] Indigenous peoples in Canada, also known as "Aboriginal Canadians (French: Canadiens Autochtones) are sometimes referred to by the acronym FNIM, which stands for First Nations (Indians), Inuit, or Metis."[10]

LGBTQ—Lesbian, Gay, Bisexual, Transgender, Queer or Questioning.

---

[7] CVM, "Ethnicity."

[8] U.S. Small Business Administration, "HUBZone."

[9] Dictionary.com, "indigenous."

[10] CAMSC, "Certification."

LGBTQ2—Primarily used in Canada by some indigenous people, the "2" refers to two-spirit or a person who identifies as having both a masculine and a feminine spirit.

MBE—(MeBee) Minority Business Enterprise. The definition of "minority" changes from country to country. See definitions from different countries in the glossary.

Native American—"A person who is an American Indian, Eskimo, Aleut, or Native Hawaiian, and regarded as such by the community of which the person claims to be a part. Native Americans must be documented members of a North American tribe, band, or an otherwise organized group of native people who are indigenous to the continental United States, and proof can be provided through a Native American Blood Degree Certificate (i.e., tribal registry letter, tribal roll register number)."[11]

Service Disabled Veteran—"A ... person who served in the active military, naval, or air service, and who was discharged or released under conditions other than dishonorable, and whose disability was incurred or aggravated in line of duty in the active military, naval, or air service."[12]

Small Business—The U.S. government has different definitions for what makes a small business depending on the type of business that it is. They have a table of standards that looks at the type of business, the number of employees, and the gross revenue. Visit https://www.sba.gov/document/support--table-size-standards to see where your business lands on the small business scale.

Veteran—A person "must be a Veteran of a branch of the United States military (Army, Navy, Air Force, Marines, Coast Guard), or served in the National Guard or reserve under Title 38 U.S. Code 4211."[13]

---

[11] NMSDC, "MBE."
[12] Office of Small Business Programs, "Veteran-Owned."
[13] NVBDC, "Veteran."

WBE—(WeeBee) Woman Business Enterprise. A person who is female or a person who identifies as female (depending upon the definition of a given company).

If that list isn't vague enough for you, let me further muddy the waters. Not all companies that have a business strategy provide advocacy for all groups. Some only track disabled veterans, not all veterans. Some only track minority- and woman-owned businesses. Some companies haven't committed to the LGBTQ business community. Those who do business with the U.S. government also track 8(a), HUBZone, and small businesses. My point is this: they have all made a choice, and to not include a group is a choice. If you are creating a supplier diversity business strategy, you too will make a set of choices, whether by inclusion or exclusion.

Not all companies refer to what they do as a supplier diversity business strategy. Some use the terms "initiative" and "program," which I strongly dislike. They sound temporary and social. Supplier diversity is a business strategy and, from this point forward, it is how I will refer to it.

If you want to know what a given company supports, here are some ways to find out:

- Go to their website, find the search icon, and type in "supplier diversity" and see what you get. If nothing comes up, that's an indication of a big "no" to your question. Alas, not all companies have mastered the art of the website yet (I know, I know), so you can't take that as gospel.
- If they generate results, look for a supplier diversity page on their website and look at the dates on the results. Are they all 2016 or before? That's not a result that inspires confidence.
- If they have a webpage for supplier diversity, does it have more than an introductory paragraph and a registration portal? If not, you are slightly better off than above, but the support is

questionable. I'll have more on registration portals later, but suffice to say, the existence of one proves absolutely nothing other than their ability to generate a registration portal.

- Go to the website of the group that supports the group you are curious about and search their corporate member list. For example, if you want to know if Coca-Cola supports woman-owned businesses, go to WBENC and find their corporate members list: https://www.wbenc.org/wbenc-corporate-members-list. You will find not only are they a corporate member they are also a board member. For example, the National Minority Supplier Development Council (NMSDC) lists 417 corporate members on their website as of July 25, 2019, so it's not as if you are looking for a unicorn.

CHAPTER 2

WHY IS DIVERSITY STILL A THING?

This is one question I am asked often enough that it needs to be called out here. While it comes to me in many forms, the gist of the question is this: Why is diversity still a thing?

This is not a political book, so I am not going to dive into the socio and economic states that make up the United States or any other country on our great planet. What I will do is address the main reasons why diversity is still a thing—primarily disadvantage and improved results.

The term "disadvantaged business" is one that no one feels particularly comfortable with, yet like many truths, uncomfortable is accurate. It is a term used for businesses owned by those groups of people who are placed at a disadvantage due to how society in general has treated them over a period of time. In the United States, unfortunately, the list is long. Native Americans who were scammed and forcibly removed from their homes to make way for the European settlers who felt entitled to whatever land they wanted. Black ancestors who were kidnapped, taken from their homes, and forced to work in the institution of slavery. Chinese who were paid slave wages to build railroads and then discarded and shunned. Women who were not allowed to vote, own property, or even inherit the money of their husbands when they died because of their gender. LGBTQ persons who are treated as some sort of blasphemy because who they love is different from some perceived "majority." Veterans who give up some of their most productive years in service to their country and then try and make a living upon their return to civilian life.

The next question I receive, usually in a somewhat whiny voice, is, "But that was so long ago, how long before it's not a thing anymore?" My initial response is that it was not so long ago. In fact, in many cases, it is happening right now today. For those who believe the Native American disadvantage was done when we "settled" the West, I invite you to visit a Native American tribal reservation. No, wait, I invite you to go live on one and make a living. For those who believe that the Civil War took care of slavery, I urge you to read up on Reconstruction, the Civil Rights Act, and your daily newspaper. My grandmother was a teenager when women received the right to vote in the U.S. LGBTQ are now suffering under what Blacks endured in the 1960s (also during my lifetime, still going on, and having a resurgence, btw) by those who do not feel they have to service LGBTQ because it goes against their beliefs. As a child of the South, that rings on the same note as not serving Blacks because they believed it was a sin against God for Blacks and whites to mix. Sorry, folks, I hold my faith as close as anyone, but there are some decisions you just don't get to make on a one-off or even state-by-state basis. Oh, and by the way, *all* of what I talked about above is *still* ongoing in one form or another. It's not "so long ago."

These arguments have been made as often as the tide rolls and rarely make headway. So, I will attempt to provide an example, a business parable, if you will, of what disadvantage is and why diversity is still a thing.

THE TWO BROTHERS

Suppose we have two brothers, Al and Abel, of similar stature, knowledge, and strength. Each brother is given 40 acres to farm to provide for his family and build his business. All is equal except that Al will have one of his arms tied behind his back. In addition, any children Al has or hired help who Al brings to his farm will also have one arm tied behind their back.

Over the years, the tied arm will wither and atrophy. As hard as Al works, he will not keep up with his brother Abel. Abel will, over time, have additional time and resources to invest in things like education on how to get the best results from his crops or equipment that will make the planting and harvesting go faster. He may purchase additional acres of land so that his yield is even higher. Al, on the other hand, cannot afford the same equipment as his brother and he may have to sell off some land over time to make ends meet.

Al's children have to help on the farm and they are also doing so with only one arm. As such, they will not have the time to invest in their schooling as Abel's children have. There is no time or money for them to participate in after-school events. Even when they go to school, they are tired from the hard work. They are not as well fed or cared for, and that will show in their grades.

Now, assume at some point after several hundred years of these two families operating in this fashion, someone comes along and says, "This is wrong, it isn't fair." So, all of the arms are untied. Do we now say that these two families are equal and our job is done? Do we expect that these two businesses can compete on an equal basis? Do we expect that because the thing that provided an advantage to one and not the other has now been removed it will no longer play a role? Will the great-grandchild of Al with the withered arm be able to compete for the same work? Play football on the team at school?

No, of course not. You don't need a SWOT (strengths, weaknesses, opportunities, and threats) chart to see the differences and who has the advantage. Whether the withered arm in this scenario is gender, skin color, who you love, or how you worship, the longer it takes place, the wider the gap in the advantages. The wider the gap, the longer it takes to even it up again. And, while you personally may not feel you have done anything to widen the gap, as you have the advantages, the tab for those advantages will also eventually come due.

Oh, and by the way, if you descend from one of Abel's children who made terrible decisions and partied his inheritance away, you are not exempt from your portion of the tab because you don't have what your cousins have. If you descend from one of Abel's children who accomplished a lot by working hard and applying diligence and discipline, that does not remove your advantage. It doesn't take away from what was accomplished, but it doesn't reduce the advantage you had going in. That is the difference between having choices and not having them.

If you still have doubts about how much this scenario does or does not represent real life, I'll give you a few references from the United States. I love my country and, like anything you love, there are things that delight you and make you proud and others that make you wince and shake your head.

A few examples of the definition of equality from our history:

All men are created equal
All men
All white men
All white men who own property
All white men who marry women and own property
All Christian white men who marry women and own property
Religious freedom
Christian religion
Christian Protestant religion

Southern New Hampshire University puts it best in one of their commercials: "The world in which we live equally distributes talent, but it doesn't equally distribute opportunity."

MY PERSONAL AND COMPLEX ADVANTAGE

Now, my roots in the United States go waaaaay back. In fact, I'm about as white European American as you can get. I have ancestors who landed at Plymouth Rock, were in Jamestown (which was before the Rock), and helped set up cities and towns from Massachusetts, Rhode Island, Connecticut, and Virginia well before anyone thought about having a tea party in Boston or crossing the Delaware with Washington. I would love to tell you that they left their country of origin eager for freedom for all in religion, beliefs, and living. My Rhode Island ancestors were pretty close to that, but the rest, not so much.

They were looking for *their* flavor of freedom and most of them took quite the exception to those who did not like it. You might think that after being pushed around by the English, French, Scottish, Irish, Welsh, and Danes, they would have wanted a place where everyone had a say. Nay, nay. They wanted a place where *they* got to say how it was going to be, and if anyone was going to be pushed around, they fully intended to be the folks doing the pushing. This is where the land of the free started to fall off the rails a bit.

Most of the relatives who created my branch of the family tree ended up in the South. Here, the one flavor of freedom took on a whole new meaning. I live today on land that was taken from the Cherokee before sending them on the Trail of Tears to get them out of the way. Slavery and all that it represents is as prevalent on my family tree as blooms on a dogwood in springtime. This stayed the course through the Civil War, where more than 90% of my ancestors fought on the wrong side (that's the Confederacy, btw). Most of those relatives', descendants were still in the South in the 1950s and 1960s, when the hopes of Reconstruction that were killed off in the 1870s and 1880s began to be addressed for real through the civil rights movement. By this time, most of my family was toiling away in fairly remote parts of the South, too poor and too busy to oppress anyone. But they don't get off for that. Racism flourished in all parts of the South, and there isn't a civil rights documentary that I view or pictures in an article I read where I don't look at the white faces hoping I don't know them or I'm not related to any of them. Making as much peace as is possible with that is a complex conversation. Suffice to say, racism in all of its flavors has been going on since the country began and, unfortunately, will continue into the foreseeable future. And that, dear reader, is why diversity is still a thing.

Elephant alert! Those tables are now beginning to turn in the United States. In a few years, the class of people who have ruled the roost for the past 400 years will no longer be the majority (that's Caucasians, in case you skipped that part earlier).

It will be interesting to see what the new majority does with their turn in power. Will they look for freedom for all or will they take their turn calling the shots for everyone? Even more interesting, will those fighting for the status quo today go quietly, or will they be the next diversity advocates, fighting for what they chose not to provide? Only time will tell.

DOING NOTHING IS ALSO A CHOICE

> *"In the end, we will remember not the words*
> *of our enemies, but the silence of our friends."*
> —Dr. Martin Luther King Jr.

I was about 12 when I put off a term paper that was due in my English class. At the last minute, I cobbled together a poor excuse of a paper and handed it in. My thinking was that, overall, I got better grades than many of my classmates and the teacher would take that into account. Imagine my surprise when I got it back with a C- on it. At that point in my life, I could count on one hand the number of grades below a B I had received ... EVER. I stayed after and demanded an explanation. Even last minute it couldn't have been *that* bad. My teacher explained that it was obvious from my previous work that I hadn't taken the assignment seriously and that I chose to spend my time doing other things (the football game, talking in study hall, etc.) instead of putting together a quality paper. And he was having none of it.

"I didn't *choose* to do a bad paper," I reasoned. "I just didn't spend enough time on it."

"Choosing isn't just an activity, Jamie," he pointed out. "Doing nothing is a choice too." Checkmate! He had me and I never forgot that.

EVERY DOLLAR WE SPEND IS A VOTE

Earlier in my supplier diversity career, I had the privilege of attending training that NMSDC and UPS put together at a UPS facility in Atlanta. One of the speakers, Ralph G. Moore, a maestro of diversity and founder of Ralph G. Moore & Associates (RGMA), talked about putting your money where your beliefs and strategies lie. He spoke about taking his granddaughter to the grocery store and her picking out a breakfast cereal that she liked. He knew that the company that made it did not support supplier diversity. He talked to her about it and got her to try one made by a company that supported diversity strategies. That resonated with me, and I have tried to adopt it in all of my purchases. It takes some effort, but I know, for example, which brands of gasoline support diversity strategies and which do not. My husband has commented on my commitment (or stubbornness, depending on how big of a hurry we are in) to go to the next exit or a few miles out of my way to buy gas from a company that is supportive versus one that is not or simply silent on the subject.

In April 2019, it was announced that Beyoncé had signed a deal with Adidas for a shoe and apparel line. What may have made more headlines was that Beyoncé first met with Reebok and it looked like it was going to happen until Reebok sent their team in to meet with her. Beyoncé listened and then asked if the team that was present is who she would be working with. They answered yes and she took a step back. No one on that team looked like her, had her background, had anything in common with where she came from. Reebok was out and Adidas was in. Beyoncé doesn't just talk the talk. She walks the walk, and she walks with a larger crowd every day.

The fact is that people do business with people they can relate to, who look like them, sound like them, are like them. If your company is a B2C (Business-to-Consumer) business, then you want a company and supply chain that is made up of a demographic similar to your customer base. If your company is B2B (Business to Business), then you sell to companies that likely have their own definition of what diversity means to them and will want to know how you measure up in their supply chain. If your company does both, then you have both groups to satisfy.

Social media has made it easier for consumers to make more informed choices about where they spend their money. If everyone who supports diversity only spent their money with companies that have the diversity business strategy, a lot more of them would pick it up.

Whether it's a huge star stepping away from a deal or buying gas for your car from companies that have a strong diversity strategy or choosing breakfast cereal from companies that look to do business with diverse-owned companies, we all have a voice and a choice. Every dollar is a vote. More and more consumers are looking to make that vote count, so they are getting smarter about what companies invest in behind the curtain of their profit and loss statements. What type of company and business strategies does your money help underwrite? Because even if you aren't paying attention, you are still voting every time you spend. If you aren't making a statement with your dollars, you are making a statement with your silence.

Let's go one layer deeper on why diversity is still a thing. For the purposes of our discussion here, diversity represents any group or ethnicity that has been disadvantaged over a period of time. I know that may sound intentionally vague but bear with me as we look at a few of the categories.

Minorities: The definition of this group tends to change from country to country. In the United States, it includes "Asian, Black, Hispanic, or Native American."[14] In Canada, it includes "Aboriginal peoples and/or visible minorities."[15] In the UK, it includes Black and Minority Ethnic (BME) or Black, Asian, and Minority Ethnic (BAME), Asian (Pakistani, Indian, Bangladeshi, other), Chinese, and Arab.[16] In Japan, it includes Burakumin (a caste, not ethnic minority), Chinese, Koreans, Ryukyuans (including Okinawans), and Ainu.[17]

Women: Easier to define than minorities, the struggle for their rights remains as difficult as with the others in these categories.

LGBTQ: Our brothers (he), sisters (she), and siblings (they) of lesbian, gay, bisexual, transgender, queer, and questioning. In Canada there is a "2" at the end of the acronym that designates those indigenous people who identify with their two spirits.

Veterans: This is a group of people who have put their own lives on hold to serve their country. So, while I was going to college and getting started in the corporate world, my veteran counterpart was serving in the military. Depriving military personnel of some of their prime earning years is just the beginning of the disadvantage. Service-disabled veterans have suffered a life-altering injury as a result of their service. There is also a patriotic

---

[14] NMSDC, "MBE."

[15] CAMSC, "Certification."

[16] Institute of Race Relations, "Definitions."

[17] Minority Rights Group International, "Japan."

part to this category in wanting to give something back to those who have already given so much.

SUPPLIER DIVERSITY STRATEGIES ARE LIKE RESTAURANTS

There are those who make amazing seasonal dishes using only the freshest ingredients, while others offer menu items that are bland or not quite what you expected. Then there are other places where you don't want to know how that hot dog was made. It is like most things in life. Some do it really well. Most are adequate. A few are less so.

At the end of the day, it can be difficult to know how committed a company really is to any of their business strategies unless results are measured and reported on. Look for reporting on their website, their annual report, or an annual report on diversity. If it's not being measured, if progress (or lack thereof) is not being reported, or if it's not in the basic principles of the company, you may find yourself stretching to see the benefits. That doesn't mean one should give up, but understand your market relative to the time and bandwidth you are willing to put into chasing it.

Another thing to be on the lookout for are their goals for the upcoming year and beyond. If they think they've peaked, chances are pretty good it will become a self-fulfilling prophecy. When a company thinks they are done; when they think all they can do now is tell everyone else how to do it, they have begun their downward trend.

A supplier diversity business strategy, even a well-thought-out one, isn't a silver bullet or the panacea. It is one tool in the toolbox that makes up a supplier diversity professional's (SDP's) overall business strategy.

 The C-Suite: As the head of your organization are you a benefactor, a bully, or do you silently empower? You are, indeed, one of those three whether it is intentional or not.

Are you a leader or a follower? Do you put your business strategy in place after all of your competitors have already done it or are you the first in your industry or space to set the best practice bar? Do you roll it out before or after you take a hit in the media? If we were talking about the newest technology or a cleaner carbon footprint, would it be a completely different conversation? Only you can decide which one you are or will be. And no action? Well, that is a decision as well. Just understand that in this day and age it's not a secret; everybody from employees to customers knows, so you should too.

What does diversity mean in your company? Does it mean your Human Resources (HR) processes meet the minimum standards of the law? Do you view it as a competitive advantage? What are your competitors doing in this space? Most C-suite folks can tell me where their competition is in terms of technology, service level, financials, you name it. Often, they have no idea what they are doing relative to supplier diversity or even diversity in general. Is there any other facet of the business where both a large percentage of your customers and the employees you want to recruit and retain care about something that you don't have a constant feel for?

The Supplier Diversity Professional (SDP): SDPs, let's begin with the same question I just asked your C-suite. Do you know where you are compared to your competition in this space? At every company I've worked for, I knew which competitors were doing it better than me, not doing it, starting it, and what events they were at. I was reporting it all back to the home base. Don't just talk about the awards you win, let them know when the competition is winning as well. I remember meeting with the executives of one client who wanted to cut back on their supplier diversity activities. They had won several awards and everyone in the C-suite thought they had pretty much taken care of this one. What they didn't realize was that their competition was winning three awards to their every one; was outspending them in every category, and was garnering far more public relations coverage on the creative ways they had found to move the needle on their diversity spend. How had they missed this? Because no one, including their own supplier diversity group, ever talked about it. Letting your company know where they stand in the field of both their competition and companies in general is part of a basic SWOT analysis. You can bet your company has this for every other facet of their business strategies. Where are yours?

Everyone in your company looks to you for all things supplier diversity related—we know this. This often includes those poorly phrased questions that you've heard a million times. Here's the thing: if they don't feel safe asking you a dumb question, or even one that borders on inappropriate, whom do they ask? I'll tell you, they either ask someone who isn't going to give them the real deal like you would, or they don't ask at all. You have to be a safe place, and that means you don't talk about it inside or outside the company. People move around, things change. I worked with one client whose supplier diversity business strategy had just died on the vine and no one could figure out where things went wrong. What I found was that the SDP had shared all of the horror stories about her executives and how little they knew with her fellow SDPs. Eventually, one of those fellow SDPs ended up in the supply chain of her company and guess what? That person wasn't as discreet as she had been. Her credibility with her senior management evaporated and it did not return. She eventually moved on, but people still whisper about the story. The world is so much smaller than it seems. Be discreet and, as Olympia Dukakis said in *Moonstruck*, "Don't shit where you eat."

 The Supply Chain Professional (SCP): Supply chain professionals (SCPs), this is a place where you can not only increase your results, you can actually expand where you have a seat at the table. Can't get marketing to take you seriously when they are bidding and spending money? Ask to see their diversity spend report. HR doesn't want to include you when looking at new technology? See what their diversity and inclusion status is and then match that to their supplier diversity status. Your SDP isn't another obstacle you have to overcome, they are your entry point to some of those areas you are having difficulty penetrating. Wake up and smell the opportunity.

Please understand, more than 85% of my career has been spent in supply chain. It is my chosen profession and I love it. But, honestly, y'all give me such a rash when you start pushing back on how you can incorporate supplier diversity in the supply chain process. Adding one diverse-owned business to each of your bids is paltry lip service at best. It depends on the category and how many are out there. What is the demographic of your customer base? Of the geographic footprint of your company? You should be looking for a percentage mix that reflects that. If you are operating on an enterprise resource planning (ERP) system and you can't add one or three or several bidders to your list, you need to go back and renegotiate that piece of software. Now, if your SDP tells you there aren't enough to do that, then fine. I'll talk more later about who is a viable potential supplier, but for now, let's say there are more than one. Limiting your potential supplier list to one, or only those *you* think are good enough is one reason why diversity is still a thing. Step up, coach, and put them in.

 Diverse Business Owner (DBO): Diverse business owners (DBOs), as the CEO of your company, what is your supplier diversity business strategy? I am always taken aback when I ask a DBO about their strategy and they clarify for me that *they are* a DBO so they don't need a strategy. Excuse me? You acknowledge the importance of supplier diversity, but you don't practice it? If you don't have a strategy, then clean up your act. DBOs, you should be the poster children for how this is done.

As to your prospective customers, do you understand what the definition of supplier diversity is for them? What is their global footprint? Who are they already doing business with that you do business with? How much do you network with other DBOs? How about DBOs outside of your certification category? I had a veteran DBO who had never been to anything other than veteran events. Even though veterans come in every single one of the 31 flavors, she had never looked outside the area that had gotten her the first contract. There are two critical comments on this.

First, if you can check off more than one box, run, don't walk to certify in them all. If you are a Hispanic female veteran who happens to be a lesbian, what are you waiting for? Get all of the organizations working for you. As a corporate, I can then choose which category I count spend with you in—MBE, WBE, or LGBTQ. That kind of choice is like catnip to a corporate.

Second, even if you are a single box, network and do business with the rest. This is an entire group of companies that already believes in the supplier diversity business strategy. Why on earth are you not marketing to them? Every one of these businesses do business with their own supply chain. It's not like there is only one dollar to spend and it has to be you against all of the other categories. And, if you come across another DBO that hasn't figured that out yet, move on. There are plenty that have.

The End User: End users, understanding who supplier diversity is in your company or in your own household is worth some pondering. I have pointed cousins, friends, volunteer colleagues, fellow students, lady at the grocery checkout, and the guy who delivers my mail to how supplier diversity might help someone in their circle who is in business. The spirit of this whole undertaking is to provide opportunity … wherever we can … not just 9 to 5 … or when we are buying something at work.

I get that you don't think about supplier diversity very much, so here is an opportunity for you. If you own a budget, project, or order the office supplies, you can contribute to this business strategy.

Ever feel like it is difficult to make a connection between what you do every day and the pillars or chevrons or building blocks your C-suite talk about? When you are picking out highlighters or coffee or giveaways for the next sales meeting, do you know which ones are provided by a DBO? If it isn't marked in your e-store or online catalog or Vulcan mind meld that you use to order, ask. Make that informed choice and contribute to something that matters to your customers and your bottom line.

CHAPTER 3

THE BUSINESS OF SUPPLIER DIVERSITY

I find it interesting that, in most things, everyone has no trouble agreeing that diversity is a good thing. We like choices, options, 31 flavors. Yet, sometimes we struggle with it when we look in the mirror or sit in a crowded room.

Everyone can agree that diversity is the gold standard when it comes to financial success. You wouldn't dream of having an investment portfolio of just one company's stock or investments from just a single industry. As a consumer, you want product choices. Whether you are selecting if you are a fan of Starbucks, Dunkin Donuts, or Tim Horton's or what flavor of Ben & Jerry's is your favorite, having options is a good thing.

Areas of the United States have learned that putting all of your economic eggs in one basket is not a good idea no matter how nice an egg or basket it might be. Skeptical? Go look at Flint, Michigan; Detroit; Gary, Indiana; or Pittsburgh. They concentrated their efforts on a single industry and, when it fell on hard times, the entire infrastructure of once-thriving cities was destroyed.

The same is true for a company's supply chain. When the magnesium manufacturer Meridian had an explosion at their plant in May 2018, Ford Motor Company, who was using Meridian as a sole source in their supply chain, had to shut down their F-150 truck production for over a week. Early in my career, I did expediting at a welding supply that was a supplier to Buick. I still cringe when I think about the calls I took when a line was shut down for 12 minutes because a shipment of welding contact tips was en route but had not arrived in time. You can bet that after the Meridian event, meetings took place at Ford over the next several months to review the magnesium situation and any others that were sole sourced. In fact, Ford wasn't the only one having those meetings, many other companies that read about it went in the next day and asked the same question of their Chief Procurement Officer (CPO). Even if a company decides to sole source, knowing what you would do if that sole source were interrupted or went away is powerful. As I said, options are a good thing.

THE INTERSECTION OF POPULATION AND PROFIT

There are a lot of data that show that companies that have greater diversity are better run and more profitable.

Back in 2009, the *American Sociological Review* published a study by sociologist Cedric Herring who found that "... a workforce comprised of employees of both genders and varying racial backgrounds resulted in positive business outcomes."[18] Herring found that "companies reporting the highest levels of racial diversity brought in nearly 15 times more sales revenue on average than those with the lowest levels of racial diversity. Gender diversity accounted for a difference of $599.1 million in average sales revenue: organizations with the lowest rates of gender diversity had average sales revenues of $45.2 million, compared with averages of $644.3 million for businesses with the most gender diversity."[19]

---

[18] American Sociological Association, "Diversity."
[19] Ibid.

And here is the headline news: "For every percentage increase in the rate of racial or gender diversity up to the rate represented in the relevant population, there was an increase in sales revenues of approximately 9 percent for racial and 3 percent for gender, respectively."[20] So, in short, the closer your company reflects the population, the closer you are to your peak potential revenue. Anyone who thinks peak potential revenue is a bad thing, please raise your hand. I thought not.

In 2017, *Business Insider* did a story on why diversity isn't just important, it's profitable. They referenced research done by McKinsey in 2015 and Credit Suisse in 2012. To sum up, they reference an article by Dr. David Rock, who says diverse groups are 1) better at focusing on facts; 2) think about facts more carefully; and 3) are more innovative.[21]

In 2018, *Harvard Business Review* did their own study to find if there was a correlation between innovation and performance and diversity. "They surveyed more than 1,700 companies across eight countries (the U.S., France, Germany, China, Brazil, India, Switzerland and Austria) and a variety of industries and company sizes, examining diversity in management positions, measured with respect to gender, age, national origin, career path, industry background, and education."[22] What they found was a statistically significant relationship between diversity and innovation outcomes in every single country. And "… the more dimensions of diversity were represented, the stronger the relationship was …"[23]

McKinsey has been studying this since 2015 and publishing their findings. Their 2018 report, *Diversity Matters*, examined proprietary data sets for 366 public companies across a range of

---

[20] Ibid.
[21] Dodgson and Ward, "Diverse companies."
[22] Lorenzo and Reeves, "Diversity."
[23] Ibid.

industries in Canada, Latin America, the United Kingdom, and the United States.[24] The findings were pretty clear-cut. "Companies in the top quartile for racial and ethnic diversity are 35 percent more likely to have financial returns above their respective national industry medians."[25] That means they are getting beyond the plateau of what everyone else in their space is doing.

But, perhaps even more importantly, "companies in the bottom quartile both for gender and for ethnicity and race are statistically less likely to achieve above-average financial returns than the average companies in the data set (that is, bottom-quartile companies are lagging rather than merely not leading)."[26] So, not only does diversity help you achieve at the top of the revenue stream, not having it puts you at a disadvantage. Ain't karma a bitch?

THE CURRENT STATE OF SUPPLIER DIVERSITY (AND INCLUSION)

Since diversity has "been a thing" for so long, it begs the question of what opportunities are still out there? Has all of the low-hanging fruit been harvested? This is where there is news that is both sad for the state of affairs and good for those mulling the opportunities.

McKinsey found "women-accounting for an average of just 16 percent of the members of executive teams in the United States, 12 percent in the United Kingdom, and 6 percent in Brazil-remain underrepresented at the top of corporations globally. The United Kingdom does comparatively better in racial diversity, albeit at a low level: some 78 percent of UK companies have senior-leadership teams that fail to reflect the demographic composition of the country's labor force and population, compared with 91 percent for

---

24 Hunt et al., "Diversity."
25 Ibid.
26 Ibid.

Brazil and 97 percent for the United States."[27] Clearly, there is plenty of low-hanging fruit to be had here.

So, let's say for the sake of our discussion, we can agree we are in favor of having more than one idea on the table. Let's say we can agree that diversity is a good thing. As of this writing, there is a lot of discussion about diversity and inclusion happening. Most of the business discussions are being held in Human Resources and you are seeing more positions like Diversity and Inclusion Officer at numerous corporations. That is needed and overdue, but that isn't what we are discussing here.

In a 2014 research report *Diversity and Inclusion in Canada: The Current State* from Bersin by Deloitte, diversity is defined as follows: "… the variety of people and ideas within a company. Organizations often define the diversity of their people according to unique and/ or legally protected differences, such as race, gender, age, disability, sexual orientation, maternity status, and other 'non-visible' qualities and backgrounds."[28] So far, so good.

But diversity doesn't guarantee inclusion. The report goes on to define inclusion as "… creating an environment in which people feel involved, respected, valued, and connected—and to which individuals bring their "authentic" selves (their ideas, backgrounds, and perspectives) to their work with colleagues and customers."[29]

That makes sense. You can have the most diverse group ever assembled but if they don't feel like they can speak up with their ideas the value they represent is, at best, diluted and, at worst, missed altogether.

Now, take all of that knowledge and think about applying it not just to the employee base of a company, but to that company's entire supply chain. If all of the supply chain partners that provide

---

[27] Ibid.
[28] Bersin by Deloitte, "Diversity."
[29] Ibid.

goods and services to the company also had this competitive advantage, what would that mean for company innovation, revenue, and performance? That is the starting basis for the business strategy of supplier diversity.

CVM Solutions, a third-party diversity reporting company defines supplier diversity as: "The business practice of consistently including small and diverse-owned businesses in an organization's procurement activities to improve bottom-line results, such as decreased supply costs via supplier competition, and product innovation through the entrance of new products, services and ideas."[30]

Back in the 1990s, every company was debating whether or not to recycle because there was an extra fee involved in the beginning. They debated whether to buy recycled copy paper because it was a little more expensive. Eventually, we figured out that there were bigger issues at play than the unit cost of a sheet of copy paper. Oh, and when we did that, the paper suppliers figured out how to get the price competitive. Now you would be hard-pressed to even find copy paper that isn't recycled. Funny how that works.

PIVOTING A "DISADVANTAGE" INTO RESULTS

The good news is that supplier diversity is past that extra fee for recycling. Business is about results, and do we have results! So, when my colleague says she wants to raise the community up with supplier diversity, I'm all over that. When a peer says they don't want to talk about cost savings, that is their prerogative. The fact is there are solid business reasons for having a supplier diversity business strategy and no one should apologize for that.

Several years ago, I attended a conference in Canada hosted by an organization that I was thinking of buying membership into. There was a coffee break between the presentations and I found

---

[30] CVM, "Supplier Diversity."

myself standing next to a Hispanic gentleman dressed in expensive slacks and a polo shirt from a nearby golf course. I found he owned a business for the past 20 years and this was his first supplier diversity event. I asked what he thought so far and he said, "I must admit, I am a little offended by it all."

That was the first time I'd heard that, so I asked him to tell me more. "This isn't the U.S. Canada doesn't have the same history. I don't feel like I'm disadvantaged in any way. Why would I want to be certified as such?"

I nodded to the logo on his shirt, "You like to play golf?"

"Very much," he answered.

"Do you ever take potential clients golfing?" I asked

"When I can, yes." He nodded.

"Do you find the one-on-one time is a benefit?"

"Absolutely! It's difficult to get that kind of time with a client," he said. "It's a relaxed atmosphere, it really helps build relationships."

"So why are you so willing to use that tool in your toolbox and turn this one away?" I asked motioning to the event.

He smiled. "You know, I've had a similar conversation with several people today. You are the first one who put the benefit in a business context instead of a social or political one."

Ignore the business strategy and you might as well try and build a house without using a hammer. My point is this: Use everything at your disposal and don't get so caught up in what everyone's motivations are; concentrate on the results. At the end of the day, I don't need to sing *Kumbaya* with everyone at the company or have cocktails together over the holidays. What I do need is for them to understand this is as much a business strategy for success as having inventory available when needed or having a successful logistics program to move product from point A to point B or paying a competitive wage.

This is not just about ensuring that everyone in your supply chain has a diverse workforce. This is about bringing actual diverse-owned companies into your supply chain. Before we dive into who these diverse-owned companies are and how one gains the benefit they can provide, let's take a closer look at our starring cast members.

The C-Suite: If your company is like many, you may not have a senior-level person working your supplier diversity business strategy. We can debate how long-sighted or shortsighted that may be at a later date. Suffice to say, if you don't, you shouldn't expect a full-blown business strategy from this person without some assistance. If you were going to invest in a new CRM (customer relationship management) software solution, you wouldn't have your top salesperson go out after lunch one day and buy it for you. You would have technology involved, supply chain, users at various levels and types of use, and so on. And so it goes for your supplier diversity business strategy. Supplier diversity professionals (SDPs), supply chain professionals (SCPs), end users, marketing, sales, technology, whoever keeps your website up to date ... let's just say there should be a number of people weighing in on how to create it, implement it, maintain it, and grow it. Do those other groups understand that you expect them to help when the SDP comes calling? Does your SDP know it's not just okay, but expected that they do that?

The Supplier Diversity Professional: SDPs, you represent supplier diversity for your company, internally and externally. Rightly or wrongly; fairly or unfairly. You might as well take ownership of this business strategy because you will be judged by how well it does or doesn't work. That's true even if you aren't the chief diversity or inclusion or whatever officer. What your company does (or doesn't do) in this space reflects back on you. Can you answer, "What's next?" for your supplier diversity business strategy? You're only done when the strategy isn't needed any longer, so until then, you have work to do.

The Supply Chain Professional: SCPs, the SDPs may be in the spotlight, but your area is being watched as well. There are fewer and fewer companies that don't care about integrating supplier diversity into their supply chain. Please don't tell me how you don't support this because you only evaluate each company on what they can do for a specific bid. This is about bringing people to the table. Once there, yes, then you can talk to me about how everyone is evaluated fairly. But, until your bid list represents the overall demographic, you are just part of the problem. And this is one SCP to another.

 The Diverse Business Owner: Diverse business owners (DBOs), know if you are ready to play in a particular corporate or government space. I'm not saying you don't call on them, bid on a project, or engage with the SDP, but be real about where your company is with them. Unless the project has specifically outlined working with you to get you ready to do business, that is not the purpose of the bid exercise. The assumption is that you are already there. If you're not, it's a training opportunity. Take that, if offered, and then come back and tell them what you did with it later. Whatever business you are in, as an SCP, I assume it's your core competency including providing it to my size and type company.

 The End User: End users, you have every right to expect that any company presented to you is ready, willing, and able to take on your business and provide outstanding service. But please don't lose sight of the fact that any business you've ever brought in likely needed some sort of level setting and assistance to get where you wanted them to be. For some reason, there sometimes seems to be this thought process that, if the end user can find anything that the DBO cannot do or cannot do better than everyone else, they are automatically disqualified. Whether this is part of that unconscious bias you keep hearing about, or whether it's how the SCP or others presented it, don't fall for it. Suppliers are evaluated as compared to the bid first and then as compared to each other. This is not a one strike and you're out, unless it's that way across the board. Btw, if it's that way across the board, best of luck finding a solution because that is rarer than a unicorn.

ACT II

CHAPTER 4

THE CAST OF CHARACTERS

Like most things worthwhile, it takes a village to create a successful supplier diversity business strategy. Understanding the various roles will make success that much easier. At its core, it looks something like this:

At the center of this universe is the internal client, or end user of a given product or service. They secure funding from the C-suite for the solutions they need. As such, they pay for everything that is purchased by the company. Until they have a need, nothing is funded.

Supply chain is in the business of providing what the business needs. They take the requirements of the end user and help them make informed choices to select, implement, and maintain solutions for the business. To do that, both the end user and the supply chain professional interact with the remaining cast members.

We will look at each of the cast members in turn, but for now they are:

STARRING CAST:

 The C-Suite: Supplier diversity is a top-down type of program and the C-suite members will play a role individually and collectively. Like any business strategy, they approve, support, and contribute to its success. They remove obstacles and provide leadership and accountability.

 The supplier diversity professional (SDP): This is the person whose primary role in the company is to make supplier diversity successful. They are client-driven, advocate on behalf of all of their clients, and provide the reporting that lets the rest of the cast know whether they are up for an Oscar or a Razzie.

 The supply chain, procurement, or sourcing professional (SCP): This is a group of people who source, procure, and contract the goods and services used in the company. They provide the opportunities that diverse business owners (DBOs) will pursue. They also support the business strategy with their metrics and accountability.

 The diverse business owner (DBO): This is the owner of the diverse business you may be doing business with or who wants to do business with you. This is someone who started, owns, and runs a business. That means they are a pretty smart cookie to start with.

The end user of the goods and services (client): This is the person who provides both the needs and the feedback on the solutions. And, like my mama, if they aren't happy, ain't nobody going to be happy.

SUPPORTING CAST:

Peripheral internal clients at your company: These could be people who make buying decisions, people who make funding decisions, people you report progress to, and on and on.

Certification and outreach organizations: There are a number of organizations out there that support some portion of the diversity population. These organizations often offer some sort of certification to validate that the business is owned and operated by the diverse faction (more on that later). These same organizations have events to put DBOs with SDPs and, hopefully, eventually others within companies to secure business.

Publications and content sites: There are a number of magazines and online sites that cater to the supplier diversity community. They may interview you or your company, include your company on one of their lists, and you may advertise through their venue to let DBOs know you are looking for them. They also provide a host of information on everything from best practices to new technology.

Third-party reporting and research providers: There are several companies that specialize in the reporting that companies need as to what their diversity spend is in a given time period. The companies usually also have other services that range from spend analytics, website registration portals, and other research items.

Government groups: If you are doing (or would like to do) business with the government, there are a number of groups you can connect with who will help.

Other internal company support: Interactions with legal, marketing, public relations (PR), information technology (IT), sales, and other business units within your company will be critical to a successful business strategy.

Members of the supplier diversity supply chain: Depending upon what your company does in house and what it assigns to suppliers and agencies, you will make purchases for booth setups for trade show booths, marketing agencies to draw up advertising copy and sales collateral, promotional products for handouts at shows, and shipping services to get your stuff from event to event. Need I remind you that you should be walking the walk when you look to hire these services?

Each of these cast members has a part to play in providing a first-rate production. Most of the people who make up your cast of characters are dedicated professionals who take pride in a job well done and value added. They will work with you in a professional manner and will be mindful of the work you are doing. Then there will be those who you will wonder how, in the name of all that is real, did they find their way to work this morning? Or how did they fit in the elevator with that chip on their shoulder? Or with that ego and a head the size of Manhattan? These people are not the majority, so we will not spend much time on them. But you do need to know how to spot them so you can move on quickly.

HOW TO INTERACT WITH EACH CAST MEMBER

For each of our cast members we will look at five things:

1. **What do they bring to the table?** Why are these cast members relevant to our success or failure? Each cast member contributes

to the overall production by moving the story along (aka progress). Understanding how they do this will help utilize their contributions to their full potential. We will look at how they interact with the other cast members as well as things you may not see because they happen behind the curtain.

2. **What is the lowdown on their area of the business?** You need to understand your client, your audience, if you are going to provide value to them. Have a sense of what is happening over there in that group before you try to align with them.

3. **How do they get paid?** If you know how someone is paid (and how they get that number to go up), you know what their priorities are going to be. Understanding what incentivizes people goes a long way in getting them to read your script. We will look at how each of the cast is rewarded for their work and how that can tie in (or conflict) with your own goals and objectives. That helps you frame your strategy discussion with them.

4. **What are their challenges?** Understanding what challenges people face in getting that previous number to go up, or even to get their job done can pave the way for a lot of discussions on where there is common ground in solving problems for both of you and having a successful strategy. Each member has their own set of challenges they are battling and questions they may or may not ask but are wondering just the same. We will familiarize you with the challenges so you can help clear the way to remove or mitigate them.

5. **What are their blind spots?** We all have them, that area that is not our core competency but is still part of what we do for a living. Identifying, dealing with, and getting past the blind spot(s) will speed the progress along and make the production much more enjoyable for all the participants. The sooner you can understand theirs (and your own), the sooner you get past them and start making progress.

6. **What are best practices?** For each group there will be a few tried and true things that may help to either remove a challenge or inspire you as to how you might address a challenge. These are things that have actually worked in the real world.

Ready? Action!

CHAPTER 5

CHARACTER:
C-SUITE EXECUTIVE

You would be hard-pressed to find anything written about how to have a successful supplier diversity business strategy that doesn't tell you that this is a top-down process and you must have senior leadership on board to be successful. That seems like a given, right? You wouldn't try and kick off an online retail store without the executives in the C-suite signing on. Yet, I have seen many companies kick off a supplier diversity strategy with little or lukewarm senior-level support.

Make no mistake, this is not something that you can make happen through sheer force of will. There are those who will tell you that you can "do a good job" or "make a difference" and you may be able to. But, let's face it, no one was ever promoted or won an award for creating something that was practically adequate. And, before everyone gets all excited, I'm not saying that is why you are doing this. However, let's not forget that you, too, are a for-profit entity. Why shouldn't there be career goals here? No one ever questions that for a sound financial strategy or marketing strategy. Let's aim higher than ground level and go for a strategy that can benefit the company, a lot of diverse business owners (DBOs), and your own career. For that, you need everyone in the C-suite.

Before we dive in, a couple of comments about the term "C-suite." The term sounds singular even though it refers to a collection of individuals who make up the executive level within an organization. There is a reason for that. The C-suite, or at least those who do it well, acts as a unit. There may be much ugly battling going on behind closed doors, but when the doors open, they operate as one. Having seen some of the battles that take place, I have a lot of respect for the one executive presence and treat it so, grammar be damned.

There are four things that the collective I refer to here as the C-suite has the power to bring to the supplier diversity table that you won't get elsewhere:

First, they have the checkbook, and without that, you are beyond limited. They have to be convinced to write a few checks to get the strategy off the ground and then a few more to keep it going.

A supplier diversity business strategy costs money. Money for people, corporate memberships, education, trade show materials, travel, advertising, third-party reporting, sponsorship/support of events and programs, mentoring, it *all* costs money. If you are approached by your company to "see what you can do with it" without time allotted and budget to support it, run—do not walk—to the nearest exit.

No C-suite worth their salt would plan to roll out a new website without a budget and expertise to back it up. This is no different. I have seen people who have passion for the strategy have the lifeblood sucked out of them because they are trying to make it work on a shoestring or without C-suite support or without the supply chain. This is not an accommodation someone in the company is making for you, this is a business strategy. And, just like the website that falls flat without support, this strategy will surely fail if it isn't properly supported.

Second, they bring the support of the strategy. If they don't think this is important, you can be assured many other people won't either. Any best practice (or even mediocre practice) document will tell you that if you don't have C-suite support you should abort your program. Do what you can within your realm, but have a day job that management has some skin in. The only thing worse than no supplier diversity presence is having it and doing it poorly. Seriously, a poor program just advertises that your company doesn't really support it. With no program at least people can wonder what the commitment is.

Third, and never underestimate this, they have the power to remove obstacles to success. Money and support are important, but this last one is the difference between a strategy that is successful and makes a difference and one that is periodically dusted off. Stubborn supply chain colleagues, ambivalent internal customers, data needs, and other challenges can all be parted like Moses on the Red Sea if your C-suite lends a hand to remove obstacles to success.

Fourth, and finally, they bring accountability. If you want people to pay attention to something, it has to matter. Accountability is different from support. Support means that the C-suite has your back when you go forth and helps to spread the word. Accountability means that there will be consequences for those who don't get on board. If you are the only one accountable, you are swimming upstream against a fierce current.

THE CHALLENGE OF SITTING IN THE C-SUITE

When I started my career, I wanted to be CEO of the world. Over time, I learned a few things. For one, it takes a certain personality to even want the job of CEO or C-suite inhabitant. Understanding some of the day-in-the-life will help you in getting and maintaining the support you need for your supplier diversity business strategy.

Here's the thing about being at the top of the heap, the higher you are within an organization, the more isolated you become. Your world becomes smaller, even though it may appear like you are around more people than ever before. You speak to thousands of employees, attend more meetings, and read more reports and pitches, but you are also further away from the action. That isn't connection. A connection means that you are present and can hear what people have to say. You know what their concerns are. You understand the impacts that affect the decisions you are making. Those connections become fewer and further apart. It isn't necessarily planned that way, it just happens. Executives get further removed from the day-to-day because they have to focus on the big picture. No astronaut ever gazed out of a spaceship and wondered if the parking lot at NASA was properly plowed because it snowed that day. The perspective is much different. That isn't a bad thing. You want the astronaut focusing on that spaceship they are in and you want your C-suite focusing on the bigger picture. But not to the exclusion of what's going on elsewhere in the company. Finding that balance can be a tricky proposition and many C-suite inhabitants struggle with it.

Regardless of the balance they find (or don't find), they tend to spend more time with like-minded people and, let's face it, a fair number of suck-ups. Most of them are decent guys. Yes, the majority are guys, *white* guys, who want to do well for the company and themselves. Some become spoiled tyrants but, for the most part, they are just trying to get the company through a successful year/quarter/week/hour/minute.

The isolation can have a number of impacts. My favorite writer, Doris Kearns Goodwin, has talked in interviews about the isolation of political figures. They thrive on the interaction with thousands of constituents while running for office, focus groups, shaking hands, going to BBQs, etc. When they win, they become isolated from what drove and fed them. This can leave a winner disoriented and unsure, not an ideal situation.

Very early in my career, I was appointed to a board of directors for an IBM user group that put on two educational conferences a year attended by 3,000 to 5,000 people. I was congratulated by a former board member and I asked if he had any advice for me. "Write down the reasons you agreed to do this," he said. "Write them down soon because you will start to forget." That sounded a bit dramatic to the twenty-something-year-old me, but I did it anyway. Great move on my part. I carried that piece of paper with me until it literally fell apart. Any time I had to vote on something and I wasn't sure what I should do, I would read that paper and I always knew which way I needed to vote. It's scary what can sound completely reasonable if you aren't properly grounded or if you are too isolated from the activities you are voting on. If you can understand how grounded (or not) your C-suite is, it will help in fashioning your dialogues with them, even if that dialogue is a few steps removed from direct contact.

HOW TO SEE THROUGH THE C-SUITE LENS

C-suite people view the business and most of the world through an entirely different lens than you do. **This is important!** If you aren't on their wavelength, you will leave opportunity on the table. For this reason, if no other (and there are other reasons), any time you can get a look through their lens, take it. If your C-suite is speaking at an event and you can get a copy of the deck, dial into the event, or see it later on video, do it. If there are employee calls, dial in and listen to them. Get familiar with their vocabulary, the issues they bring up over and over again, the things they take pride in. The better you know what matters to them, the better you will be at showing how that is connected to your business strategy. Know your audience and tailor your message to that audience. That doesn't mean you mis-represent. Quite the contrary. You can be completely authentic and craft the message in a way that will get attention and persuade.

The C-suite is extremely focused on the priorities. The priorities are about the overall health and welfare of the company. They are playing (or should be playing) for the long game. It's about what will sustain and be profitable for the company, now and in the future. Since the title doesn't come with a crystal ball, there is an enormous amount of risk and talent involved in getting the strategies accurate and the execution on point again and again over time.

It should be noted that these are mere mortals in C-suite positions and, like everything else in life, there are those who excel, those who are solid but not outstanding, those who do some parts very well and others not so much, and those who you shudder to wonder who the second choice was after this person. Regardless of where your C-suite folks fall into the categories above, you still need them for your business strategy, and it will still be next to impossible without them. If all of yours aren't perfect or 1,000% on board, buck up, buttercup, that is why you are here.

Once a company's strategies are set, the C-suite is dependent upon a lot of people to execute the strategies properly. You can have creative, fresh, and the most accurate strategies in the world, but if they aren't executed it's just a dream on a PowerPoint. If you can execute, you will almost always be able to find employment. If you can execute without it being painful for the majority of the people involved, that employment will most likely be meaningful and interesting. Good execution is far harder to come by then it should be. The intricacies of that will have to wait for another book, but it is a leg up and, if you have it, flaunt it and your C-suite will love you for it.

It should also be noted that priorities shift and change, so don't give up on a strategy you believe in. Sometimes it is a matter of timing. Other times, there are more important things happening. If you are homeless and hungry, you are probably not spending much time trying to save the spotted owl. Win the lottery, and now you are volunteering time and money to save endangered species. It doesn't make it less authentic, it's a matter of priorities. I have dusted off more than one strategy over the years. Three years ago, it was a no-go, now it's a winner. There is nothing like an idea whose time has come. Don't bemoan how long it took, just go do it.

The C-suite also makes a lot of decisions. So many, in fact, that they have to depend upon a lot of other people to get the information they need to make those decisions. They can't know it all. I once worked for a company that produced a lot of patents. I was responsible for a number of operations throughout the company. Of the 600-plus buildings, including the headquarters and the hangar for the company planes, every building had the same level of service except for one. The exception wasn't the HQ or even the airport for the executive air fleet. The exception was the building that housed the folks who created all of those patents. That building had a completely different level of service. Why? Because they couldn't master even the most basic administrative tasks. They didn't make their own coffee, they didn't put paper in the printers when they ran out, they didn't do anything to their cell phones when they arrived like everyone else (including the C-suite) was expected to do. The patent builders needed to be concentrating on their area of genius, not figuring out how to dislodge a paper jam in a copier, which, let's face it, only a few hundred people on the planet can actually do anyway. So, C-suite may be making decisions about things they only have a conceptual knowledge of … or less. If you find the C-suite having difficulty making a decision for you, then chances are you haven't presented the issue clearly enough as a business strategy. Don't take it as a "no." Take it as a "back to the drawing board" on how you present the strategy.

Next, time is their most valuable commodity. Actually, time is the most valuable commodity for all of us, but the C-suite is usually pretty good at getting optimum utilization from theirs. Because there is so much being thrown at them, they can't spend an inordinate amount of time on anything. I once worked for a COO who would schedule meetings from, say, 2:12 p.m. to 2:27 p.m. He didn't do that to be an ass (well, that wasn't his only intention), he didn't want his time wasted. That meeting schedule gave a sense of urgency to the time you spent with him. He had a few other tricks, too. If you gave him a write-up on a single page with a fair amount of whitespace, he would get back to you within 48 hours. If it was longer than that, it went into his briefcase and he read it when time allowed. Time rarely allowed. Know what you want, know why they should want you to have it. Get in and get out. If they need more answers, trust me, they will ask. No shy and wistful wallflowers at this level.

HOW TO DECIPHER THE C-SUITE CUES

In addition to priorities, decisions and time are cues. C-suite folks give you a lot of cues, you just have to pay attention. At one point in my career, I had the opportunity to head up part of a company-wide project for all business units under the COO. Every other month, I went before the CEO and all of his direct reports to provide an update with three of my peers from other groups. We each had 15 minutes. That's a pretty expensive hour for the company. I enlisted the Controller to advise me on my presentation. Any time you can get feedback from people who are interacting with the C-suite, take it! I gave five minutes on results, two minutes on something cool or unusual we had done, and four minutes on what we were doing next. That left four minutes for questions or comments.

Alas, one of my peers would run 20 minutes or more on something akin to a play-by-play. "We decided to hold a contest to name our new communication strategy," she would begin. "So, we made a locked box that looked like our new headquarters building, we put it in our coffee station between the pots and where our donuts go on Fridays and we sent three different e-mails asking people to participate. The first email was …." And on it went, an agonizing crawl to the point. They tried to give her feedback. When that fell on deaf ears, they tried reverse psychology telling me (just before her presentation) they appreciated my presentations that were succinct, to the point, and always under time. No change. The CEO would get up and leave when she began her presentation and come back in just before she finished ... with a Diet Coke. Nothing worked. And then one day, we had a new representative from that group. The moral of the story: Watch what is going on in the room around you when you talk and take that cue. You will not be able to, and I cannot stress this strongly enough, convince them of anything if they aren't listening.

HOW TO CONNECT WITH THE C-SUITE

Now that we understand this client a little better, let's assemble our intelligence on how to get the results we seek.

First is to understand how they get paid. The short, romantic answer is that they are paid for returning value to the company owners and investors, the shareholders if it's a public company.

If it is a public company, the price of shares of stock will be closely watched as is EBITDA (that's earnings before interest, tax, depreciation, and amortization for those of you who may not be fluent in C-suite), which is also a popular measure of a company's operating performance. Pull the last annual report and/or the last presentation they did for Wall Street and you can see what the priorities are for the company and the vocabulary they use to discuss it. You can find this information on the company website, usually under Investor Relations or About Us.

If the company is private, then the amount of profit made for the owners to divvy up will be the yardstick. However, you won't hear much about it if the company is private because they don't *have* to tell you anything and so they rarely do.

Regardless of public or private, there is always some presentation about how the company is going to succeed. It may be the four pillars, six chevrons, eight steps, or a partridge in a pear tree. Whatever it is, study it. Now, think of it in terms of your supplier diversity business strategy.

Are there items about how important the customer is? Some of your large customers have supplier diversity strategies of their own. How do you help your company provide the service elements such as tier 2 reporting for that?

If you sell to the general public, what are the demographics of your customers? Marketing can likely tell you if you don't know or can't find it. Or maybe your supply chain needs to better mirror the demographic makeup of your customer base.

Maybe there are items about how important the employees are. Employee recruiting and retention is something a lot of companies struggle with. Did you know that those pesky millennials everyone is trying to figure out are demanding diversity in all facets of their company? Rich Jeanneret, Americas vice chair and northeast region managing partner at EY was quoted in *Diversity Professional's* Winter 2018 issue talking about hiring and keeping talent. "EY hires a lot of people not much older than my son," Rich shares. "They don't just expect EY to have best-in-class policies on diversity and inclusion, they demand it. It's required to hire the best talent."[31] Did you know studies show they are not afraid to move on if they don't find it at your company?

How about revenue generation? Does your tier 2 reporting help your company receive higher marks from their biggest customers? Do you help your sales organization on Requests for Proposal (RFP) responses when they are asked about supplier diversity? Have you worked with sales so they have some of those answers in their sales collateral tool box? Do you do business with the U.S. government? If so, you have contractually committed to supplier diversity spend goals.

My point is that there are a lot of good business reasons why your supplier diversity strategy is a contributor, and chances are at least part of what your C-suite is getting paid will benefit from them. When you go in asking for funding, or resource, or anything,

---

[31] Diversity Professional.

tie it to a couple of their pillars, chevrons, or pear trees and you will have less trouble keeping their attention.

 Elephant Alert: Economies are cyclical and, sooner or later, whatever is feeding your company will take a downturn. When that happens, almost all parts of the business will take some sort of budget hit. Whether it is the "10% reduction across the board" or "no one travels ever again" or "every expenditure now goes on a requisition," there will be some belt tightening. I accept that. What I don't accept is "we can't afford to do supplier diversity anymore." Bear with me here.

My dad worked for General Motors Parts Division. He was not in the C-suite, he was in the trenches. But he recognized that when car sales were down and his buddies on the production line were being laid off, he was working overtime because people were fixing the cars they had instead of buying new ones. His work time was rarely interrupted by economic downturns.

When I began looking at whether I wanted my procurement career to be in direct (what you are making and selling) or indirect (the infrastructure that supports a business), I took a lesson from my dear old dad and chose indirect. Every company needs IT, facilities, consultants, staffing, health benefits, utilities, etc. I wasn't tied to any specific industry. I've worked for a bank, a pharmaceutical company, welding and medical supply, heavy equipment, insurance, and the telephone company. And, when sales are down, companies are even more interested in getting the price of all of that to go down. They may cut back on capex (capital expenditure), but if I can take points off of SG&A (selling, general, and administrative expenses), I'm probably going to get to stick around.

If your supplier diversity strategy contributes to what drives the business, that strategy will be part of the overall business through the ups and downs. I'm all over the good that the strategy does, lifting up the community and making the world a better place. So is your C-suite. But this is a for-profit entity and you will need to align with *that* strategy in addition to the others if it's going to be around for the long haul.

TIPS TO WORK EFFECTIVELY WITH THE C-SUITE

Every cast member in this business strategy production comes with their own set of challenges and the C-suite is no different. Here are a few they wrestle with and some tips on how you can ease the way to the support your strategy needs:

1. Help them ask difficult or embarrassing or stupid questions. First of all, there are no difficult or embarrassing or stupid questions, but you know what I mean. Not only do they not know what you know about this space, chances are they don't remember everything you covered in your last presentation. Do you remember everything they talked about in their last presentation? Of course not. If they are going to ask anyone why diversity is still a thing, make damn sure they are asking you and not someone else who is going to muck up the answer. More than once, I've been asked what the role of supply chain is in a company and my answer is always the same—it is to allow the internal client to make informed choices. My role in supplier diversity is much the same. If they are comfortable that you are willing to have an open dialogue without getting offended, you become an advisor. Whether you are a supplier diversity or supply chain professional, you should be able to have an open dialogue with your C-suite. Most of these folks don't dance around the issues, so be prepared for blunt, candid questions. And answer them in kind. Know your business strategy and be ready to defend it in business terms.

2. I know we have already covered that your business strategy should align with other company strategies, but this bears

repeating. This can be a real challenge for the C-suite no matter what level of support they have for your strategy. Why? Because they seldom see it in business terms. Connect the dots, as one of my COOs used to say, "So simple an executive can follow it." Don't assume that because they know what it is or even are in favor of it that they understand the business strategy.

I had the opportunity to attend a panel discussion once that included Lee Iacocca when he was at Chrysler. One of the questions he was asked at the end was what mistake people make with him most often. He said that people tended to take him too literally because they assumed he always knew exactly what he was talking about. He gave the example of having a conversation with a VP in the elevator one morning about a project the VP wanted to undertake. Iacocca said he said something to the effect of, "That sounds interesting." One of them got off the elevator and Iacocca forgot about it. Months later he learned that several hundred thousand dollars had been put into this project because he (Iacocca) liked the project. While that gives pause to the funding process, it also shows that people can take that literal thing too far regardless. I've seen people give up on a strategy because of one comment or pushback. I've also seen them barrel ahead with even less. Ensure you are understood. Provide everything the C-suite needs to feel they fully understand. 'Nuff said.

3. What if your C-suite isn't fully on board? This can be a slippery slope, so let's take a moment. I'll be the first to tell you that I suck at being unhappy. It's not a core competency for me and I have no interest in it becoming one. I love what I do and, therefore, I spend a lot of time doing it. If I don't enjoy it, or if I'm constantly banging my head against the wall of someone who is just not going to get on board, I'll try and fix it and if I can't, I'll move on. That said, I've worked for companies that I thoroughly enjoyed except for the *&#$% in the CFO

office or HR or whatever. A company is like family, you don't get to pick all of them. So, as much as you enjoy Thanksgiving or Christmas, you know at some point Uncle Roy is going to put the lampshade on his head or tell that awful fart joke he tells every year. If my Uncle Roy at work isn't on board but the work is getting done, I can live with that. Everyone doesn't have to be a convert ... as long as they aren't in the way. Why engage in a philosophical debate when you can be done in a quarter of the time with a business strategy debate? Life is short and I have things to do.

4. The C-suite doesn't always stay the same. In fact, in some companies it turns over with shocking regularity. What do you do when that happens? Be prepared to start from scratch. If you have tracked your progress (more on that in Chapter 13: Reporting) and kept your strategy up to date, it shouldn't be too difficult. If the C-suite people are new, chances are everyone is having to do some version of what you are doing. Don't get so offended that you endanger the strategy. If I had a dollar for every time I have explained the sourcing process to someone, I'd be sitting on a sandy beach somewhere sipping something with a little umbrella in it. Oh, and definitely be prepared to do the same thing when a new consulting company is brought in.

EVERYONE HAS BLIND SPOTS—EVEN THE CEO

Every one of us has blind spots. It's called being human. If you can be aware of what they are in the people you need for your strategy to be successful, then you can get out in front of many of them.

Here are a few from the C-suite that I have seen most often:

1. Jumping to conclusions too quickly.

Some C-suite people are in such a hurry to get to the end, they will jump past you if you aren't careful and reach a conclusion before you even ask for one. I think this happens a lot because people tend to do presentations that build up interest and suspense to get to their finale. That doesn't work with the C-suite. This isn't a Hallmark movie and you aren't Nicholas Sparks. Start with the bombshell in your thesis sentence and then back it up.

I once worked for a CFO who arrived ten minutes late to every meeting and then picked up the deck and went to the last two pages, regardless of what was being presented at the moment. Not only did he read it, but he started asking questions. They've no time and, in most cases, no tolerance for the dramatic build up. Get in and get out. Oh, and if you can do it in 20 minutes when most people ask for an hour, you will be likely to get another meeting when you want one.

2. Ready, fire, aim.

This is different from jumping to conclusions. This is making a decision or directing activity without all of the information because they are "action-oriented." There is a fine line between talking something to death and taking action just to be taking action. I've been known to do this one myself from time to time. One CEO at a company I worked for said he would rather take action at 80% sure than do nothing until 95% sure and I agree with that approach. Certainly, the consequences will have an effect on the acceptable percentage, but don't go along with the wrong approach because you think it's the only chance you are going to get. Sometimes doing nothing for a bit is the right answer.

3. Believing their own press clippings.

Now and again, you get a C-suite individual who forgets the company is paying someone to generate those press clippings. This may not have a direct effect on your strategy, but it's still worth knowing. This happens most often to C-suite individuals who are new in the position or have been there for a very long time. For whatever reason, they think their decision compass is the true north and never wavers. Whether it's an inflated ego or a successful run of good decision-making, it can lead to ready, fire, aim or to the next item below.

4. In for a penny, in for a pound, in for a graveyard mound.

We've all heard in for a penny, in for a pound, which means that if I'm on board I might as well be completely on board. Mamaw added "in for a graveyard mound," which meant you'd sooner let it die and be buried than to change your mind on something (Papaw could be awfully stubborn). Let's face it, it's hard for any of us to admit when a decision, direction, or strategy just isn't working. Cutting our losses and moving on can be expensive, difficult, embarrassing, and career-limiting. Who wants any of that? Once the C-suite begins moving in a certain direction, it can be difficult to get them to change direction. If they do change direction, chances are it won't be a nimble turn in the water. If you find yourself watching your company ship move ever further away from you, it might be worth putting a strategy aside and waiting for a better day, or at least letting some time pass before you put a different spin on it and present it once again.

5. What does this have to do with me?

In the movie *Beaches*, Bette Midler's character has been going on and on about her career success. Finally, she says "But enough about me, let's talk about you. What do you think of me?" Funny in the movies, not so much in real life. I put this in the C-suite chapter but it could easily go in any chapter about our cast of characters. You hear a lot in business about WIIFM (What's In It For Me?) and how you should answer that in any sales pitch. That's true, but you may find some people struggling to find the benefits of a supplier diversity business strategy for themselves. It can be more difficult for folks to personalize, especially if they are coming across it for the first time. That doesn't mean they don't believe in the strategy, diversity, or both, they just don't see it. Take some time to show it to them. Patience and persistence, grasshopper.

6. Sorry, I don't get it.

Finally, there are folks out there who will struggle to make the connection on your business strategy; they just can't seem to make the leap. That does not automatically equate to not supporting your strategy. Sometimes it takes time to click, like when you were learning to ride a bicycle or your multiplication tables or algebra theories. It's not there … it's not there … it's there! A couple of hints here, don't give them the same explanation over and over again. It may be the magic key for you but clearly isn't for everyone. Be willing to restate, use analogies, give it to them a different way. If that's not working, back off and try again later.

THE C-SUITE PLAYS TO WIN—AND SO SHOULD YOU

The C-suite doesn't play to come in third place. Let them know what it takes to build a championship supplier diversity strategy.

Here are a few items to get you started:

1. Goals and objectives should be aligned. That means it helps determine raises and bonuses of not just the supplier diversity professional but also the supply chain professional. Ideally, it will also be part of the yardstick for the internal clients, sales organization, etc. But if you aren't quite there yet, get the first two. Anything less will leave a lot of dollars and opportunity on the table. It is hard enough to accomplish without low (or no) expectations attached to the strategy, so aim high.
2. Ensure funding covers overlap. Make sure you have enough travel dollars to get an internal client and/or cheerleader to an outreach event if there is one that takes place close by. If possible,

get one of the C-suite executives to spend two hours walking the trade show floor of a national event. Let them see how many of their customers are there (and the companies they wish were customers but aren't). When you have someone attending, be sure to set up a couple of conversations with a customer or prospect. Let your C-suite hear from someone other than you about the business benefits. Don't be afraid to identify these items in your budget plan. If they get cut, put them back in next year and take a different tack.

3. Give the C-suite an easy yes opportunity. This is the opportunity I see wasted the most. They want to help. Time and again I see a huge opportunity blown when the C-suite asks, "How can I/we help?" and they get a vague vanilla answer like, "support the program" or "let us at the table" or something equally nondescriptive. Ask for something specific.

Do you have a PMO (Project Management Office) that reviews funding requests? Ask to be put on the distribution list of the minutes. It's an easy way to see what projects are bubbling up so you can ensure you have vetted supplier prospects when the time comes.

Ask to sit in on a budget meeting so you can see how things get funded within your organization. Just be a fly on the wall. You'll be surprised how much you can learn watching executives pitch ideas and projects.

Having a hard time getting traction with a business group? Ask to attend one of their staff meetings or business review meetings. Find out their pain points and get some candid insight into why they aren't playing ball with your strategy.

Specific requests that are easy to accommodate set a tone on both sides of the table. Involvement provides insight and, if they support any request from you, that sends a message to the recipient of the request and all who touch it. Don't go away empty handed.

4. Ensure there is accountability and that includes your own. Develop measurements that articulate both the results and the value of your strategy. Run those measurements by the C-suite and ensure they consider them valid measurements. Then agree on when you will report. I like quarterly. You don't want to go in so often that you repeat yourself, but you don't want to slip off the radar either. These people should hear from you more often than when you need a budget request approved. If they are receiving updates on progress, it's an easier sell when you do go in for that budget meeting. Be sure those measurements tie into more than just the amount of dollars spent and the diversity categories. We will cover that in more detail in Chapter 13 on Reporting, but don't make it a one-trick pony.

5. Don't send someone who doesn't understand your strategy to report on it. This can be dicey because our own executives/managers often don't want to bring in anyone else. Go with your gut. Ideally, you are presenting results at least two of those four quarters. If that just isn't going to happen, then see if you can get your direct executive to spend some time with you to better understand the reporting. I've seen so often in these meetings—if the person presenting doesn't feel comfortable with the information, they blow through it or by it and move on to topics in their happy place. That doesn't generate questions, interest, or support.

6. Share successes. Have a ready e-mail list for when the company is mentioned in an article online or in a magazine. I worked for one company where the chairman was female and supportive of the supplier diversity business strategy. Each time I shared a success, she would respond with congratulations and encouragement. She would forward it to the board of directors, several of whom would respond. The CEO would then chime in with his congratulations. It sends a message to all of those on the distribution list. This is not the time for humility. There is a

difference between "Look how great I am!" and "Look at what the company has accomplished!"

7. Study your C-suite members. If they do company calls, attend them. If the company posts presentations they give to investors, listen to them. You will get a sense of what is important to them, words or phrases that they use on a repeated basis. One C-suite member would often ask if something passes the sniff test. What he was asking was if it could be audited, did it have integrity? When he pushed back on funding for third-party reporting, I responded that if we did it, it wouldn't pass the sniff test, and he was in.

8. Treat them like a client. This is one of your most important internal clients, treat them that way.

The C-Suite: Put your ready, fire, aim weapon down for a few minutes because you may not have heard about supplier diversity as a business strategy. You don't have to give the weapon up, but stand down long enough to see the business benefits. If you still don't see how it can help your business, give me a call.

The Supplier Diversity Professional (SDP): Supplier diversity professionals (SDPs), there is nothing like an idea whose time has come. Have your story prepared and ready to tell all of the time. My resume, which has been current since the 1990s, is a six-page document. That isn't what I send to anyone. That is what I edit from. If I'm going for a job that is heavy in marketing work, there is no point in my sending a lot of accomplishments I had in transportation. I keep the long document up to date and then I edit it down to a two pager that is tailored to the position in question. You should have the same presentation for your supplier diversity business strategy. Then, when you have new members of the C-suite, or new sourcing managers who haven't worked supplier diversity before, or salespeople who don't understand what their customer is asking for, you have something you can edit to their particular needs. Keep it as up to date as the resume so you don't have to go looking for numbers, dates, awards, etc. There is nothing worse than having to present a practically adequate presentation because you ran out of time. Look at the other major business strategies in the company, they always have them ready to go. As should you.

The Supply Chain Professional (SCP): Supply chain professionals (SCPs), is the supplier diversity business strategy part of your supply chain business strategy? If not, you've got some work to do. Supply chain is all about providing value to the bottom line. Here is one more way you can do that. Include what you are doing with your SDP and how it impacts the business. If you don't have anything to add, schedule a meeting with your SDP and find out where you are missing the mark. Then do something about it.

The Diverse Business Owner (DBO): DBOs, we are all taught that sales are only for the decision makers. DBOs are constantly annoyed/concerned/perturbed/insulted that they aren't introduced to the C-suite or the decision maker by the SDP. The truth of the matter is that the C-suite doesn't meet with that many suppliers and far fewer potential suppliers. I can't tell you how many times I've had DBOs meet with me as an SCP or SDP or both and make it clear they are somehow "slumming" by presenting to me instead of someone higher up. Do not underestimate the ability of the SCP/SDP/anyone else you meet, to have an impact on *your* business strategy. Whether that impact is positive, negative, or meh has a lot to do with your relationship with them. Remember, that person you think you need to get to may have hired them. Don't make them feel like you think they made a bad decision.

The End User: End users, regardless of what business unit you reside in, chances are pretty good that positive acknowledgment from the C-suite is seen as a good thing. Invest a couple of hours and meet with your SDP and SCP and see how you, too, can benefit from their business strategies.

CHAPTER 6

CHARACTER:
SUPPLIER DIVERSITY PROFESSIONAL

The next of our starring cast members is the supplier diversity professional (SDP). The SDP is a multi-faceted professional who understands different aspects of their own company as well as the diverse business owner (DBO), the organizations that support supplier diversity, and business needs as a whole. For those of you who haven't walked in the shoes of the SDP, this is way bigger than attending conferences and doing matchmaking. The good ones bring a lot to the table, including the five things I've outlined below.

First, this person is a communication channel. They are the conduit between the diverse-owned business, member organizations, company supply chain, and the rest of the corporate environment. These are two-way channels, by the way. They are constantly taking in information, feedback, and requirements and getting them where they need to go to multiple points on the other side. If you think there isn't much involved in passing information along, you've obviously never played the game where you whisper one thing at one end of the table and get something entirely different at the other end. But the SDP does even more than this. They take the communication in, find the right place for it, and package it in the voice and vocabulary of the recipient. Seriously, if the marketing folks ever figure out what a great SDP does, they will hire them all and we will be back to square one on our strategy.

Next, they are an advocate. It makes sense that they are an advocate for the DBO but they also advocate on behalf of their company, supply chain, and, at times, other internal clients. Sometimes, the answer for a DBO is no and a good SDP may well be part of that conversation, not just the introduction. The SDP will also help vet suppliers to determine if they might be a suitable fit for the company. They act as an advocate for supply chain and only bring forth a source of qualified suppliers. They are an advocate for the end user to receive the goods and services they need to be successful, and also they must convince the end user to buy into the business strategy. In short, it's complicated. And yet, the best of the SDPs make it look easy because they have relationships with all of their clients.

Third, the SDP is a persuader. They are responsible for establishing relationships with supply chain. Finding great suppliers is not enough. If the SDP doesn't have credibility with the supply chain folks, the success margin goes way down. A colleague of mine, when complimented on help he had provided, would often reply, "It's the least I could do. (Pause) And never let it be said I didn't do the least I could do." It was funny for him because he always gave 110%. But we have all been subjected to the person who is in a constant search for the bare minimum. If that is what is happening in supply chain, the results of the business strategy will suffer. The SDP has 50 ways to tell the story of the business strategy and will find one that will resonate with whoever they are speaking to.

Fourth, they are a rich data source. They provide reporting, both on the spend and strategy as well as tier 2 reporting for the company's customers if needed. The SDP will sell the strategy to the company. They coordinate and usually attend various diversity events throughout the year. They are the go-to within their organization for anything related to supplier diversity. As such, they bring a number of things to the table.

The SDP understands the various certification processes and the bodies that conduct certifications. They build a network of contacts at the various organizations who can answer questions they may have or provide insight or assistance as they work through their supplier diversity business strategy.

The SDP is aware of the companies out there that can assist with their business strategy for hire. Whether it be training for internal clients on supplier diversity, third-party companies that provide reporting, or the latest technology in the space. This is part of the external network that the SDP maintains, regardless of whether their company is utilizing the services or not. They know their field and keep up with newcomers, mergers, etc.

This cast member brings a deep knowledge of what makes up a successful supplier diversity business strategy and they demonstrate that to their internal clients and externally to DBOs and the community at large.

Fifth and finally, they raise awareness about opportunities. Never complacent or satisfied, they are always looking to up their game and improve the business strategy and related results.

THE SDP'S JOURNEY

A supplier diversity professional typically started out their business life somewhere else in the organization. One doesn't go to Yale and get a degree in Supplier Diversity and then go look for jobs in that field, although formal and thoughtful education is getting easier to come by. Often, they come from somewhere in the supply chain, procurement, or finance organizations. With diversity and inclusion getting more attention, sometimes they come from Human Resources. Sometimes they have worked in the government sector and then move to the corporate side of life. Suffice to say, a lot of roads can lead to supplier diversity. That's good, because an SDP needs to be good at several things to be a success. Here are a few of those things:

SDPs need to be client-driven because they have *a lot* of clients. All of the other players in the starring cast are their clients. A lot of the supporting cast members are their clients. I'll explain.

It's easy to recognize that the DBOs are their clients. It's the reason they have a job, to find DBOs that their company can do business with. If the DBOs didn't exist, their job wouldn't exist. You can also understand why the C-suite is their client. They are providing the funding, the support, the kick in the … well, you get the idea. The C-suite drives the accountability and helps keep everyone focused on the big picture and that includes a strong supplier diversity business strategy.

The supply chain professional (SCP) is also their client. To be completely accurate, they are each other's client but we will cover the other side when we get to SCPs. You can have the best suppliers on the planet, but if you don't have a relationship with supply chain and if they don't view SDPs as a place to get suppliers they need, it will bear little fruit. I've been treated as a necessary evil and as a client and Mama knew what she was talking about when she said you get more flies with honey than with vinegar. If you are helping me fill a need, you are way better off than if you expect me to fill one of yours. It's not that I don't want to help, I'm just saying. So, honey or vinegar?

Finally, and most importantly, the end user who sits at the center of this particular universe is also their client. I know there are SDPs out there reading this whose eyebrows just raised waaaaay up. Indulge me, there is a method to my madness.

It is important that, as the SDP, you know who is buying and using these goods and services that you want the DBOs to provide your company. You should understand as much about it as possible. How does the end user use it? What are the pain points? How does it contribute to how your end user gets paid? How difficult is it to change suppliers? Why or why doesn't the supply chain bid it out? What does the end user know about supplier diversity? Are they a supporter? An adversary? A silent neutral (aka an adversary)?

You should also get to know the end users who use lots of stuff (that's a technical term) in your company. How do they feel about supplier diversity? Do they even know what it is? Do they understand the benefits of the business strategy? How involved do they like to be when their stuff is being sourced and negotiated? How well do they work with supply chain? *Do* they work with supply chain?

A successful SDP is also an advocate. Guess for who? Yep, all of same folks. SDPs are not just representing the DBOs, they are also representing their company. Don't forget whose logo is on the paycheck. Sometimes they advocate for their company or that end user to the DBO. Sometimes they advocate for the DBO to the SCP. Sometimes, they advocate for all three to the C-suite. This is what makes the SDP so interesting. There are not many roles within a company where you get a front row seat to big chunks of the business, all across the business. If you are in finance, you are dealing with the numbers; in sales, the customers signed; in facilities, the physical buildings. Supplier diversity and supply chain get to look at all kinds of pieces/parts of the business up close. You can gain a pretty in-depth understanding of your company and business in general from the people who have the budgets and make the decisions. Not many people have that opportunity. Don't squander it. If you treat them like a client and advocate for them when needed, you are an informed and vital part of the team. If you don't, you're just that person who's always whining about not having enough diverse companies in the supply chain.

THE SDP'S SUPERPOWERS

The SDP is a networking connoisseur. Supplier diversity people have never met a stranger and can strike up a conversation almost anywhere—an elevator, standing in line for coffee, sitting in a hotel lobby, you name it. And the good news is that they will have people to talk to at a supplier diversity event because it is a welcoming and supportive group. No one (well, practically no one) is keeping their successes close to the vest. This isn't the Coca-Cola recipe; it is meant to be shared. You won't find supplier diversity people standing off in a corner saying they won't share a newfound supplier with someone because that company's spend might then be more than theirs.

By the same token, the SDP has excellent antennae for those who are authentic and those who are playing the game, or think they are playing the game. Their BS-ometer is on hyperdrive most of the time. I worked with a company once that had not started out as a woman business enterprise (WBE) but had recently become one. They were looking to leverage their status and I was working with some of their executive management. I encouraged them to not filter their thoughts and questions with me so we could accurately determine how to leverage the WBE status. One executive had the same answer to every question I posed: What answer will get me the order?

I pointed out that approach would be seen as inauthentic. He scoffed, "I am in sales, I can appear authentic doing anything." I will admit, some of the role-playing characterizations I gave him during the workshop were as much for my own amusement as for his education. But, to his credit, he did admit at the end of the day that he probably wasn't fooling anyone. And spoiler alert: he wasn't getting many orders with it either.

There are companies out there, big ones, that buy the memberships every year and do nothing more. Some are unaware that they get a free booth at the annual event as part of their membership. Year after year, there is an empty booth with their name on it. It's one thing to be inauthentic, it's another thing to advertise the fact. It's not a secret ... everybody knows.

For reasons that continue to escape me, many companies feel that the SDP comes with all of the skills and methodologies necessary to fulfill their job. No one balks at the technology folks going off to learn how to code better/faster. Financial folks are expected to need seminars about the latest finance laws and processes. The mechanic in the shop gets lessons in the new engines coming out next year so they are familiar with them. But time and again I hear management push back at sending SDPs for training and development. Maybe it's because they don't view supplier diversity as a business strategy, maybe it's because the SDP goes to so many events already, maybe it's not a priority when doling out the training dollars, regardless, it happens a shameful amount of the time. SDPs need training over and above what they pick up at sessions at supplier diversity events. They need to keep up on all kinds of skills—sales, presentation, communication, marketing, financial, technology, negotiation, pretty much anything you would expect a good manager, director, or VP to have.

THE SDP'S CHAIN OF COMMAND

SDPs may report into supply chain, finance, operations, or HR. If they don't report into supply chain, they will usually report up to the same people supply chain reports to. I say usually because, well, it's all over the map across corporations.

When I was responsible for strategic sourcing and supplier diversity at my last corporate gig, everyone wore both hats. It's my personal preference. I believe that supplier diversity should be a goal and objective along with cost savings, streamlining of operations, total cost, add value, supplier relationship management and the other things that supply chain is measured on (more on that in the next chapter). If I'd had the budget, I would have had an FTE (Full Time Equivalent) on the same team whose sole job was supplier diversity. They would have reported into supply chain and coordinated the myriad of details that are needed to pull off events, reporting, and proper outreach, but it wouldn't have changed the both hats philosophy.

The majority of organizations have an individual, or group of individuals, who are exclusively supplier diversity. They work the events and coordinate with the supply chain group, advocating for vetted DBOs. This structure works well as long as supplier diversity and supply chain work well together and have at least a few similar goals and objectives.

SDPs are usually measured on some combination of:

- Dollars spent with DBOs
- Number of DBOs dollars are spent with
- Diversity among the groups and ethnicities that make up the diverse spend
- Bringing new suppliers into the supply chain
- Perception and/or recognition of the company's strategy as best practice, leading edge or otherwise noteworthy
- Providing proof of good faith effort where spend amounts are less than ideal or spending has plateaued over time
- Various activities that make up the outreach, reporting, and other aspects of a successful program.

This is by no means an exhaustive list, but it gives you the gist of what drives them. They are likely also measured on some percentage of the total of spend, or addressable spend, as is currently in vogue. I have all kinds of opinions about what makes up spend, but I saved that for the chapter on reporting.

As with most things in life, SDPs don't have control over everything their success or failure depends upon. There should be some sort of reporting metric(s) to help identify when the percentage outside of their control comes off the rails. The best time to establish that metric is when it isn't a critical situation. Priorities and people change over time. Don't let your success as an SDP rely on the support of a given individual or group, no matter how high up they might be. As Papaw used to say, "You don't shop for a gun when the bear traps you in the barn."

UNDERSTANDING THE SDP'S PAIN POINTS

Some days, it seems like there are nothing but challenges that SDPs face. They include:

- Educating their colleagues on supplier diversity: There are tons of employees in some of the best companies that do not understand supplier diversity, why it is important, and more importantly, how it impacts their role in the company. This group, which ranges from the blissfully unaware to the consciously biased, needs to know this is a company initiative and not the latest program du jour from one business unit or group within their organization. Sometimes, the biggest challenge is letting people know what they don't know. There is also a steady flow of new employees coming in. Is the supplier diversity business strategy part of the onboarding and/or orientation material? If not, you are throwing the uneducated at this strategy on an ongoing basis. Help your SDPs stem the flow of those who don't know.
- Maintaining support for the strategy. For some, it is a tougher sell within their company than other ongoing strategies (hiring and keeping the best talent, customer retention, best technology, etc.), but like any ongoing strategy, vigilance is key. It's a strategy, which connotes something ongoing rather than a program, which suggests there is a start and finish to it. I've been asked on many occasions, "When will this supplier diversity be done?" My answer is often something like, "When the need for marketing is done." However, like any strategy, when the priority recedes, so does the attention to it.

- Avoiding cutbacks when there is a business downturn or economic slowdown. If your company doesn't view supplier diversity as a business strategy, you will most certainly take hits on this. Even if it does, there are times when all of the company takes a budget decrease. If your cutback is the same percentage as the other business strategies, it's hard to argue with. There are times when there just isn't as much money to go around. But, if your budget is getting hit and others are not, you need to look hard at that.

- Communicating the successes are important but communicating how far there is to go yet should also be a part of the strategy. I recall one company who thought they had arrived because they had received an award for their program. When a company meets their sales goals for the quarter you don't hear them talking about shutting down the sales force. This is no different. When I first began reporting the percentage of total spend at one company it was less than 2%. My manager, concerned about how it would look, asked me if I really wanted that on the dashboard. "Yes," I answered. "They need to understand how much we have left to do." I wanted them to know that a couple of awards and mention in a magazine didn't mean we had reached some sort of summit.

- One of the touchiest topics is separating people's politics from supplier diversity. At this writing, it is not in vogue to be able to agree to disagree on much of anything but certainly not politics. Some view supplier diversity as a political belief and, while I can see where that might be a conclusion drawn, it is so much more than that. And regardless of your political beliefs, this is a business strategy that makes up the overall company strategy. I find most people who try to engage me in a political discussion are more interested in finding a reason not to support supplier diversity. It's like the conversation about company owners refusing to serve gay clients because they don't believe in the lifestyle.

I don't see them refusing a wedding cake to an alcoholic, an abuser, or someone who cheats on their taxes because they don't adopt the lifestyle. This is why we cannot leave it all up to the individual. The last time we did that, only whites got served at the lunch counter.

I have yet to hear someone demand to know how I feel (or more invasively, how I voted) on the last gas tax increase and yet I have been perfectly qualified to manage the fleet category for more than a handful of companies. It can be difficult to not get drawn into a discussion you may feel passionate about. But at the end of the day, it is not relevant to this business strategy. Have the discussion if you must, but not on the premise of supplier diversity. This is a business strategy, so unless you are debating whether for-profit entities should exist, there is no place for supplier diversity in the conversation.

- The previous topic notwithstanding, that is not to say there are not some uncomfortable discussions that will be had on the topic. If you have someone out there in your orbit who is questioning why diversity is still a thing or is simply looking for education that might sound like a taboo topic on its surface, I still want to hear about it. In addition to my previously stated preference of the answers coming from me rather than from who knows who, I need to understand if I'm missing something in my messaging. That is not a license for someone to be a tool, I'm talking about genuine curiosity. It can be a tough line for an SDP to walk. You want to be available to people, but you're so over some of the questions that keep coming up repeatedly.
- If an SDP doesn't have supply chain experience, it is going to hurt them at some point. That's not to say they need to go do the job for X years, but they need a thorough understanding of what happens in the process. At a minimum, that should include sitting in on several different types of bid processes and I mean the

entire bid process. A process map and a conversation with an SCP is great, but there are many, many (did I mention there are many?) nuances that will only be experienced by being part of the entire process, from engagement by the internal stakeholders to the sourcing process for viable companies, the requests for proposal (RFP) creation, the bid responses, the short list meetings, the contract negotiations, and the implementation. This process can vary widely depending upon what is being sourced. Raw materials do not follow the same process as the outsourcing of the accounts payable function, as software licensing, as uniforms, as capital expense, and so on.

Every SCP will tell you that almost every client they have ever had thinks they are unique to every other client the SCP has had. Honestly, there are far more similarities than differences but differences are there and you can't pretend they aren't or that they don't matter. I was once taking on the centralization of supply chain in a company where it had never been done before. Not for lack of trying, mind you, but it hadn't been done. I was meeting on Monday morning with one of the VPs who had been the most vocal about not going with the centralization strategy. Over the weekend, I went on to the company website, located the VP's business area, and found they had online training about what they did. I spent a few hours taking the first two classes and passed the tests with an 87% and 91%. It was interesting and I could tell there were some things there that could make the difference in how bids would come back. On Monday, I met with the VP. His first question was how much I knew about his portion of the company business. I admitted not much but I told him what I scored on the tests. He was so impressed that I took the time to learn about what they did that he ended up being one of my first converts. People don't have to be convinced so much as they have to be heard. That is the same no matter who your client is.

FOCUSING ON THE SDP'S BLIND SPOTS

All of us have blind spots. The key is to find them, acknowledge them and eliminate them. Here are my top selections for the supplier diversity professional.

1. In addition to the DBOs for whom you are an advocate, you have several important internal clients who can make or break your success. This is regardless of how much support you have from the top or how committed everyone is to the process. Treat them like the important clients they are. On the top of this list is the supply chain group. They likely control the largest dollar amount that is being awarded to suppliers within your organization. In other words, they are your biggest customer.

2. Next, as good a customer as sourcing is, the chance that every dollar is being spent through them is unlikely. Understand where sourcing does not rule the roost and cultivate a relationship with the owner of those dollars. For example, there are areas that sourcing has traditionally had difficulty getting into, such as marketing, legal, Human Resources, etc. If sourcing doesn't manage the spend for print, no print supplier is going to get a contract if you only introduce them to sourcing.

3. The most common and impactful blind spot is not understanding how and where your company spends its money. If the SDP gets a periodic list from supply chain of what is going to be bid in the next X months and goes off to find suppliers for that list, there is a tremendous amount of money being left on the table.

   Here's the thing: if your kitchen catches on fire, that is a really poor time to go out shopping for fire extinguishers. It's the same with your supply chain. If your procurement group is going to bid out, say, the maintenance of your vehicle fleet in 90 days, now is a terrible time to meet potential suppliers for the first time. Sure, if you are attending a supplier diversity event next week, you want to put the word out for companies that provide that type of service but that shouldn't be your A-game play. A good SDP needs to be on the lookout for potential suppliers who provide everything their company buys … all the time … every event … even if it's just been sourced and contracted. It's like meeting someone at the train station today and hooking them up with your sister on a date a week later. Sure, it might be her soul mate but what are the odds, really? Don't be ships passing in the night with great suppliers. Get to know them now.

So how does an SDP go about finding out what the company spends its money on? First, get on the distribution list of any updates supply chain provides to senior management. If supply chain thinks it's important enough to report to the C-suite, chances are you should know it, too.

Second, ask for the last review of spend analytics. For most companies, this is a comprehensive list of things the company spends their money on, how much money, and usually who is providing it now. This not only helps you understand what is being purchased, it also will likely show you the areas where sourcing is not running the contract awards.

Next, find out if your supply chain has a calendar of when current agreements expire. If they have a contracting tool, the answer is yes. It could also be yes if they are using an Excel spreadsheet. If they do, don't just get what's coming up in the next year, ask for a complete listing. This tells you not only where dollars are being spent but provides some insights into where supply chain isn't currently managing the spend. No spend for marketing? Time to go make friends with marketing.

4. If you have a Project Management Office (PMO) or other group that manages large projects across your company or evaluates funding requests, ask to be put on the distribution list of any meeting minutes or project updates. This provides a list of who

is seeking funding (aka the end user), what type of new projects are coming up (new or unique needs for suppliers), as well as a handy list of the people you should get to know within your own organization and build relationships with.

Whether an SDP has sourcing experience or not, they should be familiar with what the company buys, who provides it now, and how that's working out for everyone. How do you get up to speed on that? By engaging with the sourcing group on a regular and ongoing basis.

This includes things such as:

- Understand what the goals and objectives are for your sourcing brethren (see how they get paid). If your list has any conflicts, get them resolved soonest.

- Learn the sourcing process for your company. Sit in on a sourcing project from start to finish. Offer to take notes at their meeting or be a fly on the wall. Regardless, ask for a debrief with a sourcing person post meeting and ask questions. Once you have done that, sit in on another project for a different type of product or service. Learn why there are differences in the sourcing process for raw materials to software licensing to bulk fuel products. You don't need to be able to run a sourcing project or negotiate a contract, but you should know what's important to the sourcing group … and why.

5. You are one channel for DBOs into your company, you are not the *only* channel. You will see this more than once. That's because it is that important. I sat in a meeting once with a DBO and the SDP of a very large (we're talking Billion Dollar Round-table large) company. The DBO was excited to report that she had been paired with the treasurer of said large company at a golf outing taking place the following month. The SDP proceeded to instruct the DBO not to talk to the treasurer about

the business. "I am the only door into the company," the SDP told her. There are so many things wrong with that statement, the mind reels, but here are three that should be sufficient to keep any SDPs out there reading this from ever making it, or from ever making it again.

First, this is a for-profit entity and we are not playing games here. If a DBO has the opportunity to utilize a channel within a company, you use _every_ channel you can get your hands on. If you have the opportunity to meet someone in the sourcing organization, do it; C-suite individual, do it; someone in the marketing department, do it; the mailroom, do it; accounts payable, do it. Because I can guarantee you that is precisely what your competition is doing.

Next, the SDP doesn't know everything that is going on in the company. SDP, if you think that you know all from your internal clients, from supply chain, from the supplier diversity community as a whole, you really need to get over yourself. That's like saying you won't accept paying the sale price on something you're buying in a store if you didn't know it was on sale when you arrived today. Why would you throw away free money like that? The spend counts on your report whether you made the introduction or not. If any of them can find spend without you having to lift a finger, delight in it.

Finally, the SDP is an advocate and is neither kingmaker nor puppet master. This is not how an SDP controls their channel or any other channel, for that matter.

6. Not everyone is in this for the same reasons, beliefs, or passion as you and that's okay. You've heard that success breeds success? Well, that is absolutely true with a supplier diversity business strategy. There is nothing like taking one of those "grumble, grumble, I can't believe there is something _else_ I have to do to be compliant …" people and having them be part of a success story. Early in my career, I would cringe when someone started off a

success story with, "I wasn't very excited about this initially …" or "I didn't really believe in this at the start …" or something equally underwhelming, but now I seek them out. Why? Because no matter what people say (or don't say) or do (or don't do), some of those people are going to be in whatever audience this person is speaking in. So, do it because you believe, do it because the company wants it, do it because Joe did it and got promoted, just do it and I'll be a happy gal!

There are no silver bullets to a successful business strategy for supplier diversity. There are too many factors involved. Company culture, supply chain structure, the criticality of the business need, it's about people after all, so there are as many scenarios as you can imagine. However, there are a few things that, if considered against your company backdrop, can push your strategy from the practically adequate to truly successful.

BEST PRACTICES

Some of the best practices and success I have seen for a supplier diversity business strategy includes the following:

1. No apologies needed. Never, ever apologize for making the company better, more competitive, and more financially sound. Clients are like animals; they sense fear and trepidation. If you approach this as, "I know, another thing you have to think about to get your job done," you give license to second guess the credibility of your strategy. This may sound like something that belongs in a pep talk and not a best practice strategy I respectfully disagree. If you want the rest of the company to give your supplier diversity business strategy the respect it deserves then you, at least, should do the same. It really chaps me off to hear people apologize for training, like we are all too cool to be

talking about this. If that is your mantra, go get a mirror and have a session with yourself.

2. Tailor your message to your audience, but don't dilute your message. I remember a new client who asked me to attend a presentation he was making to his management about building out a strategy for the company. He spent ten minutes talking about what he wanted to do for veteran-owned businesses. Great. He then spent about 90 seconds talking about women- and minority-owned businesses. Hmmmm. He made no mention of LGBTQ businesses at all. When I asked him about it afterward, he said he knew what his manager would buy into and so spoke to that. I advised him that his role was to allow his management to make informed choices. That meant they needed to understand what was needed to have a best practice strategy. He was surprised when his initial request was turned down. Why? Because the company was already doing a lot with veterans. His request was viewed as a duplicate of that work. It took us three months to revive the request. The second time we went in with the entire story. I may take what I can get at budget time, but that doesn't mean I don't ask for everything else again next year. Management needs to know what makes a good and a great strategy that will provide the biggest payoff for the company.

3. Believe in your strategy. This may seem like a given, but it is imperative and, like every other job out there, not everyone is on board with what they are doing at any given point in time. I believe with every fiber of my being that having a diverse supply chain portfolio is critical to the success of that supply chain. I believe that DBOs, whether small or huge, bring something to the table that will be absent if they aren't there. I believe there are fantastic DBOs, there are DBOs who are pretty good, there are DBOs who are phoning it in, and there are DBOs who should go home. You know, like life, companies, families, whatever other type of group you can come up with, the level

of expertise varies. I want to introduce the fantastic companies to as many people as possible. I want to help the pretty good ones become fantastic. I want to have an intervention with the ones phoning it in and see if I can get them back on track. And I want to avoid the ones that need to go home. If you don't believe, and there will be times when you don't, go have your own intervention before you try and sell it.

4. Be prepared to defend your message. I feel all of the SDPs rolling their eyes on this one, but bear with me here. Every SDP dreads the DBO that doesn't work out. It's like introducing what you think is a great guy to your sister and then he breaks her heart. Certainly, there should be debriefing on what didn't work and what adjustments can be made on future vetting. But here's the thing, everyone sitting in whatever room or call or conversation you are having has had the same thing happen. The only person who will never bring an imperfect supplier to the table is someone who brings no one. Don't make a habit of it, obviously, but it should get no more attention than any supplier in the same situation. We've all been there. If someone isn't seeing it that way, then remind them. Unless my batting average is worse than almost everyone else who is batting, I don't expect to get a lot of crap about it. Help me improve my average—now that I will always have time for.

5. Don't look for good suppliers for a certain category, look for good suppliers. Even if I don't purchase what a good DBO has to sell, I likely know someone who does. If you focus your scope in so narrowly that you only pay attention to what is needed today, you will never be ready tomorrow. Good suppliers, diverse or otherwise, are hard to come by. Make note when you do. If you think you may have found one, take the time to look closer and find out. Have a conversation, keep in touch.

6. Give constructive feedback. A good friend of mine tells the story of how mean I was to her when we first met. I was one

of her first cold calls to get me to advertise with her company's publication. She had dialed my number and I was in (which didn't happen often), so I took the call. It was clear she was reading from a script. I asked a few questions and she had no answer. Rather than give her my email address and fade into the sunset, I could tell she was smarter than the average bear, just not prepared. I asked her to put the script away and just talk to me. I told her a few things I wanted to know when looking at potential publications. I told her she wasn't ready to talk to me, but when she was, to call me back. She could have taken my email address and likewise faded into the sunset. But, she didn't. She did her homework and then she called back. It took a while, I was usually on the road or in a conference room, but we reconnected and we did some business. We have continued to do business even though both of our situations have changed since that call. You hear the security ads "If you see something, say something." Well, that can work for when you see potential, too.

7. Allow time to build your network. Be selective. There is a reason there are 31 flavors. Not everyone is a fit. People can be smart, successful, can have things they can teach you, but you aren't having cocktails with them over the holidays. There is a wide gap between acquaintances and trusted advisors. It doesn't mean their way is wrong and yours is right or vice versa. It's just not a comfortable fit and that is perfectly okay.

8. Stay curious. Ask questions. You need to understand why you are getting pushback from an internal client or elsewhere. If you don't, you are setting yourself (and your strategy) up for getting no over and over again. Find out what the issues are. Then give them a diligent thought process. Do you need to change your messaging? Are you missing something that is important to this person? Are they just creating smoke because they don't want any part of it?

9. Ask for what you want. I have what I call the fair ask. If I'm asking for something and the answer is no, then I usually ask why. People don't always want to tell you why. It can be uncomfortable and they may not want to take the time. So, I ask them if understanding why I'm being turned down is a fair ask. I don't do that so that I can argue with them on each point they give me. Take your "no" like a grownup. No one wants to give feedback if they are going to have to defend and debate it. But listen to what they are telling you and then use that going forward. Also, remember that "no" can mean "not now." If I believe in a request, I'll go back and rework it and come back again. Sometimes it's just timing. There is nothing like an idea whose time has come. Have your best foot ready to put forward when that happens.

10. Be creative. The sky is the limit on how you can creatively impact your area. A few that I have seen/done and loved include:

    Do something creative to drive traffic to your booth at the trade show. One corporate had a professional violinist at their booth at NMSDC in 2019. It was like having the Pied Piper, people were drawn to it. They stopped to listen, they read the material, they met.

    Have an internal group that is difficult to penetrate? Set something up for just them. At one company, I struggled to get suppliers into the legal group. So, I made a deal with the Deputy General Counsel. Give me one day a year, I said (one day is a fair ask, no?). You come to my office (she would have been interrupted every five minutes at her office) and I will set up a series of 15-minute conference calls with potential companies. We have five minutes between calls for breaks, you can provide me with feedback on the choices. If you like them, you'll do a nondisclosure agreement (NDA) so you can talk to them when and if the time comes where you might use them. We had 90 minutes off for lunch and I took her to lunch, where I was able to tell her more about the strategy.

The first year yielded three strong possibilities, two intros elsewhere in the organization, and a couple of follow-up conversations. But I got a lot of feedback that I was able to use for even better candidates on the Legal Day the following year. Counsel was so intrigued that she took a day and attended a supplier diversity event later in the year.

Many companies are doing their own events. They can invite prospect companies that are tailored to their business. That is an awesome way to make it happen. They have their SCPs on site and the companies learn about the corporate. If that is not in your budget, consider a webinar about doing business with your company. Some of the publications and marketing groups will help as part of their marketing plan for you. Webinars are cost effective for you and for the prospect companies that don't have to make the time or travel commitment of a live event. They can be recorded and placed on your website to continue to bring in potential suppliers.

Need some new ideas to meet executives and get some free mentorship? One year at my annual review, I asked my CPO (Chief Procurement Officer) about training plans for the year. He asked if I had any ideas. Well, yeah (always have ideas). We had a new SVP who had joined the company and she was making some changes on the operations side of the house. I asked to carry her briefcase for a couple of days. My CPO was intrigued so he made inquiries. Not only did the SVP say yes, she actually hauled me around with her in her car from meeting to meeting. I got to see her in action and then ask questions afterward. She also wanted to know about what I did. It is still one of the best development experiences I've had. And I had an SVP who was also a huge supplier diversity supporter.

Speaking of supporters, don't forget to ask supporters to tell their family, tell their friends. One colleague did that and the Chairman of her company called her and the strategy out at the annual management meeting. You want to get the attention of your internal clients? Let them hear it from the board level.

These are just a few things I have seen. But it's really about paying attention and speaking up when the opportunity presents itself. What's on your short list of creative ideas?

11. Stay hungry. I had a few rules with my team that worked conferences and trade shows. First, I didn't fly everyone to a city so they could hang out together. I expected to see them each sitting at a table where they didn't know anyone. The whole idea is to meet people, new people. So, you go to all of the meals and you sit at a table where you don't know anyone. Next, when you are working the trade show booth, you put your phone away. Nothing chaps me more than to walk up to a booth where someone has their nose in their phone and is trying to not make eye contact. "Those booths are expensive, people! Reel them in!" Strike up conversations, especially with people wearing a first-time ribbon. If you are a repeat, you are an ambassador for the new folks coming through. Ask them how it's going for them, if they have any questions, what they do, who they do it for and, before you know it, it's a real conversation. Some of my best contacts have been made in line at Starbucks or in the buffet line at lunch or sitting in the hotel or convention center lobby. One year, a colleague commented on a woman who had an amazing jacket on. When she saw her again later, she commented on it. Ran into her later still, and she remembered. They started talking and the next thing you know …. Just stay away from the restrooms. I once had a woman slide her business card underneath my stall because she had been after me and saw me enter it. That just creeped me out. Boundaries, people, but you get the idea.

Yes, you need to understand your supply chain. Yes, you need to know how to engage with your management. Yes, you need to be persuasive with your internal clients (all of them).

But you are also running a small business of your own with a budget, and a mission, and goals. Run it like one and your business strategy will have you humming along to successful spend numbers in no time.

The C-Suite: Whatever your training and development strategy is at your company, be sure to include supplier diversity in that planning. There are not many places in your organization where people have this much unfettered access to your customers, your suppliers, and your senior management throughout the company. It *would* be nice if they were familiar with the things most important to your company. If you aren't leveraging your SDPs, you are leaving a pile of money on the table … a pile of money.

The Supplier Diversity Professional: SDPs, you are a very important communication channel for all of your clients, but you are not the *only* channel and I'm going to say it out loud: you shouldn't want to be. If DBOs can get business at your company without you being involved, why on earth would you have a problem with that? There are lots of non-diverse-owned companies out there and your friends in supply chain will tell you they don't have a problem utilizing any channel they can get their hands on. Last time I checked, those companies had more business than your DBOs had.

If DBOs have been asked by someone in your company (translation, not just you on your own) to only deal with you or to not call them, well that's different. If they don't follow those directions, they deserve the result they get.

However, to make a DBO think they have to choose between the support of supplier diversity and ever speaking to anyone other than supplier diversity? Sorry, that is just another form of exclusion.

The Supply Chain Professional: SCPs, if you want to leverage the full power of your SDPs, you have to engage with them. By engagement, I don't mean a list of what you think will go to bid next year. Invite them to sit in on your bid projects, negotiations, department meetings, and the like. Help them understand how sourcing requirements are different for different types of categories and end users. Let them see how many people it takes to implement a large-scale contract and also a small one. Then, get your own butt out at least once a year and attend a conference. And by attend, I don't mean go to the cocktail reception one evening and spend an hour at your booth at the trade show. Attend it like you are evaluating it for a contract; understand the different offerings at a conference and how your SDP interacts with potential suppliers. Then afterward, schedule time to sit down with your SDP and discuss what you saw, what you didn't see, and what you'd like to see. Don't be one of those people who complain how lame the party is and then never have a suggestion to improve it. This will also allow you to see what your SDP is faced with and help them get to the end results we all want, more opportunities for DBOs.

The Diverse Business Owner: DBOs, please respect that SDPs know more about their company than you do. Their job is not just to introduce you to whoever you feel you should meet at the company. Business owners have DNA that screams that if they can just make the right connection, they will make the sale, but that voice lies to you sometimes. SDPs put their own reputation on the line for you when they make the introduction. Often, it has nothing to do with the quality of your product, your service level, or your abilities. Sometimes, it's not about you at all.

The End User: End users, regardless of how much money you do or don't spend on behalf of the company; regardless of whether you and supply chain work well together or not at all, the supplier diversity business strategy is not a piece of some other strategy you have bought into or not. Unless you have an aversion to good service, competitive pricing, client and talent retention, you can learn something here. Invest a couple of hours and see what it's all about.

CHAPTER 7

CHARACTER: SUPPLY CHAIN PROFESSIONAL

If the commitment of the C-suite is the train that drives a successful supplier diversity strategy, the supply chain professional (SCP) is the engine that makes that train go. They bring a number of things to the table, not the least of which are:

1. They are a touchpoint into the largest amount of dollars spent in the company. You notice I didn't say "the" touchpoint (more on that later). Most of the dollars a company spends on goods and services (collectively, the "spend") passes through supply chain in some form or fashion. They have relationships with all of the supplier diversity professional's (SDP's) internal clients. That includes the C-suite and that all-important end user that the world of spend revolves around.

2. They are driven by, contribute to, and are compensated based upon business results. This means that they should understand the business strategy of supplier diversity. This makes them a first line possibility of an early adopter. SCPs understand the economics of a business strategy as well as the benefits of improving a process, streamlining, automation, or other methods of taking cost out of the process of getting goods and services from point A to point B.

3. They keep track of what's important when it comes to awarding a particular piece of business. A good bid process will identify the objectives that must be met for a successful solution well before the bid responses are ever read. A good SCP will get input on this from everyone involved in the process. They will document the items and have the group weigh their importance. Those requirements will be called upon again and again as the bid results are evaluated, a selection is made, a contract is negotiated, and a solution is implemented and measured. They are the shepherd and when some of the flock starts to wander off into other areas, the SCP will nudge them back in line with the initial requirements.

4. They are paid to not care who wins. SCPs are the objective third-party in the room. End users, business unit heads, and most everyone else will have some sort of favorite going into a bid process, and that is not just because they like someone in the group. It may be the incumbent because it is going to be a lot of work to change out an existing supplier. It may be the company with the latest and greatest technology because it's something an internal client wants to learn. It might be because there is a comfortable business relationship (not inappropriate, that's something different) and they trust the incumbent because they understand the company and how it operates. There are lots of reasons to have a favorite, no matter how hard someone tries to not have one. It may be an account representative that you just click with or a piece of software that seems more intuitive than the others. Regardless, having the objective third-party in the room keeps the focus on where it should be: on the things that were determined up front that count the most. A good SCP will guide the group back to those concerns without favoritism.

5. They know what stuff should cost. SCPs understand the various ways and touchpoints where cost is added to a product or service. They have a bevy of tools they utilize to drive cost down to

where it should be. One of the most critical of their skills is the ability to calculate what a product or service should be costing the company, or the "*should cost.*" Almost anyone can pressure a company into shaving a few percentage points off an existing price. Supply chain professionals are knowledgeable about what the company should be paying and then getting the price to that point.

I once had the head of IT tell me that the reason he didn't invite supply chain into a meeting with a supplier was that he had negotiated the price himself. Last year, the company had paid $50,000 and he had gotten the price down to $42,000. What he overlooked was that the company should not have been paying more than $30,000 (the should cost) in the first place. Congratulations! You are overpaying $8,000 less than you did last year.

How is should cost calculated? It is a combination of knowing what makes up the cost of a given product or service (cost of raw materials, labor rates, level of knowledge required, service, support, distribution, profit margin, updates over time, technology, etc.) and what those pieces/parts add up to. The should cost can also be impacted by what costs are over a given geography. For example, you may reduce the cost of making something by creating it closer to the delivery point, thus eliminating distribution and transportation cost. However, if you are creating it in New York city versus Iowa, where the cost of living is much lower, you may find it more expensive to make closer to home.

6. They are professional negotiators. Let's face it, there is a lot of persuasion involved in a successful supplier diversity business strategy. Why not have trained professionals assisting in that? Bring the SCP on the team and you get the negotiating skills as a bonus. Understand, negotiation is not about having your way with your "opponent." Negotiation involves research, understanding both sides of an issue, and then being able to gain

consensus to what you think is a fair and equitable resolution. Regardless of how much of this you think you need for a successful business strategy (spoiler alert: it's all of it), there is much more to be gained from a good SCP than an upcoming bid list.

THE STATE OF THE SUPPLY CHAIN

The thing about supply chain is that they have a lot in common with supplier diversity. For one thing, they are trying to convince their colleagues to do things that they don't always want to do. They are often trying to get more support than they have received. And they deal with a lot of "exceptions" to whatever the policy is. In fact, the farther up the food chain you go in a company, the more exceptions to the rules supply chain often finds.

It wasn't too many years ago that supply chain didn't get a lot of respect within companies. When I started my career, you couldn't go to school for it. It was often where people ended up when a company couldn't find another place for them, but couldn't or didn't want to fire them. Then they were seen as the people who drove the cost of goods down. They weren't considered very strategic but rather negotiated the cost of something within an inch of its life. It took longer for supply chain to be recognized as a strategic part of the business, a group that could affect far more than the unit price of something. That has changed over the past 15 to 20 years, but supply chain people tend to carry the memory of it. It's not even a memory because people who weren't in the field back in the day know it, so it is more a lackluster part of the legacy of the career that has been carried forward.

Most companies begin building their supply chain in the direct area, or the products or services the company sells. That is often manufacturing, or OEMs (original equipment manufacturers). These days, that requires a lot of interaction on a global basis since so much is made outside the U.S. and Canada. But most companies also spend about as much on indirect spend, or the things they don't

make or sell. The infrastructure, which can be anything from physical buildings to technology, office equipment, software, employee
needs, health benefits, consulting services, and on and on needs to
be purchased strategically as well.

We talked earlier about should cost, but it's more than that.
When looking at what something costs, one must look beyond the
item itself. How much does it cost the company for the department
to order it? How much is transportation to ship it to your location?
What are the labor and equipment costs to unload, inventory, store,
and then move it? How long do you have to keep the item, or carry
the cost of it, before it gets utilized? How are things maintained?
How about repaired if they become broken? How do you safely and
legally dispose of it when you are done using it? All of this and much
more goes into what we call supply chain, or the chain of events and
costs that are the life of an item from when it is desired until it is
paid for and finally used or out the door.

There are a lot of terms used in the supply chain field. Purchasing, procurement, sourcing, strategic sourcing—and a lot of folks
who will give you different definitions for each of them. Purchasing
is transactional, procurement is ordering and paying for something,
to-may-to, to-mah-to. Not all of my colleagues will appreciate my
take on it, but it all boils down to the same thing. As a supply chain
professional, my job is to help my internal clients make informed
choices. That means that I look at the entire supply chain and where
the cost, improvements, and risks exist. I then provide options for
my internal clients to select from. Call it what you will, it's some
piece/part or all of that process. For the purposes of my discussion
here, I refer to it as supply chain and it consists of all of it.

UNDERSTANDING SUPPLY CHAIN STRUCTURES

Supply chain teams are not all put together the same. Some are
structured by spend category. For example, you may have people

who are responsible for fleet and fuel. That could be semi-trucks you buy or lease to transport goods to cars for salespeople to drive to fuel cards to buy gas for their vehicles to bulk gas units that are installed at branch locations. Another member of the team might be responsible for travel, meetings, and events. They have the airline contracts, hotels, meeting venues, trade show materials, rental and for-hire cars, limo service, and planes if the company has their own (or the planes might belong to the person who has fleet). The categories are typically broken up so that similar skills can be optimized, similar supplier bases optimized, and that align with the skills of the people internally buying various goods and services.

Another approach is to structure the group by the internal groups they service. Those people may or may not be co-located with those groups they service. For example, you may have the person who does technology sit with the technology group. The person who handles advertising, media, and customer demographic materials sit with the marketing group. Whether co-located or not, the larger business units have the same folks who take care of them. This lets them develop a relationship and hopefully a trust factor that will make the supply chain process easier.

Groups may also be split into the pieces/parts of the supply chain process. One group handles the spend analytics, one takes care of contract negotiations, another the project implementation. Others have a cradle to grave ownership of a given category or section of the business.

I have worked on teams that had fewer than 20 and others that had closer to 1,000. I have been in groups that owned the category from A to Z and others where there were specialists for each piece of the supply chain. Each one has its pros and cons. It depends on what the business is, how much is involved, and often how regulated the industry is. I've worked in telecommunications, pharmaceutical, and banking, all of which have their own regulators and processes that go along with them. They tend to have larger teams because there are steps that cannot be skipped. I've also worked in retail and technology, where there was a lot more open to the business owner to determine. They tended to run leaner, but it's different from company to company. The bottom line is that there isn't a silver bullet for everyone. The key is to understand what your company is doing, whether you are supply chain, supplier diversity, or anyone else in our cast of characters. The better you understand it, the more successful you will be with your piece of the supplier diversity business strategy.

THE REALITY OF THE SUPPLY CHAIN SPEND

All of that said, here is something you won't find in the supply chain brochure. They almost always do not buy everything. Supply chain people don't really enjoy talking about that, but it's true. Sometimes, it's because whole sections of spend are handled elsewhere. It is mostly on the indirect side. Sometimes the technology group buys all of their own stuff or part of it. They feel they have the best handle on what is needed and it is too complex for a supply chain person to grasp and stay up on, so they handle it themselves. Sometimes the marketing group does their own stuff. They are about the revenue of the company, so everything they do has a due date of yesterday and it is complex, so they need to own it themselves. Very often, HR does their own stuff. Their stuff involves personal data and they can't afford to have someone outside of their department possibly getting any of that data. Hiring practices, salaries, and layoffs, are all just too important to let out of the department. Then there are health benefits, prescription plans, various types of insurances (life, short-term disability, long-term disability, pet, etc.) that are just too complex for most supply chain folks (this is HR talking, by the way, not me). They will often let recruiting companies or temp agencies into supply chain, but that's it. Then there are departments like legal, treasury, mergers and acquisitions, board of directors, etc. They just plain don't have to go through supply chain very often, so no thank you.

Of all of the things supply chain does purchase, they aren't always involved every step of the way. Most of the time, once supply chain has a contract in place for something, they keep it. But sometimes, a business unit will bring a proposed contract to supply chain for something they have already selected and just want the contract done. Sometimes, the business unit has talked to a number of potential suppliers and gotten down to two or three and want supply chain to help them select and contract with the final company. On other occasions, the business unit may ask supply chain to conduct a bid for them, but they have the list of potential companies and don't want to look at any others. In short, there are a lot of things that supply chain is involved in at various points throughout the process. The later they become involved, the more difficult it will be for them to include the supplier diversity business strategy. If you think all you need is supply chain to access the company's entire spend, it just isn't so.

The earlier supply chain is involved, the more they can impact the total cost of a good or service. While it may seem illogical to many to not have supply chain at the table, impacting the total cost isn't always the company's objective. When Hurricane Katrina hit, no one was bidding fuel, bottled water, plywood, excavators, etc. If you hadn't already made provisions for your provisions as part of your business continuity plan, you paid whatever folks wanted for what you absolutely had to have.

There are also times when only one solution will do. When I worked clinical trials in pharma, you sometimes wanted a specific doctor to review trial results because they were the preeminent thought leader in pediatric diabetes ... or whatever the topic was. You get the idea.

It's also not just about cost, despite what the majority may think. Just as important are solutions that reduce labor (automation), make things easier (intuitive processes), respond faster (increased customer satisfaction), or otherwise make the world a better place (sustainable, eco-friendly, make customers—internal and/or external—happier). Supply chain *does* contribute to all of those, so they are still needed, but it can blur the objectives for the internal clients from time to time.

The SCP must be able to take clients through the process and identify the requirements that are most important, put together a bid process, put together an evaluation process, combine the results, coordinate the short list, negotiate the agreement, help coordinate the implementation plan, and manage the ongoing results and relationship. Whether that is SCP of one or of many, they are still responsible for it.

But there is another skill the SCP is responsible for, one that puts them squarely in the sights of the SDP. A good SCP knows all of the suppliers who are good prospects and figures out who should compete in the bid process. That is the sourcing part of supply chain and that is the part to which the SDP wants a golden ticket.

Sourcing is one of those pieces of the pie that sounds simple enough but can get complex in a hurry. Opinions vary as to the best way to approach this portion of the process. Years ago, supply chains would limit the number of companies that could compete. This was due mostly to the amount of work that was being done manually behind the scenes to compile and compare the participants. That argument doesn't really hold water now that most of the process has been automated, but you will still find resistance to having a lot of suppliers in a bid.

You may have heard companies talk about how they need to have three bids before buying. I'm not sure where the magic number three came from, but that has pretty much gone the way of the dodo bird. The right number depends upon what is being bid, how many players there are in the space, and what differentiators those players have. For example, if you are bidding utilities in a certain geographic region, there may not be any DBOs. If you are bidding temporary staffing, there are more suppliers than apps for an iPhone and about 45% to 65% of them will be DBOs depending upon the area of expertise and the geographic footprint.

I bring all of this up because getting a reasonable number of DBOs on the bid list often means adding to the total number of suppliers bidding on a project. If you understand what your company's bid process is, you will understand how much work you are (or are not) adding to the supply chain group by adding suppliers to the bid list.

Elephant Alert! Just as women are no longer accepting that to have a single position on a board of directors is a best practice, so having one DBO is not sufficient where they make up a higher percentage of available companies or a higher percentage of the demographics your company sells to. If an SCP tells you they will require a DBO on every bid that goes out the door, push back! You want DBOs in everything, not just the formal bids. You want a representation of the demographic in the bids. In the U.S., the Census Bureau has tons of data on company and industry demographics. Partner that up with your third-party reporting and find out what the possibilities are. Tokenism is so 1880s, people. Be better than that.

THE PRESSURE TO SPEND *AND* SAVE

Supply chain professionals are paid on a number of objectives, but the one that you hear about most, and that tends to rate the highest, is *savings*. If one cannot find ways to reduce the cost of goods and services, one won't last long in the profession.

Like the terms for supply chain, there are a lot of different types and definitions of savings. The most common is cost savings. Last year, I bought it for $3 and this year I am buying it for $2. That is a cost savings of $1 for each "it" purchased. This works okay if you are buying the same "it" year-in, year-out. But "its" tend to change over time. Last year, you were buying the millennium model. Now you are buying the plutonium model. It does more, has more storage, makes coffee, helps the kids with their homework, etc. Can you really compare those two? Cost savings work well for the first couple of times through a category. Then you begin to run into things like labor cost (that never goes down) or an increase in raw materials. You cannot expect the price of something to go down year over year forever and maintain the quality of whatever "it" is. Yet, it is the most popular of the savings because it goes directly to the bottom line and is easy to understand and calculate.

Enter benchmark or market pricing. I found myself at one point having a discussion with the C-suite on why temp labor costs were increasing. We had bid the project and put in a hybrid VMS (Vendor Management System) two years prior. It had saved the company over 40% or about $7 million on an $18 million spend. We also tracked satisfaction with the candidates and we had bumped that from about 50% to the high 80%. Now, two years later, costs were creeping up and stats were in the high 70% range. What was wrong, they wanted to know? What were my team and I no longer doing?

Well, we had three issues that needed to be addressed.

First, when we implemented the original program, the team wanted to requisition staffing based upon the hourly rate they wanted to pay. There were situations where we couldn't pay higher than X and there was no point in falling in love with a candidate who would not accept the pay rate we had in our budget. The problem was, despite the company payroll increasing 6% on average over the past 24 months, despite the cost of living having gone up about 7% over the same time period, data showed we were still requesting the same rates we asked for two years earlier.

That led us to the second issue, the quality of candidates. If you want to pay rates for two years prior, you are likely going to get candidates who are not at the top of their game. In fact, the recruiting firms wouldn't even send you the top candidates for consideration. If I am a temp agency and I can bill Susie out at $40 an hour, why would I send her resume for your $37-an-hour position? We were no longer seeing the prime candidates because we were paying bargain basement prices.

Lastly, when we had implemented the program, the economy had been in a downward trend. Over the past two years, unemployment had dropped and the economy was now in a strong recovery. Translation: it was a lot easier for the best candidates to get placed than it had been two years ago.

As you might expect, none of that made anyone in the room any happier. What to do? I suggested we move to a negotiated mark-up rather than a flat rate. This let our program remain competitive with changing economics and unemployment. We could benchmark our mark-up rates (and pay rates for that matter) against the market instead of the market two years ago. If we were beating the market and we were happy with our candidates, we were at the top of our game. That also gave us data to have discussions on those projects where we had a rate ceiling.

This meant that the temp agencies had to share what *they* were making on the person. Not popular with the suppliers in the first years, but now they have come to expect it. Let's face it, if you have a choice between someone making $70 an hour with a $30 mark up or a $30-an-hour person with a $70 mark-up, who do *you* think you will like the best? That is the gist of benchmark or market pricing. I have used it on everything from hotel rates to fuel prices to cloud capacity. It's a tougher sell, but if you've got the data, you will find your pricing competitive and your results (and client satisfaction) top shelf.

Another way SCPs get paid is by contributing to streamlined and/or automated processes. These measures tend to find their way into goals and objectives when business process outsourcing (BPO) is on the radar, but it pays in a lot of ways. If you can reduce the amount of time it takes something to happen, reduce the cost of the processing to generate same, or improve the process so it shifts from most abhorred to practically okay, that is goodness. This can be anything from consolidated invoicing on high transaction items (processing one monthly invoice instead of 3,000 individual invoices) to reducing the approval process for travel from three business days to four hours; from eliminating the cost of issuing checks by going to automated or purchasing card (p-card) payment; to allowing end users to issue purchase orders for items supply chain hasn't sourced yet (they keep the business running and you get the data), all of that reduces the overall "cost" of the good or service. Some of that can be put into dollars and cents. Another is the number of checks, transactions, etc., and still more is subjective. If SCPs are getting recognized for providing goodness in this fashion, they will make it happen.

This can be good news for SDPs. Often, you will find DBOs more willing to work with you on processes versus the behemoth who wants to fit your square peg needs in their round hole processes. DBOs have shown themselves to be more nimble and flexible in various processes that can make a difference to the supply chain and the company as a whole.

Supply chain also gets rid of hidden costs. This can be anything from administrative fees to costs that go down or are eliminated once certain milestones are met. For example, in 2019, social security taxes are paid on the first $132,900 paid by a company. After that, the tax stops. One pharma company I worked with had clinical trials contractors who were working for the duration of the trial, typically 12 to 24 months. When their earnings met the social security maximum, my rate did not decrease. That meant the contracting company was pocketing the difference as an increase in mark-up. That was over $10,000 per contractor each year.

Finally, there is one way that supply chain gets paid that can be the bane of the SDPs existence. That is in making reductions to the supply base.

On the surface, it makes sense: if one buys office supplies from seven different places, they are likely paying too much across the board. However, if they can combine what is being purchased into a single list and bid it out to multiple suppliers, they will likely reduce the overall cost of office supplies. In addition to the unit cost of say, copy paper going down, they are only processing one invoice and one check at the end of the month instead of seven. If they can do that multiple times across everything that is purchased, the savings will quickly add up.

There is also something to be said for trying to manage a supplier list of 500 suppliers instead of say, 35,000 suppliers. This process has a definite place in the SCPs toolbox, no denying. And there are plenty of categories where dealing with one company versus several can lower price while increasing things like safety, processing, and satisfaction.

This process of reducing the supply base often comes into direct conflict with SDPs who are trying to get as many diverse and small businesses into the supply chain as possible (see how the SDP gets paid in the previous chapter). Like all of the other tools in your toolbox, reducing the number of suppliers doesn't work in every single scenario.

A couple of cases in point:

> First, getting to one supplier can sometimes provide a risk to your supply chain. If something happens to that supplier, you could find yourself in a holding pattern until said supplier gets back online or you figure out what Plan B looks like. Having a second can be a Plan B and keep things afloat while you sort out whatever is happening.

> Second, there are times when having a choice can be a good thing. Several years ago, I found my category manager for MRO (maintenance, repair, and operations) was spending a lot of time mediating issues with MRO and how much

inventory was the right amount of inventory. Our MRO program called for providing the shelving and keeping the shelves stocked. This can be a very personal item for the repair crews. We found that the satisfaction rate across our 1,000-plus locations had a lot to do with their local provider—the relationship with their account representative and their inventory person.

We went to bid and stated up front that at least two companies would win a contract. Each of the winners could have up to 100% of the business if they could sell it. They would be provided with the contact information for each location. The location would make the decision on who they went with. We added provisions for a location leaving a supplier if certain KPIs (key performance indicators) and/or service elements were not met. Customers got a choice and the companies stayed competitive on the bazillion MRO parts that you can't bid one at a time. And the category manager? She had enough time to take on an additional category when we eliminated the bickering.

The last and hopefully most prevalent of ways SCPs get paid is through the total cost of ownership (TCO). TCO recognizes that there are more things involved in cost than the unit price of a widget. Those process improvements, automation, outsourcing, delivery, disposal, recycling, sustainability, customer satisfaction, and a whole host of other things all factor into the overall cost of something. The best and brightest SCPs are always looking to reduce the TCO, not just the item they are buying. Acknowledging this in how SCPs are compensated can give companies a differentiator, an edge in their market space and over their competition by being better, faster, more competitive. Reducing TCO can have a significant impact on the bottom line, and everyone can get behind that. The good news is that DBOs are usually smarter than the average bear about TCO.

THE PRESSURES PLACED ON THE SUPPLY CHAIN

SCPs face a number of challenges in their line of work. Here are five of them:

1. **Conflicting objectives.** We have talked about this before, but it's worth some additional space. If the supply chain group's goals and objectives are done in a silo, if they aren't tied to those of the rest of the company, they will often be in conflict with their colleagues. Supplier diversity is one of the first who are often impacted by this. If SCPs are being paid to reduce the supplier base, to speed the sourcing process, to satisfy internal clients at the cost of good sourcing practices, the supplier diversity business strategy will suffer. But that is just one place where that can happen. If a TCO approach isn't taken, or if the supply chain is given a single target, such as reduce cost by X%, there won't be as much time spent understanding the end users' requirements, or taking the time to automate where opportunity exists.

    If objectives are aligned, then everyone is working together for a successful outcome. If supply chain isn't part of that, they are often on the outside looking in trying to make an impact on their own. That almost never works out for anyone.

2. **A seat at the table.** Talk to an SCP for more than ten minutes about how they could do a better job, and this will come up. In order to leverage all of the SCPs skills, they need to be involved as early as possible in the project at hand. Being on hand early means they understand the requirements of what the end users are looking for. It means they are part of discussions and so can help to identify areas where automation, streamlined processes, technology challenges, and other things might occur. It also means that the potential suppliers recognize they need to negotiate in earnest with the SCPs because they are a key part of the decision-making process.

Once in my career, I had joined a company who was looking to centralize their sourcing efforts. The company spent a lot on promotional products and apparel, so we decided to bid it out. I met with the top 20 incumbents (out of the 200 or so we were spending money with) and explained what we were doing and that, as an incumbent, they would be invited to participate. One company representative sat quietly and listened, smiling and nodding. At the end of my presentation, I asked for questions and comments.

The representative, an owner of the company, said "Thank you but we will not be participating in a bid process. I appreciate what you are trying to do, but I'm not sure you appreciate how many of you I have seen come and go over the past 20 years. Every year, I have done more business with your company than I have done the year before. I don't expect that to change."

I thanked him for his time and wished him well. We met in September, and the following January he rang me up to tell me that, as expected, his sales with my company for the year just ended had surpassed all previous years. Again, I wished him well. We went to bid in February. By April, we had selected a new company. By May, we had shut down the vendor accounts for all of the incumbents. The following January I called him.

Now, if he hadn't been such a tool the previous year, I would have taken the high road. Because we were at the table at the outset, we knew what type of solution we needed to put into place. We heard our internal customer's concerns for the incumbents and did our best to offer them an opportunity that would include all of the business. We also had better buy-in from our end users because we had worked together through the entire process, not just at the end or at some point along the way.

Nothing can replace being at the table early in the process when it comes to driving success. If supply chain isn't there, the company is leaving money on the table. Yet, supply chain is one of those things that a lot of people don't see as being all that tough to do. We have all negotiated the price of our new car, or a house or with some service provider in our everyday lives. A lot of people seriously think they have it covered.

3. **Rogue spending.** Rogue spending is the ill-behaved cousin of a seat at the table. Rogue spending is deliberate. For whatever reason, people spend time and resources to skirt the supply chain processes to spend the company's money the way *they* want to spend it.

The most obvious abuser is someone who wants to keep a supplier they have because they know them or are related to them or worse. Throughout my career, I have had to deal with siblings, in-laws, mistresses, children, and best friends of my end users. This happens most when you are centralizing or doing a spend analysis for the first time.

Other reasons may be that they don't like change ("But Roy knows what we need, I don't want to deal with anyone else."). Or they had a bad experience with the supplier supply chain has awarded it to, they think buying local is more important, or they are buying from a customer and don't want to make them mad.

There are a lot of reasons out there and each one can shave spend dollars off from the total being negotiated by supply chain. Supply chain teams spend hours on compliance—how to enforce it, how to change it if it isn't happening, how to keep an internal client relationship positive when the client keeps doing it.

4. **Too much with too little.** While it may sound like supply chain spends a lot of time trying to drum up business, there is another side of the coin. Many groups find themselves stretched beyond the limits of mere mortals in what they can actually do. Whether trying to work through a centralization project that

has worked far too well, or just being grossly understaffed, having the resources to respond is an ongoing challenge for the SCP.

There is nothing worse than having some sort of edict go out that everyone has to go through supply chain and it turns out to be far more than anticipated. Then supply chain begins to slow down the business because they can't respond fast enough. It's been the kiss of death to more than one supply chain strategy.

5. **The exceptions.** No sooner is supply chain brought in than exceptions begin to be negotiated throughout the business. Here are a few of the more popular exceptions carved out from supply chain:

   A. Our stuff is too technical. This is a favorite in the technology areas. They can't articulate their requirements because they are just too technical for supply chain people to understand and be able to successfully source.

   B. We can't be slowed down. Sales and marketing likes this one. Everything they are doing has a due date of a week ago. They can't possibly stop the revenue flow for a bidding or contract process.

   C. Our stuff is highly confidential. Human Resources and legal are top exceptions for this reason. Hiring and firing, litigation, no one needs to know about this stuff. Mind you, that isn't needed to participate in the selection of a new HR system, but you get the idea.

   D. It's too complex to bid it out. There are just too many moving parts. However it is seen as being over the head of the SCP, at the end of the day, it's just messing up their hair as it goes over. Fine, since I have to begin learning it sometime, put me on the team and I'll start here.

   E. There are other forces at play here. Sometimes, there really are other things going on that prevent the usual process. Since I don't want to make the list of folks who have information that makes me an insider, you may have to trust the C-suite occasionally. A former boss of mine who was in the C-suite would sometimes say something to the effect of, "I know it looks like it should be yours, but you'll just have to trust me on this one." And you know what? I did trust him. But that was because he didn't tell me that every time he couldn't figure out how to keep me out of it. He also would remind me when things did come out, that was why he couldn't bring me in. Relationships, remember?

F. I don't f-ing have to. Hey, sometimes your executives just don't want to be told what to do or see other alternatives from what they want to do.

The point is, there are as many reasons for exceptions as there are stars in the sky on a clear night in the desert. SCPs have dealt with them all at one time or another. If they are hitting a wall, chances are the supplier diversity business strategy will hit one, too. If the SCP and the SDP are working together, they can help to reduce those instances. Just sayin' ...

NAVIGATING THE SCP BLIND SPOTS

As we have said before, we all have them and supply chain is no exception. Here are a few of the blind spots that SCPs have to beware of.

1. Too much time chasing things they don't control. SCPs can get so focused on what they *don't* participate in, they don't have adequate time to spend on what they *do* participate in. I've always tended to take the approach that I have plenty of internal clients out there trying to do the right thing for the company and that is where I should focus my time and talent. I'll worry about the rest of the clients when they come on board. Not everyone has

that luxury, however. Sometimes, management looks to SCP to build a strategy to bring the stakeholders in.

One of my life's mantras is that if I can't change, control, or influence it, it gets 15 minutes. Sometimes that may stretch to an entire afternoon if I'm really steamed about it, but that's it. Pout, vent, eat a pint of ice cream, do whatever works for you, and then, and this is the important part: **Let. It. Go.** Focus your efforts on the things you can make a difference on. You will feel a lot better about how you spend your time and you'll sleep like a baby at night (you know, like the one who steamed you in the first place does). Be very frugal about how much and to whom you give access to the inside of your head. That's true even if the engagement is part of your strategy. Know when to give it a rest and concentrate on serving the stakeholders who have signed on already.

2. Providing the latest bid list to your SDP and not much more. Shame, shame on you, first off. You know how this stuff works and yet you are doing less than the bare minimum. The SDP should be looking for good suppliers for everything you buy, not just what you are buying right now. This is a professional who meets potential suppliers on a daily basis. If you are not doing everything to ensure each SDP understands what you buy, how you buy it, and when you might be buying it again, you are wasting a valuable resource to the supply chain and the company overall. Give them the long view in addition to the short one and you will be repaid many times over.

3. Thinking that only supply chain can penetrate a business unit they don't currently have access to. Just as there are many paths to your end users, there are different paths to the business units. For example, there are a number of other business units that have the same struggle as supply chain, as in getting into a project early enough. IT struggles with internal clients who love to pick out technology all the time. Legal is notoriously called

in at the eleventh hour (often because someone has to) to get a contract over the finish line. Marketing is not always aware of what people are doing to the brand throughout the company. Human Resources get brought in when something goes horribly wrong with what someone deemed a good direction to go in for training. The EH&S (Environmental, Health & Safety) group often gets overlooked on projects even though it involves operating machinery, or driving, or increasing the carbon footprint of the company by 10%. The list goes on and on. Notice how a lot of the groups I just mentioned are those often tough for supply chain to get to? Funny how that works.

The next time you have an internal client who thinks they don't need IT for their purchase because it's on the cloud so there are no IT issues or decides to switch out the washable water bottles for Styrofoam, pick up the phone or shoot an e-mail to a peer in the potentially affected group and run it by them. Even if it's perfectly okay, the recipient of your call will appreciate your thinking of them … just like you will appreciate when they return the favor.

Now, with that thought in mind, set up a meeting with your SDP to talk about who they are working within the organization. Do they work with EH&S on the annual sustainability report because it includes diversity information? Do they work with marketing because that's where their trade show materials come through? Oh, and if you don't have a relationship with the other peers I mentioned, you have some other coffee dates to set up.

This can be hard I know. We are pulled in a lot of different directions and people are no longer just down the hall. But you can have coffee with people via videoconference or phone call. It doesn't always have to be in person. It's an investment and it's as valuable as taking the time to learn the new software or reading over your benefits package prior to open enrollment.

4. Letting one part of an overall strategy drive the bus. Strategies like centralizing supply chain, or optimizing the supplier base, or supplier analytics, or new payment terms are all important undertakings that pay big dividends to companies of all sizes. They are, however, one tool in the toolbox of a successful supply chain. And just as you would never try to build a house using only a screwdriver, even if it's the best damn screwdriver ever made known to man, you don't focus on just one tool in the supply chain toolbox.

One of my favorite examples of this is reducing the supply base. Now, I completely agree that no company needs 1,000 different suppliers selling them office supplies. I also completely agree that there are some categories where having multiple suppliers is an invitation to bedlam. What I do *not* agree with is that every category has to be all or nothing. This is especially true on the indirect side.

In one of my former lives, I had responsibility for about 1,200 locations across a wide geographic footprint. My team provided a lot of services to each location and we were working our way through the list to bid them and implement consistent service and pricing for each. When it comes to services provided at that many locations, the experience depends a lot on the individual servicing each branch. You can ask ten branches about their UPS or FedEx people and you will get ten different answers. The people in the branch don't judge UPS on what's in the contract, they judge them on their UPS guy or gal. The other services are much the same. At this company, we also factored in customer (the end user was my customer in this case) satisfaction with services. As you might expect, the ratings were all over the map and we leveled out at some median.

So, we did an experiment. The company provided company uniforms to our maintenance workers. Laundry service was also part of the service. Something as personal as the clothes you put on your back comes with a lot of opinions. We took it out to bid and stated outright that at least two and no more than three companies would be awarded the business. Each company could have all or none or any amount of business in between. It would be up to each branch to decide who they wanted. To the branch, we said they could talk to all or their favorite, but they could not hire anyone not on the list. We had the same KPIs and the same terms under which a branch could switch suppliers. We ended up with three suppliers. Our pricing stayed competitive and service satisfaction went through the roof. Part of that was because the branches felt like they had more control over their own destiny. But, part of it was also that the suppliers knew that our Plan B was already on board. Switching away from a company was far easier for us than it had been. By the way, we also ended up with two DBOs. This doesn't work for every category, but it's a tool in the toolbox.

5. Small companies are too small to service our company. If I had a dollar. Here are just a couple of my thoughts on this one. First, DBOs are not all heading up small businesses. DBOs with small businesses kick butt, win more business, and become big businesses. So, often my first question is, "What makes you think it's a small business?" Sometimes, I ask that even if it is small, just to see if they know or are just assuming.

Second, not every need of a large company is large. I may be working for a large pharmaceutical company. That company may have two locations that have a particular obsolete HVAC unit. I don't necessarily need to do business with the largest HVAC house to provide the backup motors I need for that unit.

Finally, even if the need isn't small, the biggest provider isn't always the answer. How do I know this? Because I've looked at it and a number of other companies as part of my supply chain process. That process should include DBOs, whether small or large.

6. We require a diverse-owned business be part of every bid. Gah! I know this sounds like it should be a good thing. I hear companies list this as a best practice in talks and honestly, I just throw up in my mouth a little when they do that. This rule often comes as part of a package of supply chain saying they only bid to X number of companies because it is so time consuming. I will combine the two here for brevity's sake. First, the number of diverse businesses that participate in a bid should only be determined based upon the total number of potentially vetted businesses that exist. I'm not saying all of any category should be part of the bid, but limiting it to one or two is just silly. When I bid contingent staffing, one of the first issues is how many companies to invite. The reason is that there are literally thousands of staffing companies. Off the top of my head, I would say that at least 25% to 30% of them are diverse owned. So, having a list of ten companies and one of them being diverse owned is not a very good representation. And second, if your supply chain limits the number of bids to a small number because of the time involved, your supply chain needs some new processes. I'm not saying hundreds of bids should be the norm, but there are so many ways technology can help. Technology can get past an initial long list or can help to compile and evaluate a list of potential suppliers. The time needed to vet the list should not be a key driver of how many get to bid.

FAST TRACKING THE ADOPTION OF BEST PRACTICES

The good news is that best practices are something most supply chain people are already talking about and investing in. Some may not immediately make the leap to best practices in supply chain and supplier diversity, but the gap shouldn't be a cab ride, it should be a short walk at most.

1. Sharing goals and objectives is probably the single most important thing you can do to improve the deliverables. I don't mean one line in a long list, but a real stake in the outcome. When I built my first supplier diversity strategy, everyone had the title of Strategic Sourcing and Supplier Diversity. Manager, Associate Manager, Director, etc. Followed by Strategic Sourcing and Supplier Diversity. That really made a difference to both communities. Suppliers see that on your business card and they know they are going to have to deal with it.

   I'll be honest, I did that for a couple of reasons. First, I didn't want to have to mediate discussions between supply chain and supplier diversity. If they were responsible for both, they would be more likely to figure it out (they did). Second, I wasn't entirely sure how committed my C-suite was when we started, and I didn't want to have to cut people the first quarter the company didn't make numbers. If they were also SCPs, they would be less likely to cut them (they were).

2. SDPs who understand their company's supply chain, how it works, and what they buy will do a better job at finding good potential suppliers. The more supply chain can include them, the better they will like the companies they meet. Try to get every SDP to sit in on at least one complete bid project a year of varying product and service types. I am always trying to expand the horizons and category expertise of my SCPs. It makes them source with a bigger picture mentality and it helps with retention. SCPs who feel they are learning new things will stick around. Part of that was sitting in on negotiations that were outside their everyday norm. Whether that was a more intense negotiation or one that supply chain came in on late in the game, it exposed them to a variety of situations. The same should be done for SDPs as well. The more they see, the better they understand. The better they understand, the more successfully they represent supply chain at their events.

3. Refresh the potential bid list. I often am told that there are no diverse-owned companies in the space. Sometimes that is true, but not nearly as often as I hear it. I will often counter by asking when was the last time supply chain (or supplier diversity) looked for a supplier in the space? I pride myself in coming up with excellent diverse-owned businesses in nontraditional spaces, so be sure you have done your homework before you tell me there isn't anyone available.

Here are a few examples:

The Heico Companies, LLC: https://www.heicocompanies.com Heico has a group of companies in manufacturing and distribution of engineered components (electronics and sensors, cargo control, motion and flow control, testing and measurement, etc.), construction and industrial services (commercial concrete construction, steel industry services, commercial electrical construction, heavy industrial construction, etc.), specialty equipment (tools, material handling, forestry, transcription, etc.), and steel products (long steel products, fasteners, structural steel fabrications, wire products, etc.). They are a company of over 9,000 employees run by Chairman Emily Heisley Stoeckel, a dynamo. Yep, all WBE certified and not small in size, ideas, or service.

Hovair Systems, Inc.: https://www.hovair.com/ Hovair is a manufacturing company that produces air-bearing systems and material-handling equipment capable of moving everything from your latest stock shipment to an airplane, all on a cushion of air. That also means no grease or fossil fuels, so it's good for clean room environments and sustainability goals. Based in Kent, Washington, it is a NMSDC-certified MBE owned and operated by Ron Benman.

Havens & Company, Inc.: http://www.havensandcompany.com Havens is a Women Business Enterprise National Council (WBENC)-certified WBE that provides companies with life, disability, accidental, vision, dental, and voluntary benefits. President and Owner Laura Havens Hall founded the company in 2007. She has a B.S.B.A. From Xavier University, a J.D. From the University of Dayton School of Law, a Masters of Law in Taxation with an Employee Benefits Law Certificate from Georgetown University Law Center. She also runs a successful company.

ARI Fleet Management Company: https://www.arifleet.com ARI is one of the leading fleet management services company. They are part of Holman Enterprises. They manage 1.7 million fleet vehicles in North America, the UK, and Europe. Headed by Mindy Holman, Chairman of the Board of Holman Enterprises, this company delivers best-in-class products and services at the best value. This is no small business and they walk the walk with their own supplier diversity business strategy in their supply chain.

4. For many companies, their tier 2 program drives a lot of their diversity spend. Tier 2 lets suppliers know you are serious about supplier diversity and they need to get serious about it, too. It is a big undertaking asking for, receiving, and keeping track of tier 2 reporting from the supply base. A couple of best practices I have found are to include the language in your contracts even before you kick the program off. You don't want to have to go back and try to amend programs. Put it in now. I did that at my last corporate job and, immediately, companies began pulling it out during the redline process. If they didn't have a supplier diversity business strategy, they thought it should be removed. "Nope," I responded. "You have to report in every quarter that you have nothing." There is a big difference in pulling it out once, never to be discussed again and having to turn in a report four times a year with a big fat zero on it. It also went on everyone's scorecard, too.

Speaking of scorecards, companies that did have tier 2 reporting were asked to include a couple of their DBOs in their scorecard meetings. It didn't have to be for the entire meeting and the DBO didn't have to fly in, they could do it by video conference, but I wanted to meet them and hear about what they were doing. I also wanted different companies over time, not the same DBO over and over again.

5. Let DBOs tell you they aren't ready to get business instead of you telling them. This goes back to the issue of how many people can bid. In many, many bids I included a company that I didn't think would earn the business, but who could benefit from going through the full bid process. As a business owner, you believe there is nothing your company cannot do, so it stings when some SCP tells you your company won't be invited to bid because your company isn't big enough, high tech enough, whatever else enough. Sometimes, the best development opportunity is to let that company go through the process. Many times, they will come back and tell you they weren't ready. Sometimes they are right and you get to see that. Win-win.

6. We already talked about offering choices to the end user and opportunities for DBOs, but it bears repeating and I think it is a best practice. One company I worked for did a lot of acquisitions. At one point, we bought our next largest competitor. They were almost as big as we were and their strategy had been to go with a single provider. I was a little nervous. I had done four different programs with the choices. What if our pricing was not as competitive as the acquisition was getting? I'd have a lot of explaining to do. But the strategy was sound. In every instance our pricing was more competitive, and it wasn't just a 12% or 20% difference in total spend dollars. The results didn't just provide relief. The results also provided support for the next program we did that way.

7. Road trip. Whether your SCPs have supplier diversity as part of their goals and objectives or not, get them to at least one supplier diversity event each year. Not only will they have the opportunity to meet potential suppliers, they can see what the SDPs are doing and then the two groups can determine how best to get the company's monies worth at each of the events.

The C-Suite: If your supply chain does not buy everything for your company, then sending your SDPs to supply chain is only part of the answer. It is not uncommon for there to be plenty of indirect spending that happens outside of supply chain. Be sure your supplier diversity strategy is allowed to cover all of the dollars being spent.

The Supplier Diversity Professional (SDP): SDPs, be sure you meet with supply chain as an equal. Regardless of what the reporting structure is in your company, this business strategy contributes to the bottom line as much as any strategy does. Take your story and reporting into all of your internal meetings.

The Supply Chain Professional (SCP): SCPs, you do not have to choose between good supply chain practices and good supplier diversity practices. The fact is, you need the DBOs at least as much as they need you if your supply chain strategy is going to be successful. This is a rich source of potential suppliers, mine it like you would a good data set. If you don't like what you are getting, sit down with your SDP and talk about why that is, the same as you would a sourcing manager.

The Diverse Business Owner (DBO): DBOs, give the benefit of the doubt. In my last corporate gig in supply chain, it was typical for me each day to receive over

50 phone calls, over 100 e-mails, attend four to eight meetings, and somewhere in there get my job done. After a diversity event I regularly came home with a couple hundred business cards and received a follow-up from most of them. Don't assume SCPs are being rude, don't care, etc. I had a DBO chew me out on the phone once for cancelling two calls that had been set up. What they didn't know was that I had a parent in hospice. Most of the time, it really isn't about you.

 The End User: End users, you have to live with the solution that comes out of the supply chain process, so you have more stake in this than anyone else. Be sure you are seeing all of the available options. That includes the one you fall in love with first, but also the other choices. Yes, some of us married our high school sweetheart and lived happily ever after, but most of us kissed a few frogs and the first option wasn't the love of our lives. And so it goes with business solutions. Your SCPs and SDPs are there to ensure you see all of the viable choices. Let them do that voodoo that they do so well.

CHAPTER 8

CHARACTER:
DIVERSE BUSINESS OWNER

The diverse business owner (DBO) comes from many, many backgrounds. Few are the traditional story we often hear when getting the background of a C-suite individual at a large company. Good schools, extracurricular activities, college education, travel, and advanced education, these are not always part of their stories. If they are, it is usually due to someone in their life making large sacrifices. In my case, I had to go to work out of high school. College came later at night while I worked. Almost all will tell you there was a gnawing need to do something more, something different, something that mattered. Regardless of the back story, DBOs bring a lot to the table.

1. Work ethic. DBOs are used to doing it for themselves. Early on, they don't have staff or people to do things. Later on, they know there are more important things their staff or people can be doing. They don't punch out at 5 p.m.

   Entrepreneur Al Bullock is the owner of Kayla Creative, an integrated marketing and design company that supports all things image related from brand development through graphic design and production, including trade show and exhibit support. Al talks about being there for customers 24/7/365. "A vendor has business hours, a partner is *always* available."[32] DBOs are partners.

2. A storied education. DBOs come with all sorts of educational backgrounds, from high school dropout to the local trade school to Harvard and Oxford. They also usually have some other type of education. Whether it is working through tough times or dealing with racism, abuse, or feeling like an outsider. Whatever the extra ingredient, it gives DBOs something that other business owners don't often possess and, when they use that power for good, it can be tough to beat. It may be additional insight into how people are feeling that helps them close the deal. It may be a greater sense of empathy that allows them to connect with potential clients. It may be a no-nonsense approach to what needs to be done that makes the client feel confident they are in good hands. Whatever "it" is, the DBO knows how to put the skill to work.

3. A better BS-o-meter. DBOs are usually the first in the room to pick out the BS. One of my former CEOs used to ask if something passed the sniff test. DBOs have a powerful sniff tester. Maybe that is because they have had to listen to more insincere BS than most. Whatever it is, their instincts are spot on and DBOs tend to listen to those instincts rather than doubt or ignore them. That can come in handy when they are listening to things related to your project.

4. They know how to prioritize. DBOs know a lot about having to do a lot with a little. They know how to set up a plan that can be executed within an inch of its life. DBOs don't have a lot of time to waste. If you contribute, they are committed. If you are just talking a good game, they will move on quickly.

---

[32] Ibid.

5. DBOs will bottom line it for you. They are accustomed to people trying to dress things up for them, especially before they are told no. They can be depended upon to give you the straight goods. If you want to get told what will make you feel good instead of the real scoop, the DBO is probably not for you.

6. DBOs are creative. They have to be. They have to differentiate themselves from companies that are often larger and have bigger budgets. As a result, they will often come up with the better mousetrap, the new idea, or a different approach. As the old Avis ad used to say, they try harder because they aren't number one. The large companies often come in telling you, the customer, how you can fit your square needs into their round hole of a solution. DBOs will tailor a solution for you. They will file the edges off their solution instead of expecting you to do it to your problem.

7. DBOs are fearless. A large company will protect their solution, their "that's the way we've always done it" approach to business problems. A DBO will throw the template out the window and have a conversation about what needs to happen. Part of that is because they don't have as much infrastructure, so they aren't so set in their ways. Part of it is that you are dealing with the owner of the company or close to the owner of the company and they are risk takers, they are comfortable putting some extra skin in the game. Part of it is they can make alterations and change directions faster. If the big corporation is the Titanic trying to change direction in the ocean, a DBO is a speedboat bouncing across the waves and moving in whatever direction works best.

Regardless of what the differentiator is for the DBO you are talking to, you can be sure there will be one. Some people, especially supply chain professionals (SCPs) can sometimes mistake this for thinking they aren't focused on what they do. There is a certain level of comfort when people stroll in with all of the answers and the SCPs just have to follow the chevrons on their

PowerPoint. But don't be fooled, DBOs are smart, insightful, and know more about your business than you may give them credit for. Take the time and have the conversation. You won't be disappointed.

CONSIDERING THE DBO'S POINT OF VIEW

There isn't much the DBO hasn't seen or heard by the time they meet with you. They know all about the companies that have supplier diversity programs (notice I didn't say strategy) where the needle hasn't moved on their spend in ... well ... ever. They have attended more matchmaking events than a serial dater. They have sat through more how to do business with ... sessions than a high school teacher through graduations. It can be hard, at times, to do it all gracefully. They especially rankle when the keynote tells them they will have to earn the business or to be professional when meeting with potential customers. This from someone whose answer to getting more business ends at registering on the company portal (I'll rant more on portals later).

You see, DBOs don't have a lot of time to waste. They have a business to run and they are wearing many, many hats. They understand busy, because they are. So, when corporate people tell them how busy they are, they smile and give a little bit of an eye roll on the inside.

What DBOs don't always understand is what is going on within the corporate offices. How they can demand a bid be completed in 48 hours and then sit on it for six months. How they can be asked to have specific insurance amounts before the business is awarded. How they can require everyone to fly in for a pre-bid conference even though that is a $5,000 trip that doesn't even guarantee a copy of the RFP.

But you won't hear much about this from DBOs because they want the business. They are constantly hustling to keep up with websites and announcements about business opportunities from companies that want to do more business with DBOs. They understand that if they can get one or two large corporate accounts it will go a long way in convincing other large corporate accounts that they are capable of doing business with them. They hear about that a lot, worries about whether or not they can do the business. Whether it is a supplier diversity professional (SDP) who is vetting them before an introduction, or a skeptical SCP who wants to be sure they have been properly vetted, or an end user who just thought they would be dealing with a bigger company.

Some DBOs came from large companies and that's good because if they haven't, they are at a disadvantage. Several of my clients have never worked in that environment and they don't always understand what is happening beyond the conference room where they have met with supplier diversity or maybe even supply chain.

I've heard that being in sales is a lot like being an actor. You have to steel yourself for a lot of no's. You hear a lot about why you aren't a fit. The actor is too pretty, not pretty enough, too blond, too midwestern, too tough looking, not rugged. DBOs hear a lot of that as well. They aren't big enough, they can't scale fast enough, IT is worried about their technology, risk is worried about their insurance, legal is worried about their indemnification capabilities, the list goes on and on. You see, it's often not enough for a DBO to check the box that they have something, they need to prove to someone that they have it. That's not a problem for things like insurance certificates when everyone is providing it. But it does grate on them when the big companies can check the box and be okay. The DBO has to prove it to someone.

All that aside, while the DBO wears a lot of hats, it is the sales hat that they are seen in most often, since that is the engine that runs their business. And DBOs know how to do sales. They do all sorts of business that has nothing to do with the color of their skin, their gender, their orientation, or their service to their country. They do all sorts of business because they are good at what they do. So, it can sometimes take them aback that, when they meet with companies that are supposedly there because they are seeking to do business with more companies that are diverse, they have to prove themselves so much more than when it's not an issue at all.

UNDERSTANDING THE DBOS UNRELENTING FINANCIAL PRESSURE

DBOs get paid like everyone else. When they sell their product or service and turn a profit, they get the benefit of that profit. It may go back into the business or may pay the electric bill at home. The biggest difference is that they are juggling the costs of building and running a business, paying the mortgage, buying things like health coverage, and paying for their daughter's soccer lessons and son's music lessons all from the same money. There is no weekly paycheck with a percentage (a small percentage it turns out) deducted for insurances and coverages. There is no expense account that covers travel expenses, the cost of training for themselves and their employees, or memberships or subscriptions to stay on top of their industry or the industry of their large customers.

DBOs likely will find it difficult to get a line of credit to ensure that payroll isn't missed while their client takes some extra time to pay their invoices. DBOs are often making up those gaps with their own personal savings or credit and that results in their credit scores often being lower than the norm because they are using a higher percentage of available credit. It's not that they don't pay the credit cards off, it's just that they don't fit into that template of what is good credit usage all of the time.

As a result, DBOs have a constant stream of decisions they have to make about how to spend the money they have (or have borrowed) and sometimes the choices are tough ones. That's not to say that larger companies don't have some of those same struggles but, let's face it, they are doing it with a regular paycheck. Imagine doing all of that and no paycheck at the end of the pay period. Now, add to the list of how to spend it the decisions DBOs are making about the business versus the soccer and music lessons for their children. DBOs are figuring out how to cover it at work and at home. Granted, if you don't make budget you might lose that regular paycheck, but this is a more day-to-day and week to week issue for DBOs.

All of that said, most DBOs wouldn't trade their situation with a regular paycheck for anything. They love building their own vision into a company. They don't mind the day-to-day risk because they are doing something bigger.

So, why do they do this? What do DBOs want? They want an opportunity to compete for your business.

A COMPLEX BUSINESS MODEL

Small business owners in general and diverse-owned business owners in particular face a number of challenges including cash flow, recruiting and retaining talent, and keeping up with technology needs. But there are challenges that are specific to working with companies' supplier diversity strategies and that is what we will concentrate on here.

Supplier diversity has its own set of requirements that you don't find elsewhere. Capability statements are needed in addition to whatever has been done in the way of brochures, website content, or other sales collateral. Opinions abound on what makes a good capability statement, so DBOs can count on lots of feedback on theirs, regardless of what they have done with it. Many DBOs have more than one capability statement and that works great if you are sending it to a prospective customer after a meeting. Like a resume, you can tailor it to the needs of the discussion or project.

Certifications are necessary for almost all of the corporate strategies. Depending upon the situation of the DBO, there can be one or many needed. Having multiple designations can be a blessing or a curse. Some companies are far more interested in multiple designation companies (shame on them) and that can give one an advantage. On the other hand, each certification comes with its own share of information, forms to be completed, and, of course, related fees to obtain and then maintain certification. DBOs should conduct their own ROI (Return on Investment) analysis to ensure that the time, effort, and dollars are worth it. Certification isn't for every DBO. If you own a bakery, it's probably not worth it. Unless you specialize in custom cakes that businesses use for their events, in which case, certification can be an additional differentiator.

Along with certifications come the associated organizational memberships and events. All the designations have multiple organizations that are designed to assist DBOs in obtaining business and business prospects. Not all organizations offer certifications, but all have some methodology of putting DBOs together with companies that have a supplier diversity business strategy. Which is better? Well, that depends upon the needs of the business. Again, it is left to the DBO to determine what they need and who has the best solution for them. Chapter 11 has a list of organizations, certifying or otherwise, that may help in that endeavor.

Years ago, DBOs struggled to find events that supported their objective of obtaining more business. Now, there are too many events to attend them all. NMSDC for example, has national events and regional events put on by each geographic chapter. Multiply that by the number of organizations that specialize in whatever designation(s) a DBO has, and it could be a full-time job just going to all of them. Galas, business trade shows, matchmaking, there are as many events as your calendar and travel budget can withstand. Many of the events also offer educational sessions where a DBO can learn about the latest changes in the law, technology on the rise, how to step up their marketing program, and many other topics of interest to a small business owner. The most important aspect of the events, however, is the unbridled access to many large companies at one time. So, how does a DBO decide? The challenge becomes determining what a DBO needs at a given point in time to move their business to the next level or to gain access to a particular business prospect.

Once the calendar has been laid out, the next challenge is in covering the event itself. Go on your own or take staff with you to divide and conquer? Booth or no booth? Attend every invitation for an offsite reception or after party or steer clear and stay with the business at hand? Schedule every minute or leave free time for serendipity to play out?

Another challenge is the matchmaking events. Most of them now allow DBOs to request meetings with companies ahead of time so they can know who one is meeting with. But which companies should they request? Someone you've already met that you can reinforce the meeting with? Someone you can't seem to get introduced to no matter how hard you try? Someone you've done a little business with but think you could do much more? And once invitations go out and you start to get a few no's, what then? Who are your Plan B invites?

How about the trade shows? Which booths are the right ones to visit? Do you stand in line for 40 minutes to meet with a popular company or cover six other companies in the same amount of time?

It may seem like it should be easy peasy with these events to get all kinds of business going but each presents their own challenges to get the most for the time, money, and resources spent. And, once the event is over, there is the time of following up after while still taking care of the backlog of work that accumulates any time a DBO takes a day to do something other than what they do every day.

So, if a DBO doesn't clamor to accept your invite or attend your RFP prep meeting or whatever else you may offer, don't take it personally and for Heaven's sake, don't think they aren't interested. There are just so many slots on their dance card and, believe me, they are dancing as fast as they can.

MANY HATS AND MANY SHADES OF BLIND SPOTS

As many hats as the DBOs wear, there are a few blind spots, too. Here are a few that can hamper their progress in leveraging their certifications to the maximum.

1. Funding for their business strategy. Building out a business and a related business strategy takes expertise, commitment, and some dollars. Whether it is the cost of a good attorney, a marketing specialist, or their own consultants, DBOs frequently try to do this stuff on the cheap. Like LASIK surgery, there are some things that shouldn't be shopped only on price, and the help they need for things like legal issues, HR policies, a sound marketing strategy, etc., are not places to skimp on quality. Just as you insist on quality materials going into the products they sell, they should likewise insist on the best strategists and advisors they can obtain.

2. Time management. While I've sung the praises of the DBO's ability to prioritize, they do tend to have a blind spot around how many hours there are in a day and how much a mere mortal can accomplish during that time. There is nothing worse than getting overcommitted and missing a deadline with a client. DBOs can overcommit themselves right into bankruptcy. Know your limits and work within them. Also, understand that every day cannot be a take-it-to-the-limit day.

3. Refilling their own cup. You cannot keep being the well from which everyone draws without it having an impact. At some point, DBOs need to refill the well. Whether that is playing golf, taking a vacation, reading a book that isn't related to their business, playing Barbies with their four-year-old for a day, or sitting on a mountaintop watching the sun rise and/or set, DBOs must invest in themselves, health wise (that's physical and mental, by the way) and otherwise.

4. Knowing how to grow. Just like all small businesses, one of the biggest killers can be success. Companies that are in a growth mode, particularly at a fast pace, are at one of the most at-risk points in the business life. I had a client recently who had a successful business. She had built a successful model, was increasing her sales and profits each year. She wanted to take it to the next level. She and I spoke about how I might help her do that. She was excited about the prospects and so was I. She was in a position to really impact her industry. I made a proposal, she signed on and wrote a check, everything looked good.

    Then we began trying to meet. A 30-minute phone conversation had five to six interruptions with things she needed to deal with. She would miss appointments we set up or would make the call or meeting but hadn't read any of the materials I'd sent to prep her for the discussion. She wanted to skip steps on some of the strategies and go right to the end stuff. It quickly became apparent that she wasn't ready for me yet. This is bad enough when a DBO has hired and paid for expertise and then can't make time for it or doesn't trust the expertise they have hired to map out the strategy. It is even worse when this happens and they are taking part in programs that a client has invited them into or is paying for. Don't ask other people to invest in you if you aren't ready to invest in yourself or take their advice under consideration. Unfortunately, the client in question left feeling like they didn't get their money's worth from me, and I felt like it had been a waste of time for both of us.

5. Tier 2 snubbing. Many companies will meet with a DBO and try to get them to meet with one of their prime businesses to become a tier 2 provider and the DBO is having none of it. I get it, to a point. Being a prime is a first choice, of course. Tier 2 can be a tenuous position to be in. You are somewhat dependent upon the tier 1 supplier to do what needs to be done to keep the business. You are less in control and DBOs like to be in control.

But I'll let you in on a little secret. Tier 2 money is just as green and spends just as well as tier 1 dollars do. I can't tell you how many tier 2 suppliers have become tier 1 suppliers either in the same or in an additional area of their business. I can't tell you how many tier 2 suppliers I have introduced to other corporate colleagues, introductions that would never have taken place if I hadn't known them through the tier 2 relationship. There is nothing second class about being a tier 2 supplier. In fact, it lets you try on various companies without having to take on the burden of being responsible for all of the relationship.

6. Bid dates are a moving target. I tell DBOs that it is a fair ask to find out when something is scheduled to be bid next, and it is. But those bid dates move … a lot. As a supply chain executive, I had control of about 40% of my project calendar at any given point in time. I begin the year with a solid plan, but then, real life has a way of taking over. Resources are moved to a new initiative within the company, the company buys another company (in some cases, they do this over and over again), an agreement that was in place is in trouble and needs to be unwound, there are all sorts of reasons why the calendar changes. It is one of the reasons some SCPs hate giving those dates out when asked. So, while it is a fair ask to find out when it's planned on being bid again, don't feel like you were lied to when that didn't happen. I once worked for a company that did two massive acquisitions back to back, before data was easy to mine, and everything I had planned ended up getting moved 18 to 24 months. There was just too much going on with integration. I know it's frustrating. It's frustrating for the SCPs, too. But it happens.

STRATEGIES FOR MAXIMIZING ROI AND VISIBILITY

As with challenges, there are many best practices that apply to running and growing a business that all business owners can implement. We will concentrate on those related to successfully leveraging a diverse-owned designation for our discussion here.

1. Be an informed consumer. DBOs often feel it is necessary to join all organizations that are supportive of supplier diversity and, if you can afford that in time and dollars, good on you. For the remainder, remember that you are the customer in the membership scenario. Whether or not you need a national membership or one in every region you sell in should be an informed buying decision, not a knee jerk reaction. Each of the organizations (including regions within a national organization) are different. When I was in corporate, I never signed on for an event I hadn't attended first. See what it's about, who attends, what type of return you think you will gain from it. Then, schedule a call with the organization and tell them you are looking for ROI. Ask what the membership includes. What kind of benefit do you get over and above being able to participate in the annual event? Ask for a list of companies that attended the previous two years.

2. Have your own business strategy. I tell clients that, if they had to pay $5,000 to participate in an RFP they would research it within an inch of its life. Yet, they will pay that much to attend a conference without more than a couple of meetings set up, casting their fate to the wind. Certification is a tool in your toolbox. If you want to get the most out of your tool, you have to take care of it and, most of all, you have to take it out of the box and use it.

3. Work the long game. Occasionally, the moon and stars align and you go to your first event and land a contract. Sometimes, the ingenue gets discovered in the soda shoppe, too. Most of the time, it takes work and building a relationship. Most of the DBOs I end up doing the most business with are not those that come in at the eleventh hour to participate in a bid project. Most of them I have gotten to know over time. I see them at events (don't

forget to factor that into your ROI, how many companies do you continue to see that you want to do business with); I hear about what they are doing. I may introduce them to my category buyer to meet with. If they end up at an event where one of my internal clients are, I may introduce them, even if it's not their category. They may check in with me every six months or so and let me know what they have been up to, a new area they are servicing now, or what they have planned for the coming year.

Any contract that was worth the effort of a bid was awarded from anywhere from two to five years. That means I could be four-and-a-half years away from bidding it again.

4. Ask for help when you need it. Those who know me will laugh when they see me giving this advice out because I am terrible at it. But when you have a specific need, ask around. People by and large want to help. If they are involved in supplier diversity, they have determined it is a core relevance for their company to want to help. If you are having difficulty getting in somewhere, or you are dying to meet Suzie and you haven't been able to make it happen and you know that I know Suzie, talk to me about it. Honestly, I'm not going to tell Suzie that you are the sun and the moon of ball bearing manufacturing if we've only had dinner at the same event table a couple of times. But I'd likely have no problem telling Suzie that I have heard good things about you and having had a couple of meals I think you would be a great cultural fit. People are much more inclined to help if you can give them a specific request. Could you provide a virtual introduction to Suzie? is a better request for me than Can you help me meet decision makers at companies I could do business with? See my comments on the easy yes under *The C-suite Plays to Win* in the C-suite chapter.

5. Don't hide your light under a bushel basket. DBOs are often wary of advertising their certification status. I get it. There are still people out there who don't see it as a plus. We all just want

to be considered for the work we do. You don't have to make that your lead-in, but it pains me to see companies go through certification and then it's not on their website or anywhere in their sales or contact collateral. Here's the thing. The people who have an issue with it will eventually have that issue anyway. There are way more people out there who love finding great companies and then finding out they are also certified. What a win! Don't hide it, be proud!

At the end of the day, certification will get you an invitation to a party you might not otherwise have been invited to. But only you will determine if you have a good time at the party once you are there.

 The C-Suite: If the last ten years in business has taught us anything, it's taught us that you don't have to be around long to take over. Ten years ago, no one had heard of Lyft, DoorDash, the Apple Watch, Instagram, WhatsApp, and the iPad. And those are just a few of the items no one knew they couldn't live without ten years ago. Still think you should only be doing business with the behemoths that have been around forever? Didn't think so. If you want a differentiator in your business, look at something everyone else in your space doesn't have already. One way to do that is to have an ever-curious supply chain.

 The Supplier Diversity Professional (SDP): SDPs, I know that you know that DBOs are your lifeblood. Did you also know your network can be their lifeblood? If you meet a DBO that impresses you, even if you don't do business with them, tell your SDP peers.

 The Supply Chain Professional (SCP): SCPs, your willingness to stay curious and invest in looking at some solutions you may not need yet is the equivalent of your company investing in training and development for you. DBOs are as much a part of that process as travel budget for conferences or membership to CIPS (Chartered Institute of Procurement and Supply) and ISM (Institute of Supply Management).

 The Diverse Business Owner (DBO): DBOs, you don't get certified because you know less, you get certified because the opportunities have been less. 'Nuff said.

 The End User: End users, the small business owner has taken on more risk and done more things than you can ever imagine. The diverse business owner (small or large) has done twice that. Never mistake small or diverse for less … on any level whatsoever.

CHAPTER 9

THE END USER

The end user is the largest population of people that you will interact with in the company. The end user is typically who supply chain meets with. They hold the budget and the purse strings, and it is that person or someone from their business unit who they designate as the point person for a project. The end users are all the people who use or who are impacted by the solution that is the project. If the company is buying a piece of software to manage the selection of their outside transportation and hauling of product, the end user is probably logistics, or maybe the technology group.

The end users include:

- Technology people who will install and maintain the software
- The people who input transportation requests
- The people who dispatch transportation requests
- The people who track and expedite transportation requests
- The people who receive and process the invoices for payment
- The people who pay the invoices and get payment to the transportation companies that performed the service
- And lots of other folks I have missed in this list.

You can't and don't necessarily need to win them all over, but if you get one or two in your corner, they are worth their weight in gold. In one company I worked for, it was the Chief Technology Officer; in another several people in the sales organization. Regardless of who they are, they provide two very important roles. They help you educate and spread the word about the business strategy and they add perspective to the approach you are selling. Hearing it from you over and over is one thing. Hearing it from someone in a different position of influence can make all the difference to a team member between knowing the company supports it and actively looking at how they, a given team member, can support it.

Elephant Alert: Do not expect to schedule an introductory meeting and come away with a convert. The kind of support I'm talking about here comes from relationships not acquaintances.

HOW TO IDENTIFY THE ELUSIVE END USER

So, who makes up this mysterious group of people? A bunch of folks. The end user is the one who pays for whatever supply chain goes out and buys. Yeah, supply chain doesn't usually have any money of their own. They are spending the money of the end user. It's whoever is paying for, using, or benefitting from whatever is purchased by the company. The true end user is the person who is actually *using* the good or service, thus the name. But for supply chain and for much of supplier diversity, it is more someone in the business unit of that end user.

1. They can be a cheerleader. The end user can bring a lot to the table that will help make your supplier diversity business strategy successful. An end user who is aware of supplier diversity and supports it can take you a long, long way. Not only can they make it easier to get diverse business owners (DBOs) to the table on a given project, they can also lend support when you have things you need to support and/or fund for the business strategy.

2. They can add relevance. Supply chain works with these end users a lot and that is one of the best reasons you want to team up with them. They have entree into a lot of the folks you may know but may not know well or even have great access to. When I worked with end users, I was looking to solve their immediate business problem but was also learning about their area of the business. When I worked on the project for salesforce automation, I learned a lot about IT and about how the sales process worked at my company. I learned it was hard to get consistent information out to all of the salesforce. That was one reason why some knew about my supplier diversity business strategy and others were telling prospective customers that we didn't do anything on it. I found that they would love to be able to provide their customers with the reporting they were being asked for, but didn't think the company had any way of getting it. So, when I decided to go after funding for third-party reporting for supplier diversity spend, I went to see my peers and colleagues in sales. I offered to provide tier 2 reporting to any customer who wanted it, no matter how many asked for it. I also offered to give them some sales collateral on what the company was doing for supplier diversity that they could share in their QBRs (Quarterly Business Reviews) with their large customers and in RFP responses where it was being requested. The sales group supported my request for budget dollars for reporting and I provided reporting to them that helped them with their customers. It also positioned supplier diversity as having a connection to revenue. It wasn't just an overhead cost or nice to do. It now had a direct line to sales and revenue.

3. They want the best solution. Sure, they may have definite ideas about what that is, but if an end user gets a whiff of a better solution, they want to see it. This can be good news to the flexible, tailor your solution, makes decisions quickly DBO that has built a better mousetrap. End users are curious, one of my all-time favorite traits.

4. They can dictate a lot more of the process than you might think. While they can't (or shouldn't be able to) alter the sourcing process itself, they can pave the way for adding companies to the bid list or taking another look at something that didn't quite make the short list. If they like something, it has a better chance of sticking around.

5. They make up a majority of a cross-functional team. Almost nothing is decided by a single individual at the corporate level anymore. I mean, the day-to-day things, sure. But when the company is on the verge of spending a chunk of money and/or picking something they are likely to be stuck with for a while, the business will invoke the cross-functional team. The cross-functional team says, hey, a lot of folks are going to be impacted by this decision. Let's be sure we get input from all of these areas before we make a decision.

Anyway, if you bring together the people using a solution and building a solution and designing a solution, you stand a much better chance of success instead of the above solution. It has pluses and minuses. On the plus side, in addition to the solution itself, you typically have better buy-in (it's harder to knock something you helped create), implementation is often faster (people understand what's coming), and you don't have those pesky slow-downs while you stop and deal with bad decisions that were made when you are much further into the project.

On the minus side, it can slow things down. Lots of people have lots of calendars and just getting everyone together can be a logistical nightmare. If you don't have a strong project manager at the helm, the group can get analysis paralysis and be unable to reach a decision. For the most part, the cross-functional team is still in wide use and that puts more people in the room who have a vested interest in the best solution.

STRENGTHENING YOUR TOLERANCE FOR CHANGE

I like that I don't like being unhappy. It makes embracing change that much easier, although that has never been a problem for me. What it *did* take me much longer than it probably should have to figure out is that I am not the norm in this affinity. Most people will put up with the known unhappy for fear the unknown might be even more unhappy (it usually isn't). That's why dozens of entire companies make nice livings helping other companies with something called change management.

Supplier diversity and supply chain are, almost by their very nature, about implementing change. As a result, they become accustomed to it.

The C-suite is all about figuring out what the next changes are that will take the company to the next level. No CEO ever got up and announced that this year, they have decided it will be a status quo year. So, by their nature they are promoting change on a pretty constant basis. DBOs are the C-suite of their companies and so they are doing the same for their company and helping customers make their changes.

And then we have the end users, around which everything revolves. End users by and large are resistant to change. They have their routine. They come in and sit at their desks they have decorated according to what they want and HR will allow. The systems they work with are not perfect, but they have mastered the work arounds and have developed the relationships they need to get the job done. I'm not saying what they do is boring, I'm just saying they have figured it out. They don't need a lot of people coming in and changing things up and screwing up the system.

This is not just a bunch of people who don't want to play ball with the game changers, there are real issues here. Change can mean a reduction in staff. It can mean there is a bunch of new stuff to learn. What if I can't learn it? Right now, I'm the expert and everyone comes to me for answers. What happens if that isn't the case? The company won't need me anymore. Training may be needed. I may be working a flexible schedule that allows me to work and care for my parents. What if I can't do that through weeks of training? There are all sorts of things at play when you begin to impact the end users. My point is that when most people see supplier diversity and supply chain coming, they aren't thinking: Whoooo hoooo! Finally, that new system we've been dying to get or a new supplier we can start over with. They are thinking: change, Change, CHANGE, **CHANGE**. The sooner you figure that out, the easier your time with the end user will be.

Most of the cast of characters have been connected in some way and almost all of them shared some similarities in how they got paid. For the end users, how they get paid most likely has nothing or almost nothing to do with how our cast members get paid … on the surface. It will be part of your job to make the connections that show how you both have skin in this game and how your supplier diversity business strategy can help you both.

If you can get the minutes of the meeting or discussion that show who provided each of the requirements or evaluation items, it will help make those connections. For example, you may have a requirement on correct invoicing that you would assume is from the person who processes incoming invoices or works any problems with two- or three-way matches. But, in fact, it may be someone in accounts payable, because they are being measured on correct payment amounts. Regardless of how similar or different your objectives, understanding at least the major users' incentives can go a long way in providing the right solution and the right DBOs to be part of the bid process.

Despite any differences, we can only hope all are working toward the best total cost of ownership and successful solution on behalf of the company. If you are at odds on this piece, your C-suite has some explaining to do. And while we have pointed out the time stretch that a bid project can have while doing the day job, the primary users will have enough at stake to make it worth their while. The recurring members are those who can be difficult from a time and calendar perspective. People in the technology, Environmental, Health & Safety (EH&S), Human Resources, legal, and shared services whose business is also servicing these same end users can get a little numb to the various projects they work on, supply chain being only one of those areas. The more you can connect them to an outcome that matters to them, the more engaged you will find them.

You may be thinking this sounds more like a concern for supply chain than the supplier diversity business strategy, and that is a fair statement. However, I submit that as a supplier diversity professional (SDP), if you are working with your supply chain professionals (SCPs), the information you will gain from these discussions will go a long way in getting the right DBOs in on the project.

Sometimes, when you are talking about a project with a DBO (or anyone for that matter), you can see they are trying to make your problem fit their solution. They want to be the answer and they have something they do very well. The more they can make whatever that thing is the answer for your company, the better it is for them. But if they are trying too hard, it just comes off as disingenuous, whether that is where their heads and hearts are or not. If you are feeling that, chances are pretty good your end users and supply chain will feel it, too. After all, you are looking at it through the lens of your company's culture, vocabulary, and way of doing business. The better the SDP is at picking those out, the happier everyone will be with the companies you do bring forward. To that end, the more you understand the incentives, even though they may not be the same as yours, and the mindset of those involved, the better your participants will be.

MEETING THE END USER WHERE THEY ARE

The challenges your end users will face in relation to the supplier diversity strategy will depend a lot on how much they know about the strategy coming in. If this is their first experience with supplier diversity, they may have concerns about the size, depth, and bench strength of a smaller company. They may not understand the vetting process that has already taken place prior to their seeing the companies that will participate. If you haven't had the opportunity to familiarize them with the strategy prior to the project, take a few minutes to give them the 30,000-foot overview. Be ready for questions that may or may not use politically correct vocabulary. Most importantly, try to give them the benefit of the doubt in the early stages. More important than that, don't accept the wrong behavior in the later stages. Just as supplier diversity is a business strategy, it is also part of the company makeup and should receive the same respect. Most people know better in this day and age than to make a comment about a woman being pregnant in the workplace or someone whose orientation doesn't match their own. I expect them to be just as closemouthed about any disrespectful thoughts they might have about supplier diversity. I am there to help them with the business strategy. My role is not to validate their belief systems or their right to their belief systems.

In addition to knowledge of the process, you will be dealing with the change management fears we have already discussed. Those concerns may be increased when thinking about a company that isn't Fortune 500 or one of the big providers in a given space. The good news is that your DBO should be familiar with those concerns and be able to address them. You may want to have that conversation as part of your vetting process.

I have seen a concern, even fear, that including supplier diversity will somehow limit the control the end user has over the project. I find that by addressing it up front in the same list with financially viable, properly insured, demonstrated expertise, references, and everything else you will be looking at is the best approach. This strategy is not an also-add or something that is handled separately. Again, the closer the SDP and the SCP work together, the more fluid the process becomes. One mentor of mine says her goal is to remove all of the asterisks associated with supplier diversity and she is spot on. The more it is part of the overall strategy, the better for your supplier diversity business strategy.

Finally, the other thing a good partnership with supply chain will provide is a trusted source for your end users to get information and answers to their questions. If you are on the outside of the supply chain process, the SCPs may try to answer the questions themselves to keep the project moving forward. You want to be the contact point for information as well as a heads up for any issues as they arise, not after the fact.

END USER BLIND SPOTS

Frankly, the largest blind spot your end users may have is that supplier diversity is part of the process at all. In some cases, that is fantastic. If the inclusion of the suppliers is such a normal part of the supply chain process that no one thinks to ask questions or push back, well, that is where we are all trying to get. But if it's going to be because they don't understand, think it is complicating the process, and don't think it is part of the business, then you have your work cut out for you.

Apart from the very existence of your business strategy, a few other items that may be a concern include:

1. It's optional. If I had a dollar for every time someone sat me down and said something like, "Now, I know you have this diversity thing you need to do, but we are in a real time crunch on this project ..." I'd be vacationing somewhere in Europe

this year for three months, with high-end lodgings and luxurious spa appointments while getting my kitchen redone back home. You've heard the old adage, "Your lack of planning does not create a crisis on my part?" Well, it doesn't create an exception either. If they are allowed to skip the approvals and other signatures they need for their project, then we'll talk. Otherwise, nada.

2. It's something we went out and shopped for this morning. For some reason, a lot of end users have the view that once their project hits the radar screen, that is when we go looking for DBOs who do that. Oh wait, that could be due to so many supply chains treating it that way. Okay, if you haven't done that, then you can put this concern to rest. If it is something the company never thought they were going to need (who shopped for app developers ten years ago?), then they are looking for all suppliers the same way as the DBOs. Again, it's the same process. Again, no exception.

3. They don't see how the business strategy affects them. End users don't always have an appreciation for what diversity of suppliers brings to the table. Maybe they think only a company like IBM can provide what they are looking for. Maybe they don't see what has happened to small companies like Microsoft, Apple, Facebook, Google, Amazon, and the small companies that are now becoming the next generation of those companies. Technology is (can be anyway) one of the great equalizers. They may have to be shown some of the research that is changing the way those Fortune 500 companies are looking for board members, executives, and entry-level managers. It affects them because it raises the chances of their getting the best possible solution.

4. They don't see how they affect the business strategy. End users often don't think they can make a difference in the supplier diversity business strategy, so what's the point? They miss that the point is making it a standard part of the supply chain process.

That it is as important to the business outcomes as comparing pricing, contract language, and everything else we look at when choosing who to do business with. I had an end user once who had grudgingly gone along with "my diversity thing." When none of the DBOs who had bid on the project were selected, she came to my office to do a victory lap.

"See?" she said. "I told you there was no use in our doing the diversity thing on this project."

What she didn't see was that the three DBOs had all benefitted from the process. One went back to their office and changed out a lot of their sales collateral and canned RFP responses after that project. Another took what they got from the debrief session I had offered and won their next three RFP projects with large companies. The third, well, they ended up getting other business from us because they had impressed the technology group with their understanding of our business needs. I learned a big lesson from that. I started reporting some of that as part of our success.

Michael Jordan put it well when he said, "I've missed more than 9,000 shots in my career. I've lost almost 300 games. Twenty-six times I've been trusted to take the game-winning shot and missed. I've failed over and over and over again in my life. And that is why I succeed." Well played, Michael, well played.

CULTIVATING THE END USER RELATIONSHIP

So, what are some of the best practices we can develop to benefit our end users and our supplier diversity business strategy?

First, you can remember who the most important client is. It is your end user. I see those eyebrows going up, but they are the reason you are here. Never forget they have the same logo on their paycheck that you do. It is their needs that drive the need for supply chain, that make the business that needs a supplier diversity business strategy in the first place. Without them, you have nothing to do. Which is good because without them, the company can't afford to pay you anyway. That is why they are the ultimate client. That's why they are *everyone's* ultimate client. Yes, the customer is king, but the internal client keeps those customers happy and keeps them coming back. Sir Richard Branson, a guy who knows a little bit about success and customer service, has revealed that at his company, they do not put the customer first. They put the employees first. "Effectively, in the end shareholders do well, the customers do better, and your staff remains happy."

Next, do your best to let the company know about your business strategy. You don't really know who the next end user is going to be, so it pays to have them all know. Spread your reporting and successes around liberally. When the business strategy received any recognition or was mentioned in a writeup, I had a long (and I mean a looooonnnnnggg) list of people I sent it to. Some thought I just wanted to toot my own horn and, you know what, I can't do anything about what people think. I wanted everyone to know that the strategy existed, that it was doing well (at least in some areas), and that the company benefitted from that. I also didn't want the only time they heard about the strategy was when it needed money or support. Every time I sent one of those notes out, I would get at least one e-mail back from someone asking for information or if they could get help with an RFP. At one company, our Chairman was female and she was a great supporter. She would do a reply all to those e-mails and forward them to the board of directors. It's not just nice to do, it's a business strategy.

Speaking of recognition, I like something one of my clients began doing a few years ago. They have a recognition program for their DBOs and they also recognize someone in the supply chain and someone in their end user base for their support over the past year. If you have colleagues who are supporting the business strategy in an above and beyond way, call it out.

Talk to Human Resources about getting the supplier diversity business strategy in the new employee orientation and onboarding. Ideally, it would be part of what is already happening. If the orientation is done face-to-face or via video, get it as part of that presentation. I think making it separate just calls out that it wasn't thought of when the other training was being put together. The more it's part of the normal process, the more ingrained it will be and the more your next end user will be aware of it.

The C-Suite: When do the employees of your company hear about the supplier diversity business strategy? Is it part of their onboarding? Is it included in company updates? Annual meetings? If this is an integral part of your business plan (and it should be), they should hear about it more than a token mention once a year or a shout out that's remembered most of the time when talking about supply chain. How many clicks does it take to find it on your company website? These are things your customers want to know, too, so those end users should recognize what it is and be able to speak to it.

The Supplier Diversity Professional (SDP): SDPs, end users are the cast member I find being ignored by supplier diversity more than any other and you are passing by gold nuggets laying on the ground in open view. Have a marketing plan for your strategy and don't take no for an answer on this one. If you have to break new ground every time a new end user shows up, you will never get the business benefits where they need to and can be.

The Supply Chain Professional (SCP): SCPs, when you are having the discussion with the end user about how the process works, supplier diversity should not be a separate step in the process, it should be contained within your process.

This isn't "something else" that needs to be done or a box that needs to be checked. This is part of how potential suppliers are sourced.

I started a new position with a company once and was immediately outsourcing a lot of work. I asked one of my team members who had been with the company for a long time what advice he could give me about being successful in the company. He said, "You can have as much authority in this company as you are willing to presume." I thought that was a really powerful statement. He wasn't telling me to go boss everyone around. He was telling me that they were looking to me for guidance and it was up to me to provide that. The more you can state to your end users a matter-a-fact process, the more acceptance you will find. And, if they push back, then you have a response for supplier diversity the same as you have for checking a supplier's financial viability or references.

 The Diverse Business Owner (DBO): DBOs, consistency is the guiding principle here. Understanding what the bid process is going to be is a fair ask. Don't ask, "When will I meet the end user?" Ask, "When does the end user meet with potential suppliers?"

I know every sales technique says you have to meet the end users, establish a relationship with the end user, learn the pain points and desires directly from the end user. The fact of the matter is that as an SCP, suppliers rarely met my end users until they made the short list from the bid process. Part of my role as an SCP was to only make them attend the meetings they really needed to, and most end users don't want to meet a bunch of salespeople from every company that was going to bid.

Once the bid returns have been vetted and the strongest contenders have been identified (usually two to four suppliers), then meetings are set up. There is a personality, or cultural fit, that needs to happen as well as digging deeper into the solution. One way I get the number of serious contenders down to two to four is that the project team has to meet with each contender for the same amount of time with the same agenda and document the results.

My point is, don't get caught up in what you think should happen. Find out what the company does in their process.

 The End User: End users, this is all about using good science to get the best solution. Good science means that everyone gets the same information, goes through the same process, and is evaluated based upon what they submit.

CHAPTER 10

INTERNAL CLIENTS

When I got my first budget responsibility, a mentor gave me a piece of advice. "Whatever you do," she said, "Keep your accountant/controller and your attorney happy." Advice I have tried to consider and it has worked well for me. Whether you are responsible for the supplier diversity budget for your company or the entire budget for your company as a whole, it pays to know who is impacting the checkbook and how that's going.

FINANCE

In a corporate environment, a good controller will keep an eye and ear out for changes coming. Usually right after that six-month checkup on the operating budgets, companies will do things like make a proclamation that no one is traveling for the rest of the year or something similarly impractical. If you have already paid for a booth and registration at an event, it would be a shame to lose that because no one can fly to the event location. A good controller can help you present your issues in a way that will be favorable to those providing any new approvals that need to take place.

Finance is also where all of the funding happens for new and existing projects. This is a great opportunity for supplier diversity and supply chain to buddy up and find out who is spending money, what they are spending it on, and who they are spending it with. Supply chain is often trying to get their own seat at the table earlier in the process, before the end user has selected the supplier and started negotiating a contract. If the business unit is blowing off supply chain, chances are good they are blowing off supplier diversity being in on the solution as well. However, finance almost always knows what's happening because they are tracking the money.

Finance also usually has the shared services group who manage things like accounts payable (AP). AP is someone to make friends with as well. This is one of the most thankless jobs in all of planet corporate. They are juggling no end of legal and corporate policy requirements, paying thousands of bills each month and, if they are lucky, they won't get yelled at for doing it too slowly or for the wrong amount or not paying someone or paying someone who shouldn't have been paid (even though the invoice was approved). Respect their process and they will move heaven and earth to unwind one of those spiderweb nightmares that, for some reason, hasn't paid a company in three months. When I was in corporate life, I sent the AP team gourmet popcorn or cheesecake or something every year to say thanks from my team. Yes, out of my own pocket. Yes, it was totally worth it.

Another area that often either resides with finance or co-locates is treasury. Treasury does some very interesting stuff including the bank agreements for the company, lease versus buy decisions on assets, often credit card agreements. They can also tell you things like the cost of cash for your company. That's important to know when negotiating things like payment terms or rebate payouts.

One of the topics that comes up frequently in supplier diversity discussions is payment terms. Small businesses have a difficult time carrying receivables for the time that has become "the norm" for many companies. For years, standard payment terms were net 30 days and for professional services you could often do less than that, net 14 or even net 10. Then some years ago, businesses started to figure out they could make more money on their cash if they held onto it longer. Payment terms started getting pushed out to net 60, and in some cases even net 90 or greater. Large suppliers grumbled but usually went along. For smaller businesses with tighter cash-flows, it is crippling. It is one of those things that can put supply chain and supplier diversity at odds with each other. Supply chain often gets dinged for any contracts with less than standard payment terms. And to get less than standard usually takes St. Peter and two Archangels to sign off.

Recently, I had the pleasure of listening to a webinar from a Diversity Professional (more on them when we talk Media) on doing business with California American Water. In it, Edward Simon, Director, Business Performance and Supplier Diversity, talked about payment terms. Their standard terms are net 60 days and that's what they put in their contracts. However, they have an option for small business (actually any business) who can get paid faster if they need to by taking a small discount on the payment. How can they do that? Because they know what the cash flow costs and can let the business make an informed choice without impacting their bottom line. Brilliant! I was sitting there wondering why I hadn't been doing that very thing for the past 25-plus years of my corporate career. And how cool is it that, as a small woman-owned business, I can sign the contract with the 60-day payment terms because I know if I get in a pinch, I have some options that don't involve my going to my customer with my hat in my hand. Treasury is where the con-versations will take place to allow something as innovative as that to take place.

So, don't be put off by your colleagues in finance, their number crunching and love of pivot tables. Make friends with them and then find some diverse business owners (DBOs) who can help provide what they need.

HUMAN RESOURCES

People usually have an opinion about the Human Resources group of the company they work for. Sometimes it's good but, more often than not, they will have a bone to pick with them. In addition to hiring, developing, retaining, and sometimes firing company employees, they also tend to manage things like dress code, holidays, time off, when to call snow days, temporary staffing, harassment (complaints, not creating it), reviews, raises, bonuses, promotions, health benefits (content and cost), and a whole host of other things people have absolutely no opinion about. Yeah, AP is looking pretty good right now, isn't it?

Throughout my corporate career, I have leaned on HR for everything from the guy in the mailroom who was dating the CEO's administrative assistant—until he wasn't and refused to deliver mail to that floor anymore to the employee who dressed up like Abraham Lincoln on their lunch hour every day to protest a particular law of the land out in front of the office to the conversation I had to have with an employee who refused to shower more than twice a month (yep, the 15th and the 30th, whether he needed it or not). But don't be so quick to rush past the HR department. There may be a treasure trove of useful collaborators there.

Diversity and inclusion are big topics now and they usually reside in HR. That's good, it's been a long time coming. It does not, however, replace supplier diversity nor is it the same thing. Diversity and Inclusion (D&I) is about the demographics that make up the employee base in your company. How many women, minorities, LGBTQ, veterans are employed? How many of them are in positions of management? How many are VP and higher? In the C-suite? On the board? The truth of the matter is that supplier diversity and HR are often ships passing in the night at similar events for the same or similar hosts. HR is at a college campus to recruit seniors and talk about D&I in the company. I am guest speaking at the same campus to talk to graduating supply chain majors about negotiation and supplier diversity. HR is at the annual sales meeting to talk about sexual harassment and I'm at the sales meeting to talk about tier 2 reporting for our external clients. My point is that if you can track down that other ship and have a conversation, the two of you might be able to have some consistency in the look and content of your message. You just might save some money, too. One of the veteran organizations had different tier levels of membership. I discovered that both supplier diversity and HR had a membership in the same organization. We were able to pool our funds and get a higher level and split a cost savings of $1,500 each in the process.

Many companies also have Employee Resource Groups (ERGs) for different ethnicities, genders, orientations, etc. If you aren't involved with these groups, you should get up and move now because you have some serious catching up to do. Who better to help you ensure that LGBTQ-owned businesses get a shot at your bids than your LGBTQ ERG? Want to get the word out that you are looking for veteran-owned businesses? Go talk to your veteran ERG! Don't worry about what these people do in the company. In five years, it will all be different anyway, I'll demonstrate.

At one point in my career, I left my job and went back to school full time. This was before a lot of online education and I traveled far too much to go to night school. I kept signing up for classes and ended up dropping them because I'd have to go on the road for several weeks out of the semester. Yet I knew I was reaching a level within the company that I would have a difficult time replicating without at least my bachelor's degree. I planned on taking three years off to complete my Bachelors and Masters programs. I wanted to stay involved in things like supply chain and supplier diversity.

After I got my school schedule set up, I reached out to a few of the organizations I had worked with in my former supply chain role. I told them what I was doing and said I wanted to stay involved. I wanted to volunteer at events so I could attend without having to pay registration but was also willing to do whatever work needed to be done—stuffing envelopes, making phone calls, data entry, etc. Most welcomed me warmly and we had discussions about what would work best for the both of us. One group, however, never seemed to return my call. I had done a lot of work with them during my corporate tenure and I was certain that the message just wasn't getting where it needed to go, so I persisted.

At last, I got the head of the organization on the phone and explained to her what I was looking for. She listened and then said, and I'll never forget this: "You know, Jamie, you aren't with a corporate member anymore who can help us underwrite the cost of things we need. There really isn't anything you can do for us, is there?"

"You know," I replied, "You're right, there isn't anything I can do for you." I reminded her of the conversation five years later when she rang me up at my new gig heading up procurement wanting to get together and talk about how we could work together. If you spend all of your time only chasing the people who you think can help you today, eventually you end up with no one to talk to because they have moved on and you are left surrounded by a bunch of folks you have ignored or, worse yet, treated with contempt. It costs nothing to treat everyone with respect and you never know who will be where in six years, months, weeks even.

HR also frequently has the training and development folks. They can be a lifeline into all sorts of channels within the company. Would you like to get the word out to the salesforce that we do have supplier diversity and can provide not only reporting but responses on RFPs about it? Get it in the sales training program that is being developed. Do you need for all of your fellow team members to know about your strategy? Get a paragraph or two in the new employee orientation package.

Often, I find that companies overlook telling all of their folks about supplier diversity, and that's a shame because it can help on a lot of different levels. One company I worked for had a pretty large promotional items program. Clothing, coffee mugs, golf balls, you name it, they put their logo on it. The company that had the business was not diverse owned, but that didn't stop us from working with them to get DBOs supplying to our program. We had a private label e-store where employees could purchase the items that were then fulfilled by our promo company. We put a DBO logo on all of the items that were being provided on our e-store. It let our employees know which products supported the supplier diversity business strategy. Our spend with those companies took a jump because the salespeople who were providing tier 2 reporting, the people who had heard about it at ERGs, and others could make an informed choice and support something by which golf shirt they selected or what pen they handed out at their branch. The promo company saw the opportunity and took the idea to their other clients who had supplier diversity strategies. That's what I call win-win.

LEGAL

Nothing makes a supply chain professional roll their eyes more than to ask if they work with their legal department. Usually, you will get a response akin to, "I work with them on what *they* want to work on, but we don't do much sourcing for them, they do their own thing."

For some reason I can't exactly explain, I've been fortunate and had a great working relationship with my legal departments over the years. Part of it is that, even though I've spent many years tearing apart contracts and building them back up again, I realize that I am, in fact, *not* an attorney. That may sound like a given, but you would be surprised at how many people think a number of years doing something that involves legal documents makes them an expert. Legal, like spinal surgery, is not something you want to skimp on and buy on the cheap. It has consequences.

Legal also has a number of specialties. So, just as I don't want an acclaimed OB-GYN doc doing my spinal surgery, I don't want a contract attorney handling criminal litigation. Once you understand there is more to, well, pretty much anything legal than your part of it, you have taken the first major step in improving your relationship with your legal department. How does that help with your supplier diversity strategy? A couple of ways and thank you for asking.

No matter the source of the supplier, if they are going to be part of the supply chain, there will have to be some legal documents. This can sometimes be an obstacle. Companies often have notoriously complicated, dare I say, one-sided agreement templates they like to use. Smaller businesses don't always have an attorney on staff, so they are paying by the hour for someone to review legal documents for them, or worse yet, the business owner reviews it themselves. In no way can anyone from the company advise the small business on legal documents. That includes supply chain, supplier diversity, a company attorney, the sales organization, company archangel, or anyone else. My advice? Get into this as quickly as possible, do not leave it until the end. I have seen more than one deal go south because time ran out and the contract couldn't get done.

In negotiations, I often have what I call "the fair ask." The fair ask is a question for the other party that they may not want or like answering. But if it's a fair ask—that is, a reasonable person would consider it something they have a right to know—it should be answered. The other party in this scenario is often a potential supplier, but it can also be supply chain, supplier diversity, or our friends in legal.

A few fair asks:

1. Does the standard template have to be used in all agreements or is there a different, reduced (for lack of a better term) version that can be used in certain circumstances? Those circumstances could be a combination of type of service and dollar value. For example, if I'm contracting with a small business to come to a branch and conduct a four-hour training seminar for

$2,500, do we need the full-blown agreement? Dollar value is not a sufficient threshold, it will also matter what the seminar is about. If that four-hour seminar is about remediating toxic waste, the consequences are greater than if it's how to build pivot tables in Excel.

2. Are there Plan B responses to the standard template that I can use to move the conversation forward before having to bring it back to legal? For example, at one company I knew that even though our template said that the governing law had to be the state where our headquarters were located, I could change that to a couple of other states that might be more palatable on the other side of the table. This can be a sticking point with a small business. If they are located in Omaha and governing law is New Hampshire, it is going to be too costly for them to go to court and hire an attorney knowledgeable in New Hampshire law. In effect, it means if I sue, they will have to acquiesce. So, another alternative might be that if I sue, I go to Omaha. If they sue, they come to New Hampshire. This may seem like a small item, but it's the kind of message to a small business that says we want to play fair.

3. Can we have an NDA (Nondisclosure Agreement) that is mutual? A nondisclosure or confidentiality agreement is usually the first step to a meaningful conversation. If we are going to discuss how your company might help me, I will likely have to share some facts with you about how I run my business. Likewise, if I am the potential supplier, I will have to disclose facts about how my solution works. None of this is anything we want the other sharing at the cocktail parties attended over the holidays. But these documents can get complex in a hurry and can also sometimes be one-sided. If you have something simple that both parties can agree to (because it covers both parties fairly) then that initial conversation gets off to a quicker and friendlier start.

4. How do we get more supplier diversity opportunities in legal? You didn't think I was going to let them off, did you? In talking with legal groups over the years, I learned that while the rest of us don't really control our calendars, nothing says throw it out the window like being served with a suit. What creates a need in legal does not often allow the time to shop the need for legal. We have already talked about legal day, the fair ask of one day a year to meet potential new companies. Another fair ask is to understand what type of legal services go outside and what stay at home. There are dozens of legal specialties that can affect business. Buy someone in your legal group lunch or a cup of coffee and find out what they are. Collections, bankruptcy, patents, employment, real estate, and privacy just to name a few. Once you know the types your company uses from time to time, then find out which ones they handle in-house and what they seek outside counsel for. Then find out where there might be room for someone new. Litigation may be wrapped up with a couple of companies, but there may be room for some tier 2 or look at the rest of the list. This type of knowledge is a fair ask.

5. What would be the obstacles to a prime/sub agreement? If you do business with the government and are a general services administration (GSA) contract holder, this conversation is a bit easier to have. If you don't, or if you don't do a ton of business under your contract, it can be less so. Regardless, one of the ways that DBOs move forward is through project-based partnerships. Let's say you work for a construction firm and they have won the bid to build a new stadium in a metropolitan area. Your company will be expected to award a certain percentage of business to DBOs of various categories. This can present a challenge because, while there might be DBOs in various types of business, they may not be large enough to handle all of the business of a given type. The answer could be a project-based partnership between a DBO and a larger company. How it is structured depends upon what is being sought. It could be the DBO going in as a prime, but they

have a partnership with a large company as a subcontractor. This gives the contractor the assurance that the DBO has sufficient equipment, resources, and bandwidth to take on the project. In this scenario, the DBO deals directly with the contractor including invoicing and receivables and the large company acts as backup and advisor as needed. The good news is that it's all tier 1 being billed. The bad news is that the DBO is on the hook if the contractor doesn't pay on time or there is scope creep. An alternative arrangement is where the large company subcontract to the DBO for a certain amount of work. The good news is the DBO doesn't have to carry the risk load. The bad news is it isn't tier 1 but it will likely be tier 2 direct.

Anytime you insert a third-party into a two-party agreement, there will be challenges. In my experience, most of the time that has been around what everyone is getting paid for the work. The contractor must meet the percentages they have agreed to, but they don't want to pay extra for it. Likewise, the large company doesn't want to reduce their profitability to meet the requirement. The DBO needs to make a fair living on their work as well. Add a layer, add a cost. There is no silver bullet for this challenge. It's going to depend upon the various players and what they can agree on. Legal will play a key role in this no matter what the end result is. If they understand why this is being done and what the spirit of the arrangement needs to be, it will be a lot easier to get it done.

Whether you are negotiating an agreement or trying to get diverse-owned legal services in the front door, having a friend in legal can never hurt.

MARKETING

Marketing is an interesting part of any company. They are responsible for everything from ad campaigns to website content to the sign on the door. Their work looks glamorous from afar but can be tedious up close. They tend to get all kinds of budget money, yet often cannot give you a definitive dollar amount that was returned on the investment.

They have their own vocabulary, marketing, and they don't suffer lightly those who don't speak their language. I had the opportunity to work in the marketing department of a large company for six months as part of a cross-training initiative. It was one of the best educations I have received.

In addition to all of that creative work, they deal in data, lots and lots of data. They look at it a multitude of ways. You could do worse than spending a few days finding out how your marketing group looks at the data they use. If you were told there wouldn't be any math in marketing, you were lied to. They have data scientists on staff now who do nothing but crunch those numbers a hundred different ways looking for patterns and trends.

Think about the data that is out there on each of us these days. My grocery store knows what I buy and how often because they track it through my rewards program. Between Amazon and Apple, I am no mystery at all because they know everything else I buy, what I watch, how often I travel, you name it. When I went out on my own, I became fodder for every company with a passing interest in selling me healthcare insurance. They know I won't answer the phone if it says ABC Insurance based in Omaha so they call me on numbers that show as Blairsville, Georgia. When I travel, if I spend more than a few days in a given city, I start to get the same calls from that city. Who do you think put those programs together? Marketing, that's who.

As much as I may resent them for those phone calls, marketing can also be a great ally. They can help you with collateral that you use for the supplier diversity strategy and ensure it's tied to the message the rest of the company is putting out there. You want consistency of message and you want it tied to the other business strategies of your company. Marketing can be your answer for that.

Marketing is another of those areas that supply chain struggles to penetrate. If they are lucky, they might get the print, promotional items, and perhaps trade show spend. But according to splash copywriters, there are 159 different types of marketing. Some may be po-tay-to, po-tah-to, but not 159 of them. Is your marketing above the line or below the line? B2B (Business to Business), B2C (Business to Consumer), or B2P (Business to People)? Contextual? Drip? Test-driven? If you don't know the types, how on earth can you expect to source potential providers of it? This is not *Mad Men* marketing, this is the world of niche players being brought together by an agency or the company themselves. For each of those 159 ways, there are at least 50 companies that specialize in each one. It's enough to make Don Draper's head explode.

In addition to the myriad of types, there is an urgency to marketing that is only equaled by a zombie apocalypse. Everything that marketing touches has the opportunity to create wild amounts of revenue for the company, so they cannot be slowed down by anything (said every marketing professional ever). Contracts, deliverables, competitive pricing, it can all take a back seat to the fantastic opportunity that awaits us. Here's the really frustrating part, this stuff can work. Let's face it, the reason I can't get through an evening meal without a telemarketer calling is because someone out there is saying yes to them and actually spending money. Bastards!

So, how do you get marketing on board to spending some of that cash with DBOs and to take you (that's supplier diversity and supply chain "you") seriously? You can start by understanding how your company markets. Which of the 159 types are they using? How's it working for them? Who are their suppliers today? Does your company have an agency of record who coordinates all of the others? If so, do they have a supplier diversity strategy? No? How about a diversity and inclusion strategy? Chances are much better today than five years ago that the answer to that question is yes. If so, time to meet your agency representatives.

There is a lot of opportunity for supplier diversity in marketing. A fair number of those niche companies will be diverse owned. Why is that? It's a creative business (entrepreneurs tend to be creative types) and the cost of entry is low because you are selling ideas, not widgets that have to be manufactured. There is also a share of marketing that is specific to diversity and inclusion these days. Marketing to women, Black, Hispanic, LGBTQ, etc., are all factions that marketing pays attention to, especially in B2C or B2B businesses.

If you don't currently have any friendly colleagues in marketing, hire them to help you create an ad for supplier diversity publications, or an outreach brochure, or content on the company website. And if you can get them in a room with your supply chain colleagues, so much the better.

OPERATIONS

Operations is one of those business units that can consist of pretty much anything and the definition seems to change from company to company. When I worked in pharma, it was the manufacturing and distribution of drugs. When I was at a bank, it was the branch operations and the parts of the business that supported their daily activities like cash vaults, ATM setup and maintenance, safe deposit box installs, bank uniforms, etc.

Whether the operations are manufacturing related or a myriad of brochures and forms, operations is the center of the business. If they are humming along, chances are the business is, too. If you put the actual goods/services the company sells aside, operations is probably where most of the money is spent. In sourcing, we call this indirect spend. That is dollars spent on the things the company doesn't sell. A bank branch needs furniture, carpet, tile, a vault, safe deposit boxes, ATM systems, telephones, computers, business cards, printer paper, trash pickup, uniforms, notary stamps, lots and lots of forms, pens, mints, office supplies, doggie biscuits, and lollipops. That's just scratching the surface. I have said that the goal of indirect sourcing is to be invisible. If everything is working well, no one is thinking about us. If something isn't working, they aren't thinking of anything except us. We can screw up your day about a dozen different ways. Operations is much the same way. Whether it's an ATM lane that isn't working or not having biscuits for customer's fur babies, someone is not going to be happy if it's not working like it should.

Most of those products reside under an agreement that sourcing has done for all of the bank branches. We will deal with real estate and facilities in a different section because they tend to be more localized. Regardless, there are dozens of mundane things being purchased that could be provided by a diverse-owned business. We tend to concentrate on the big items, and that's fine. You want to be part of those discussions, but there is an awful lot of money being spent a few thousand dollars or more at a time. You know what they say, a few thousand here, a few there, before you know it, it's real money. If your supply chain folks have this stuff under contract, chances are good it's a three-to-five-year agreement, so it doesn't come up very often. If it's working well and the price isn't going crazy, they may not even bid it, but negotiate an extension to an existing agreement so they can concentrate resources on the bigger ticket items. My point is that if you wait until supply chain tells you they are bidding it and asking for potential suppliers, you may never need to look for them. However, if you know when contracts are coming up and you have already provided a number of possibilities, chances of success will improve. Most supply chain groups have a contract management system of some kind that they enter their active contracts into. Part of the data is when the contract expires, when any notices have to be in (typically X number of days prior to expiration), and for many, how long it is anticipated an RFP will take to complete. This is all so they can be notified well in advance when to get to work on a contract that has been in place for a while. Is it possible for you to get a log-in to this system so you can see what's coming up? There may be some resistance, or maybe there is a charge to add someone. It never hurts to ask. If not, then can you get a periodic report of contracts coming up in the next 24 months? If you get a list and there isn't much on it, ask for a report on all current agreements. Sometimes departments don't fill out all of those pesky fields, like when a contract expires. Or maybe they have what we call evergreen contracts. Evergreen means they never expire, there is usually (hopefully) a way to terminate the agreement, but if no action is taken, it just remains in effect forever. This is not a best practice, but supply chain groups that are short-staffed sometimes do these for operational agreements so they don't get caught with a contract that has expired before they have time to negotiate it. In other words, it's not an ideal solution but it's done more than you might think. The goal is not that you should be trying to find work for your supply chain colleagues, but sometimes a lot of these agreements can become out of sight, out of mind. This is especially true if there have been changes in leadership or a lot of merger and acquisition activity. If there is a chunk of business that is being ignored, there is a chunk of business you will never be able to get in front of potential DBOs. It's a fair ask to understand how much of the business is working this way and when that might change.

PUBLIC RELATIONS

Not everyone has a public relations (PR) group in their company. If they do, it might be a firm that the work is outsourced to or it could be done within the marketing group. Occasionally, it resides in the finance organization, especially if the primary focus is on releasing information to Wall Street. No matter where it resides, it can be someone you should know for your supplier diversity strategy. Public relations often has to review anything being presented to the public, like a magazine article or press release or even a general announcement. This may seem like a huge pain and another link in the chain of how far in advance you have to start, well, anything but it's worth it.

Each of us have a lens we see our messages through. The good news is that makes us capable of formulating a message that will be useful to our intended audiences. The bad news is it often makes us blind (or at least terribly nearsighted) as to how the rest of the world might view our message. PR people can view that message through the long list of eyes that may be viewing what we have to say. This keeps us from having to do awful things like retractions or damage control.

PR folks are also interesting to talk to because they have a unique view of the information that is going in and out of the company, whether it's to the public at large, investors, or even internally. Since a key part of a good supplier diversity strategy revolves around solid, consistent messaging, there is something to be learned here. I have also found that the more people know about your supplier diversity message, the more likely they are to let you in on ways to include it in other things they are working on.

REAL ESTATE AND FACILITIES

Real estate and facilities handle all of the building, repair, and maintenance of the physical locations your company has. Sometimes they are the same group, sometimes separate. If your company consists of a few offices that are leased, there is less for these groups to manage. If your company has a lot of branch locations, whether they be retail or internal, there will be more. Either way, there are a lot of opportunities for the supplier diversity strategy here that will be missed if you aren't paying attention.

The real estate side of the group will handle any buying, selling, leasing, and renting of space that the company owns, wants to own, or wants to rent or lease. There is not a huge amount of opportunity in the actual real estate transaction. You don't get to pick who you are doing business with and much of the work for the company is probably done by the real estate department itself if there is one. However, there are things that need to happen as part of the deal. Title searches and inspections are just two of the things that have to take place before business can be transacted. Sometimes there is a need for a local real estate attorney (remember those discussions with legal). Once the transaction has been done, that's when the work begins. Whether purchased or leased, there will be work done to make the space what it needs to be for the company. That can be anything from a fresh coat of paint and some furniture to a complete gutting and reconstruction of the property.

That work will be done by contractors. Contractors do a lot of work that already requires an understanding of supplier diversity, so they aren't shocked when the question is asked. Contractors also tend to use local businesses. Electrical, HVAC, running fiber, you name it and if you are repurposing a location, services will be needed. One of the first stumbling blocks a supplier diversity strategist will encounter with supply chain is that the DBO is not large enough to cover the amount of work they need done. This is one business unit where less really can be more. They are often looking for someone local. Even if the work is being managed by a larger company the services may be outsourced to, the outsource company is still doing business locally.

Once the property is set up as desired, there are a host of services, again, many local that will need to take place. Landscaping/snow removal, paving, roofing, security, fencing, coffee service, vending machines, plumbers, there is no end to it. And while many of these can be outsourced or given to a national firm, the truth is that they are using local business in a lot of cases. So, why not be sure they are including diverse-owned business in their work? Even retailers like Burger King and 7-Eleven use national firms for all of their equipment and location work. And those national firms have dozens of agreements with, you guessed it, local firms. When your Slurpee machine goes down you can't send someone from 100 miles away to work it, that needs to be fixed right now!

Here's another item to consider. Even the most devoted real estate and facilities folks are likely not using supply chain for everything. Whether it falls under the "they don't understand real estate transactions" or "it's such a small spend, they don't care about it" or "a water pipe broke, we weren't going to get three bids," you can bet there is some spend happening that doesn't have supply chain's name on it. If you haven't made the acquaintance of your real estate group, they are usually divided up into geographic regions. Find one and strike up an acquaintance.

SALES

Sales is the lifeblood of any company. Without sales, there is no money coming in and without money we all get sent home. Yes, they can be a little cocky in sales, but then again, they keep the bills paid, so a certain amount of bravado is allowed.

People work years for a company without understanding what their salesforce does and that's a shame. If you really want to understand how to serve your company and internal clients, you should understand what kind of business you are in and how product(s) and service(s) are sold. Your sales organization may not be in a direct line to your end customers. If you are General Motors, your distributors sell directly to the family that needs a new SUV. If you are Kellogg's, you sell to Walmart, Ahold Delhaize (Food Lion, Giant, Stop & Shop), Target, and Amazon. Understand your sales channel and you understand how your supplier diversity strategy can strengthen it (and where it cannot).

I have already talked in previous chapters about how companies that sell to other large companies that have their own strategy can help you sell to your internal clients.

TECHNOLOGY

I am basically a millennial trapped in a baby boomer's body.

The technology group is one of those mysterious places where things are done that no one understands other than to know they must have it to keep the business growing. I'm a total technology nerd and I love learning about the newest bells and whistles. At one point in my career, I became convinced that I wanted to work in technology and took a four-year tangent to work in mid-range, which ended at a little company called IBM. I was wrong about wanting a career in technology, but my time there did improve my ability to negotiate all things technology related.

From a supplier diversity standpoint, technology has several things to offer. First, they spend a bunch of money, so there are opportunities galore. Granted, a lot of that money is with major manufacturers, but more and more is being spent with small businesses that find a niche and do it really well. There is an app for everything these days and for each of those apps is someone, often a small business owner who has a great idea.

Second, there is all kinds of infrastructure associated with technology and whether a company does it all in-house or outsources the lion's share, it creates more opportunities for DBOs. Call centers that provide support for employees and/or customers come to mind. Telecommunications strategy and cost containment. There are companies that do nothing except check telephone bills and get money back for things that are billed in error. Have you ever looked at your phone bill? Do you understand what each of those charges, fees, taxes, etc., are? Can you even pronounce all of them? Well, these companies can, and they have made a living off of being able to generate more savings and returned fees than they bill out.

Third, and most importantly, they have all of the data. Well, they know where it resides anyway. When I decided I wanted to report the percentage of revenue that received tier 2 reporting,

I needed some data points. I needed the total revenue, okay that's in the financials. But I also needed sales for each of the companies in question. I rang up a bud in technology and asked if I needed that where I might find it. She told me which application that would reside in. I also found out if that application was on a subscription basis because I wanted to know if I was going to have to pay for membership or if it was something I just needed to request access to. When I went and made the request, I knew exactly what I needed and what, if anything, it was going to cost.

Technology was also my contact point when I began to wonder if there wasn't a place where all of the projects for the company were assembled before they started. My technology colleagues were able to educate me on the PMO (Project Management Office), how it worked, who was involved with it, and the fact that they had monthly calls and published minutes of the meetings. It was my technology contact who advised it was difficult to get included on the actual call because they tried very hard to keep the number manageable, but that they published minutes within 48 hours of each call. Bingo! The easy yes was to ask to be on the distribution list of the minutes, not try and push my way onto the call. There isn't much going on in a company that technology doesn't know about.

As involved as they are, technology shares a suffering point with supply chain. They, too, are often not brought into a project until it's too late to provide the best solution. One of the first questions I ask in my supply chain role is who the technology colleague is on the project. If the answer is they don't have one, I ring up my technology folks and confirm they don't need to be.

This area is moving so fast, technology has to be thinking six chess moves ahead. You could do a lot worse for your supplier diversity strategy than to get a technology colleague to spend a couple of hours to walk the trade show at your next national event. This is a big chunk of the company spend and it's also one area where bigger doesn't always mean better.

ACT III

CHAPTER 11

OUTREACH CREW AND STUNT DOUBLES

No organizations were interviewed in the writing of this chapter and none will be harmed. It is a compilation of online research and my personal experiences and observations. While I have tried to include all of the organizations I am aware of, I am sure that I have missed some. Do not interpret my oversight as a negative review of an organization not mentioned.

It takes a village of specialists to provide a quality production. A supplier diversity business strategy is no exception. There are a host of organizations that are ready, willing, and available to help. Some of them do the heavy lifting to bring the right people together for diverse business owners (DBOs) to meet and perhaps do business with. Others take things that are extremely complex, like good analytics or reporting, and make them look easy, as any qualified stunt double would do.

As you research the various organizations in this chapter, you will find that each of these groups has various levels of membership, usually for the business type being supported and for corporate and government entities (think those hiring said supported group). In other words, it's a pay to play design.

Regardless of the profit status of these organizations, they are all in business to either turn a profit or collect more revenue to help them provide the services they provide on a nonprofit basis. Some people (and, more often than not, I am part of this group), feel like the true calling gets lost from time to time in the search to pay the bills. But I have also sat where they sat and tried to pay the bills and keep the events going, so I am sometimes in conflict with myself in how I feel about the products and services I will describe here. Heck, I'm even involved in a couple of them and I will be sure to call that out.

So, unlike my role as a procurement professional, where you pay me to be the one in the room who doesn't care who wins, I am not wholly objective on this topic. I will do my best to present an objective view, provide viewpoints other than my own, and identify when I find it difficult to do so.

In the end, however, consider these disclaimers when reading this chapter:

1. Part of my business is in the same business as each of these organizations. While I don't consider myself in competition with them (so far, the supply has not outpaced the need), there are times when the lines between what is chargeable and what should be volunteer get murky. When I was a corporate member, I volunteered my time and could underwrite more things. Now, as a WBE, I still volunteer but have fewer hours to give and less money to underwrite.

2. While I have been a corporate member representing a number of large companies over the years, I have never been a member representing one of the mega companies that provide the primary support to these organizations. That is neither good nor bad, but it's easy for me to say such and such organization only pays attention to the Coca-Colas or the Raytheons of the world when I haven't been at Coca-Cola or Raytheon. Some of my comments are perceptions on my part and not from being on the inside looking out.

3. I have always been someone who likes to know where my money is going. I am far more likely to donate to a specific project my favorite organization is undertaking than write a check to the general fund. I am also more interested in helping to get X number of people to Tuck University's next session than to sponsor a lunch break at an annual event for one afternoon. Amazingly, the price for those two are often not that different. I know that both are necessary, I just have a personal preference as to where my money goes.

4. As a corporate, I often found myself taking dollars from organizations who didn't discuss ROI (Return on Investment) with me and putting them where I knew there was a return. I'm not saying that I eliminated the organizations entirely, but reduced the spend with them to afford to do some things I found more worthwhile.

5. A word about Canada. I love Canada. I grew up in Michigan and worked close to the Canadian border for years, so I've spent a lot of time in Canada. That helped when I was working for companies that did a lot of business in Canada because it's different in Canada. You hear a lot about Canadian people being so nice, like it's some sort of affliction. Canadians are savvy businesspeople, so don't mistake courtesy and respect for weakness. You are talking about a country whose biggest sport is ice hockey, where a player will break their leg on the ice and still finish their shift playing defense. Take that, NFL. Canada is not just like the U.S., with more colorful money. They are keenly aware of their historical differences from the U.S. on topics like slavery, inclusion, and diversity. There are differences, and if you want to succeed in Canada, you should research it no differently than you would if you were going to talk to Germany or Japan or Brazil. That said, I love spending time and doing business there and their supplier diversity organizations are some of the hardest working on the planet.

THE OUTREACH CREW

There are a number of organizations whose primary purpose is to support the supplier diversity business strategy in some form or fashion. They are mostly organized by the diversity type that they support—women, minorities, veterans, LGBTQ, procurement professionals, etc. Make no mistake; you will not have a successful supplier diversity business strategy without some combination of them, regardless of which cast member you happen to be. No one is an island in this production.

They each provide some kind of support to your business strategy, which may include: certification processes; host events and provide ways for corporate and government members to meet diverse business owners (DBOs); provide training, coaching, and mentoring for businesses (DBOs, corporate or both); and lobby government for changes they believe will benefit their members and help provide access to legislators.

In addition to the organizations I briefly describe in this chapter, there is a host of others that are specific to a given location, government entity, or industry. The National Association for Women in Construction, or NAWIC (NAY-Wick) for example, is for women in the construction industry.[33] Its membership is made up of woman-owned businesses that supply/provide service to the industry and large companies that are in the industry (contractors, concrete, heavy equipment rental/purchase, etc.).

Most of the organizations have a combination of paid and volunteer staff. Coordination of volunteer staff is a different set of management skills. Volunteers have day jobs that tend to have a higher priority than their volunteer work. You can't fire a volunteer. Well, technically you can, but it's usually frowned upon. My point is that

---

[33] NAWIC.

it is a different level of incentivizing someone to do work on a volunteer basis.

Early in my career, I served on the board of directors of an educational organization. It was technically oriented and had the support of a large high-tech company. Board members could serve two three-year terms or a total of six years. Members rotated so each year you had a percentage of members coming off the board and new people being elected by the membership. Executive positions (President, Executive VP, Treasurer, and Secretary) were elected by the board members each year. A board member could not serve more than two years in an executive position.

I learned early on that the year the president was completing their second term, very little got done in the final six months. The president was treated very well by the high-tech benefactor—invited to important meetings, flown to locations to represent the organization, interviewed by magazines and the press. As the final year began to wind down, the company began to look at who was going to be the next president and began to engage them. The current president received fewer invitations as their influence began to wane. They often became cranky and difficult to deal with. As a result, the working sessions of the board were not as productive. It taught me a lot about temporary power and influence. Employed and elected power and influence are temporary as well (at least in democratic societies), but the end date is not as finite as my board member example with some exceptions for things like potential re-election.

I make this point because your work with organizations will put you in contact with people who have temporary power and influence. It may be as serving a term as the head of the organization or it could be getting up on stage in front of a large audience at an annual event. It can be intoxicating, especially if the week after you are back in your cubicle at work where you may not feel special or appreciated. Understand where people are coming from and you will have an easier time of working with them and getting things done.

So, who are these organizations that you should care about? Some of the better known include (in alphabetical order):

BDR (Billion Dollar Roundtable)[34]

Established: 2001

Mission: Recognize and celebrate corporations that achieved spending of at least $1 billion with minority and woman-owned suppliers.

Overview: If you are spending $1 billion in diversity spend, you are probably already a leader in the industry and the rest of us aspire to. BDR provides a channel for those companies to get together and share best practices, not just with each other, but with all of us. The smartest thing they did was to have supply chain people front and center as well. BDR gets that these two groups have to not just talk to each other but share a strategy for the type of success they recognize.

Resources: Best practices, white papers, books, demographics, speaker's bureau, TED Talks, research, and relevant articles.

Blind Spot: I have a friend whose daughter was a nanny for a very well-off family in Greenwich, Connecticut. She tells the story of the little girl, about ten years old, who was asked to write an essay about a poor family. It starts out: "Once upon a time there was a family that was very poor. The mother was poor, the father was poor, the children were poor, the butler was poor, the cook was poor, the gardener was poor, the chauffeur was poor." Companies that spend a $1 billion or more with diverse suppliers operate in an orbit that is quite different from the supply chain of many companies that have a total spend of less than $1 billion. I have been the biggest fish in the pond and I have been a minnow. It can be tougher to get both internal clients on board as well as your suppliers when you aren't anyone's largest anything. Yet, like small business, it is the smaller

---

[34] Billion Dollar Roundtable.

companies that together will make the largest impact. Don't spin your wheels trying to do something the way that Walmart does it. Do what works for your company.

The Bigger Discussion[35]
Established: Approximately 2012

Mission: To act as a catalyst for honest, powerful dialog about diversity and inclusion.

Overview: On August 23, 2012 thought leaders in the fields of supplier diversity, economic development, and small business advocacy from across the U.S. started the Bigger Discussion. The conversation addressed the conversations that were taking place in private because publicly they might seem too politically incorrect. Scott Vowels, PhD, Phala Mire, and Alvin-o Williams wanted to tackle the taboo topics in an open and honest environment. Vowels, who has authored two best-selling books on supplier diversity and is Manager of Suppler Diversity at Apple, has done as much as anyone in trying to spotlight supplier diversity, warts and all. Mire, currently president and CEO of WBEC South has worked at NMSDC, the U.S. Department of Commerce and others, and knows as much as anyone about the similarities and differences among the organizations. Williams, a former president of the Minneapolis Regional Affiliate of NMSDC and Strategist for Qonsultum, an advocacy, social impact and all around think tank on all things diversity related, has worked in many different aspects of diversity. These three have guided some great conversations as part of the Bigger Discussion. You can find them on YouTube. But even they haven't been able to bring together the different factions to work together the way many of us would like to see. Until that day, however, this is probably as close as we are going to get and they have covered some very solid ground.

---

[35] NMSDC, "The Bigger Discussion."

Blind Spot: This is a bigger discussion for those who are already in the space. If you are going to see the bigger discussion live or probably even watching the YouTube videos, you have already drunk at least a couple of servings of the Kool-Aid. This is not The Bigger Discussion for Dummies, or skeptics, or outliers and I am not suggesting that it should be. You will hear some topics discussed more frankly than at many other sessions, but there is nothing here to make you gasp. As long as you don't go into it with the expectation of getting a reality TV show about supplier diversity, you can gain some understanding and certainly some wisdom from the participants. I also like to sit with strangers when I attend these sessions live. I almost always come away with a new business card because it does do what I think is the most important objective, it stimulates discussion. And at the end of the day, that is the bigger thing.

CAMSC (Canadian Aboriginal Minority Supplier Council) (CAM See)[36]

Established: 2004

Mission: To champion business relationships and economic growth of the Canadian supply chain through the inclusion of Aboriginals and Minority suppliers.

Overview: CAMSC is the NMSDC of Canada. I'll just get this out there, I love the Canadian organizations. I think they work hard for their corporate and diverse members and the various groups in Canada work together more than they do in the United States. They even coordinate their events from time to time. That meant occasionally I could make one trip to Canada and meet companies in more than one category. As a client, I like that. CAMSC is headed by Cassandra Dorrington, a savvy businesswoman in her own right and consummate networker.

---

[36] CAMSC.

Blind Spot: Canada is a big country. The Canadian memberships do not come cheap and part of that is because you are paying for the entire country of Canada, versus the regional affiliates of say, NMSDC in the U.S. Okay, fair enough. However, other than very small events that happen across Canada, all of the annual events take place in Toronto. I get their point, most of the companies that support them are based out of Toronto and that is where they are most likely to get the largest attendance. But as a company who had presence in all of the provinces of Canada, I would love to see the various Canadian organizations put together one annual event that took place outside of Ontario. The Toronto locale sometimes gave the impression you were meeting the same people year over year.

CCAB (Canadian Council for Aboriginal Business)[37]

Established: 1982

Mission: Their mission is to foster sustainable business relations between First Nations, Inuit and Metis people, and Canadian Business.

Overview: This organization was started by Murray B. Koffler, founder of Shoppers Drug Mart and cofounder of the Four Seasons Hotel and Resorts. An experience he had in Calgary brought him face-to-face with the number of homeless Aboriginal people there were and he found that unacceptable. Koffler went home, assembled some of his peers into a think tank, and the CCAB was born. They host about 15 events all across Canada each year and help Aboriginal businesses with everything from matchmaking to funding to understanding any government economic programs that might be available.

Blind Spot: It's easy for potential corporate attendees to overlook this group. CAMSC already certifies these businesses, so you may

---

[37] CCAB.

feel you've already checked this box. That would be a shame and a missed opportunity.

Centre for Women in Business[38]

Established: 1992

Mission: To enable women to reach their full potential as entrepreneurs through exposure, connection, and learning.

Overview: The Centre is about helping women in business make the most of their opportunities. They have a lot of different types of events that are both live and video-based. That's nice because it's not cheap to travel across Canada. They work closely with Mount Saint Vincent University and that helps them with educational content. They offer a lot of specific topics, like responding to a bid, or managing money, or measuring and improving customer service. Executive Director Tanya Priske is the co-owner of a hospitality and real estate business, so she knows how to make the most of a member's time.

Blind Spot: The Centre does some great work for woman-owned small businesses and yet they can get lost among the CAMSC and WBE Canada organizations. The Centre almost always attended events put on by their counterparts and did not try to grandstand their own agendas when they were there. I applaud their integrity in that. However, if you didn't dig, you might talk to them at other organizational events and never know what great stuff they were doing. I'm not saying they should be taking up more oxygen in the CAMSC or WBE women's rooms, but they do get overlooked at times and that's a shame because they provide a ton of hands-on, boots on the ground kind of help to women business owners.

---

[38] Centre for Women in Business.

CGLCC (Canadian Gay and Lesbian Chamber of Commerce)[39]

Established: 2003

Mission: The CGLCC fosters economic growth by supporting and nurturing LGBT+ businesses, entrepreneurs, students, and allies and by helping Canada's corporate world connect with the LGBT+ business community. It is also the certifying body in Canada for LGBT+ businesses.

Overview: Headed by Cofounders CEO, Darrell Schuurman and Vice-Chair Bruce McDonald, the CGLCC is an active and welcoming group of business owners, corporate members, and advocates. They support initiatives that help youth and young entrepreneurs, trade missions to other countries, and training and education on topics of interest to the LGBT+ and supplier diversity communities.

Blind Spot: Much like the other Canadian organizations, CGLCC is firmly rooted in the Greater Toronto area. Hopefully, they will combine for an event outside that area in the future that will showcase more businesses across Canada. Other than that, I've got nothing. I love this group.

CIPS (Chartered Institute of Procurement and Supply)[40]

Established: 1932

Mission: Think global, be local.

Overview: CIPS is a not-for-profit global champion of the global procurement and supply management profession. They are the largest organization dedicated to the profession with a global community of over 200,000 professionals. They are a certifying body for the profession and are recognized by regulatory authorities. They provide knowledge through education and research. They have traditionally

---

[39] CGLCC.
[40] CIPS USA.

been more prevalent in Europe than say, ISM in the United States. However, they have recently come to the U.S. and are making a lot of headway here as well. The not-for-profit status gives them a feel that is more university than retail sales. I love that I see them and they support things outside of their own events. To me, that means they are getting input and observations from more than what they can generate from within.

Blind Spot: When I purchased my last car, the model I chose had self-operating windshield wipers. I remember giving something of a snort when the salesperson pointed them out for me. I think I can operate my own windshield wipers. Can I just say that is now almost my favorite thing on the car? They start, stop, and adjust their speed based upon the amount of rain falling. No more getting that awful scrape when the rain lessens. No more adjusting them faster, then slower, then faster again when driving in changing conditions. CIPS is the automatic wipers of the supply chain profession. They need to somehow get that message out because you truly don't know how much you will use their site until you, you know, go out and use their site.

Disability:IN[41]

Established: 1994

Mission: Disability:IN is the leading nonprofit resource for business disability inclusion worldwide. Their network of over 185 corporations expands opportunities for people with disabilities across enterprises.

Overview: Disability:IN have a central office and 30 Affiliates who serve as the collective voice to effect change for people with disabilities in business. Formerly the US Business Leadership Network (USBLN), they rebranded to propel business disability inclusion in the U.S. and internationally.

---

[41] Disability:IN.

Overview: This group has a special place in my heart for several reasons. First, they are a very inclusive group. They work with LGBTQ, minorities, women because, let's face it, disability has no bias. Second, disability is often overlooked in the supply chain. Companies with robust supplier diversity business strategies often overlook disability and that is a shame for everyone because these are some of the hardest working, take on whatever comes-minded people on the planet. Third, and finally, I have a six-year-old granddaughter who is autistic. Let me tell you, if you are ambivalent about disability, your whole outlook will change if it comes to your family.

Disability:IN has a great website with a lot of resources on it including roadmaps and playbooks about many types of disabilities and planning aids.

Blind Spot: They need a higher profile with corporate groups and supply chain groups. Until there is the same concerted effort to get the companies into corporate supply chains, their involvement will lag. I would like to see Disability:IN at the other events. They just might be the group to bring the others on board to do a few things together.

GSDA (Global Supplier Diversity Alliance)[42]

Mission: Their purpose is to:

- Drive inclusion of ethnic minority-owned businesses within corporate supply chains across the world
- Provide single point access to research best practices around supplier diversity
- Give ethnic minority businesses access to the information, networks, and business intelligence they need in order to trade globally
- Bring together advocacy networks from across the world that champion and drive supplier diversity in individual countries

---

[42] GSDA.

- Develop a common global governance and delivery structure that effectively supports the global supplier diversity goals and objectives of multiple global partners

Overview: This is an attempt to get diversity organizations together on a global basis. It is made up of six organizations around the globe who are advocates for supplier diversity. They are:

Australia: Supply Nation
Canada: CAMSC
China: MSD China
South Africa: SASDC
UK: MSDUK
USA: NMSDC

Blind Spot: It's easy to take a shot at people trying to forge a new path, so I'm going to take the high road and not go there. So far, it appears the groups are talking to each other (that's good), attending each other's events (that's great), and contributing some research and information to the website (great initial step). Where are the women? Pacific Asians? LGBTQ? They aren't here yet. Keep an eye out for this group to see if they can provide more than a website and a conversation on a global scale.

ISM (Institute for Supply Management)[43]

Established: 1915

Mission: To advance the practice of supply management to drive value and competitive advantage and contribute to a prosperous, sustainable world.

Overview: To anyone in the supply chain profession in the United States, you already know ISM. You are probably a member or

---

[43] ISM.

have been one at some point in time. They were the first to provide education, support, and networking for the supply chain profession in the U.S. Before there were tons of events to attend, memberships to purchase, and research organizations who concentrated on supply chain, there was ISM. They are structured with a national office in Tempe, Arizona, and regional offices throughout the country. They are most known for the certification programs, quarterly economic reports, and their events but they also do research and publish on different topics. They also have a certification as a supplier diversity professional, something we haven't seen elsewhere.

Blind Spot: The organization has been through some major changes in the past several years. There has been a lot of turnover, and by a lot I mean almost everyone at the national office. There have been a lot of changes between the relationship of the national office and regional chapters. Changes that, in some cases, are causing chapters to close and members to become confused about what their membership gets them (and should get them) these days. I've no doubt they will work through it. They have been around for over 100 years. But they have their work cut out for them with the proliferation of new organizations and research sources now available to their customer base.

MSD China (Minority Supplier Development in China)[44]

Established: 2008

Mission: MSD China is dedicated to driving the development of China's minority-owned businesses through connecting minority suppliers with purchasing corporations for procurement opportunities on a mutually beneficial basis.

Overview: There are 56 nationalities in China. Han, the most populous nationality, accounted for over 90% of the population in 2005. The other 55 ethnic groups are called ethnic minorities because of the smaller population they represent. The overall total of those

---

[44] GSDA.

55 groups are increasing faster than the Han population. MSD China helps companies owned by the 55 non-majority ethnicities gain access to companies. The organization holds events, allows their corporate members access to the database, and promotes inclusion of these groups in the Chinese business environment. They are affiliated with NMSDC, CAMSC, Supply Nation, MSDUK, SASDC, and GSDA.

Blind Spot: Anyone who has done business with China knows that they aren't exactly known for their concerns for inclusion and business practices that would be viewed as ethical in the west. Things have improved greatly from say, ten years ago when this organization was brand new, but it remains to be seen what kind of impact supplier diversity can have on the global supply chain. A big measure of that global view will depend upon what happens in China.

MSDUK (Minority Supplier and Diversity UK)[45]
Established: 2006

Mission: MSDUK brings together innovative and high growth EMBs (Ethnic Minority Owned Business) with global corporations committed toward creating an inclusive and diverse supply chain.

Overview: MSDUK is the NMSDC equivalent in the U.K. There are over 300,000 ethnic minority-owned businesses (EMBs) in the UK, representing over 7% of all SMEs (Subject Matter Experts). This organization certifies EMBs and coordinates one-to-one meetings with their 125 corporate members. They have held over 120 events since taking off in 2006.

Blind Spot: All things related to the U.K. is currently holding its breath with Brexit. Until that is resolved, there will likely be a slow-down in the progress that can be made as everyone waits to see what trade will be like after they leave the European Union (EU). On the upside, MSDUK can provide an open channel for small businesses in the U.K. who may be dealing with a very different trade environment.

---

[45] MSDUK.

NaVOBA (National Veteran Owned Business Association) (Na Vo` Ba)[46]

Established: 2007

Mission: To create corporate contracting opportunities for America's Veteran's and Service-Disabled Veteran's Business Enterprises (VBEs/SDVBEs) through certification, advocacy, outreach, recognition, and education.

Overview: NaVOBA is one of two veteran-owned business certifying bodies and support organizations. NaVOBA has a presence at most of the supplier diversity events taking place in the United States, such as Business Beyond the Battlefield and the national events put on by NGLCC, NMSDC, USPAAC, and WBENC.

Blind Spot: The Billion Dollar Roundtable (BDR) began accepting veteran, service-disabled veteran, and LGBTQ certified companies toward the billion-dollar goal in 2019. However, NaVOBA certification is not accepted. This will not help build corporate membership for any company that aspires BDR membership or uses BDR as the guideline for certifications.

NAWBO (National Association of Women Business Owners)[47]

Established: 1975

Mission: NAWBO propels women entrepreneurs into economic, social, and political spheres of power worldwide by:

- Strengthening the wealth creating capacity of our members and promoting economic development within the entrepreneurial community
- Creating innovative and effective change in the business culture

---

46 NaVOBA.
47 NAWBO.

- Building strategic alliances, coalitions, and affiliations
- Transforming public policy and influencing opinion makers

Overview: NAWBO is less about the traditional supplier diversity outreach to large corporations and more about woman-owned businesses being the best business owners they can be and doing business with each other. They offer events, regional chapters, plus a virtual membership for those of us who are not in the big cities. They have an Institute for Entrepreneurial Development and a public policy arm (the organization began in the Washington, D.C. area). They have affiliations with groups like WBENC, WIPP, the Association of Women's Business Centers, and the Small Business Roundtable. They also have global partnerships around the world and with organizations based in Australia, Canada, France, Mexico, and the Netherlands.

Blind Spot: This group has a lot of stuff going on. I have to wonder how much of it is really covered from one year to the next. If you want to know, ask me when you see me. I liked the message on the website so well I joined while I was researching it.

UPDATE: In less than 12 hours from joining, I received a phone call from Lori Lemmon, Regional Membership Director out of Atlanta welcoming me to NAWBO and asking about my business and how she could help. In 25+ years on both the corporate and WBE side, I had never had that happen once. I'm just sayin' …

NCAIED (National Center for American Indian Enterprise Development)[48]
Established: 1969

Mission: To develop and expand an American Indian private sector that employs Indian labor, increases the number of viable tribal and individual Indian businesses, and positively impacts and

---

[48] NCAIED.

involves reservation communities by establishing business relationships between Indian enterprises and private industry.

Overview: NCAIED is *the* organization for American Indian business. They have events in support of Native American-owned business. The largest is RES (Reservation Economic Summit) held each spring in Las Vegas. They combine the traditional trade show with their artisans market and traditions. It is quite simply an impactful experience. Not only do you meet great businesses, but you also see (and can purchase) some of the stunning handmade items from jewelry to pottery and artwork. They have a large matchmaking event that is well run.

Blind Spot: The blind spot is for people who are attending this event for the first time. If you are expecting the traditional trade show, you may find yourself confused. This is an immersion into both the business savvy and the spiritual-ness of the Native American. Ignore that, and you will come across as trite and disrespectful. Embrace it, and you will be embraced in return and, frankly, a better person for it at the end of the event. I love this event. Enjoy!

NGLCC (National Gay and Lesbian Chamber of Commerce)[49]

Established: 2002

Mission: The NGLCC is the business voice of the LGBT community, the largest advocacy organization dedicated to expanding economic opportunities and advancements for LGBT people, and the exclusive certifying body for LGBT-owned businesses.

Overview: NGLCC has 1,100 certified business enterprises, 228 corporate partners, and 60 affiliate chambers. Cofounded by Chance Mitchell (CEO) and Justin Nelson (President), they have built, hands down, a supplier diversity advocacy organization that has the most potential of any organization anywhere. The national conference has gotten bigger every year since its inception.

---

[49] NGLCC.

Blind Spot: NGLCC has partnered well with other organizations, advocates tirelessly for their members, and supports and acknowledges their partners of all sizes. Nelson says to the effect when one group rises up, we are all lifted. As the organization becomes larger, they will struggle with the same issues the other organizations struggle with: ensuring that they aren't swallowed up by the largest corporations and make certification a business necessity for the thousands of businesses they represent. They have at least one ace in their pocket. Their national conference is the best run event out there.

NMSDC (National Minority Supplier Development Council)[50]

Established: 1972

Mission: NMSDC develops successful relationships between America's top corporations and supply chain partners from the Asian, Black, Hispanic, and Native American communities.

Overview: NMSDC is the first of the certifying organizations in the U.S. They have long been the gold standard, the largest, the one all the other organizations have looked to when forming their own supplier diversity related organizations. NMSDC has hit a few rough spots in recent years. They have had some turnover in their management and staff and it has hurt the continuity and the ability to take the organization in new directions. They have regional chapters that each serve their geographic areas with support and events. The national conference has been the largest supplier diversity event in the U.S. the majority of their history. They have hailed some of the best advocates in the space. Dr. Fred McKinney who had the Connecticut chapter, which became the Greater New England chapter under his direction, is one of the best business and economic minds I have known. He is also one of the best networking coordinators I've come across. Every aspect of an event he oversaw was

---

[50] NMSDC.

considered. I remember volunteering to drive one of the golf carts at their annual golf outing. I don't play, so I said I would do two shifts taking water to the players and selling raffle tickets. There were two people assigned to each cart. I had a different person with me on each of the shifts and both had been trying to get into my company to sell without success. Coincidence? Not even close where Dr. Fred was concerned. That type of organization may take a setback here and there, but they will always rise up.

Blind Spot: Part of being at the top of the heap is that people will take shots at the top spot. NMSDC has occasionally suffered from "That's the Way We've Always Done It" over the years and have sometimes let their attention to their largest supporters detract from support for the small and medium companies that make up the brunt of the membership. But they are the patriarch of the group and you can't argue with the numbers: 1,450 corporate members and 12,000 certified MBEs.

NVBDC (National Veteran Business Development Council)[51]
Established: 2013

Mission: The NVBDC was created for the purpose of providing a credible and reliable certifying authority that would ensure that valid documentation exists of a business' veteran ownership and control.

Overview: NVBDC certifies and advocates for veteran and service-disabled veteran owned businesses. While the Veteran's Administration offers certifications, it is only for small businesses. NVBDC ensures that the businesses that become successful enough to not fit SBAs definition of small business can still be certified. They are the certifying body recognized by the Billion Dollar Roundtable. Headed up by Keith King (Founder and CEO) and Richard (Dick) Miller (President), they have put an impressive organization together

---

[51] NVBDC.

in a short amount of time. They have events throughout the year and have leveraged the government connection with events like Doing Business with the Federal Reserve. They have formed a solid partnership with NGLCC, NMSDC, and WBENC offering a Fast Track certification to veterans who have already been certified through one of the partner organizations.

Blind Spot: At six years old, there hasn't really been time for any blind spots. The leadership has made smart affiliate partnerships, gotten in on the big discussion, and has been accepted by the Billion Dollar Roundtable. I hope to see nothing but onward and upward for this group honoring our brave men, women, and families who serve.

OMNIKAL[52]

Established: 1980

Mission: OMNIKAL is the United States' largest inclusive business organization, built to empower all entrepreneurs and small- to medium-sized businesses through a powerful social B2B platform that fuels real growth and success.

Overview: The OMNIKAL business proposition is that they connect you with potential customers. They outline a five-point membership benefit as follows:

1. Connect with millions of quality business owners
2. Build networks and key relationships
3. Generate significant new business
4. Learn to grow and scale your business
5. Gain Fortune 1000 visibility

While the supplier diversity centric organizations may be viewed as more strategic, OMNIKAL is boots on the ground, let's

---

[52] OMNIKAL.

meet the right people and learn some stuff to grow our business. OMNIKAL began life as DiversityBusiness.com and its secret sauce is its big data technology platform and collection methodologies. Headed by Kenton Clarke, who took an ad on a matchbook cover and became a programmer and then the owner of one of the largest technology companies in the northeast. Kenton decided there was too much talk about diversity and too little about getting folks together and rebranded into OMNIKAL, Omni for all-inclusive and KAL for the initials of his three children. On the OMNIKAL website, diversity is defined as "Outdated historical term used to replace the word 'minority' but still used to reference labels, classifications, or groups of people." There is an annual conference in New York City, webinars on a host of topics, and online information and research. As the name suggest, OMNIKAL is open to everyone. Honestly, this is as close to the message of Backstage Pass as you will find on this list.

Blind Spot: Part supplier diversity, part technology guru, part CRM (customer relationship management), OMNIKAL has done well. They have most of the corporate logos on their website that you find elsewhere in this space. The lack of certifications, so ingrained in the supplier diversity DNA, has put them in the position of being a choice to make *after* you have joined the certifying bodies. That means for companies like many I have worked for, the additional membership and conference to attend stretched both budget and resources too thin most years. However, there is nothing like an idea whose time has come. As other organizations struggle with their regional chapters and how to keep them all profitable, OMNIKAL is basically a virtual community. Younger entrepreneurs (of whom research has shown us are increasing in record numbers) will like this approach instead of trying to buy a regional membership everywhere their distributed workforce is. They will also like the inclusion versus this designation or that designation. When Kenton puts his technology skills to use and comes up with that database

I'm begging for, it will cause a major disruption in this space. And in some ways, OMNIKAL already is. Not so blind after all, eh?

SASDC (South African Supplier Diversity Council)[53]
Established: 2011

Mission: Through best practice supplier diversity development implementation, SASDC helps to sustainably integrate Black-owned suppliers into company supply chains—thereby directly improving your corporate brand and image, increasing market share, competitiveness and B-BBEE compliance, while indirectly growing Black businesses, employment, and the economy.

Overview: SASDC identifies five points, or their 5C approach, that moves their mission forward.

1. Collaborate
2. Certify
3. Connect
4. Capacitate
5. Celebrate

They have 28 corporate members and 761 certified suppliers as of this writing.

Blind Spot: If you aren't doing business in South Africa, it will be difficult to justify the membership and activity. It is good to see members of Cummins and Accenture on the board. With the history of the region, if supplier diversity isn't thriving here, we all need to step up our game. As the world continues to shrink with technology advances, groups like SASDC will become more and more attractive to allow companies to expand their horizons into areas they haven't been before.

---

[53] SASDC.

SDAC (Supplier Diversity Alliance Canada)[54]

Established: 2016

Mission: SDAC was established for the intention of advancing supplier diversity in Canada. SDAC seeks to provide support, guidance, and consultation to stakeholders on the direct impacts of developing and applying effective inclusive procurement policies and practices.

Overview: Remember how I said the organizations in Canada work together better than they do in the U.S.? Here is an example of that. This group was founded by CAMSC, CGLCC, and WBE Canada. It is not easy to bring different organizations together for a joint mission. They are engaging with the Canadian government to set standards for supplier diversity inclusion, similar to what the U.S. government did. They have an annual event called "Connect. Collaborate. Succeed," which brings the three organizations together. In 2019, it was held in the morning and the CGLCC's Black & White Gala was that evening. Again, working together to make the trip to Toronto worthwhile.

Blind Spot: It's been a bit of a slow mover but for heaven's sake, they are making the effort, so kudos to them. If they can get past the individual organizations needs and work together, they will knock down a wall that has existed for a long time. It would be a great benefit for both the corporate and DBO communities. Keep your eye on this one.

Supply Nation (Australia)[55]

Established: 2009

Mission: Supply Nation has a vision of a prosperous, vibrant, and sustainable indigenous business sector, and we work toward that:

---

[54] SDAC.

[55] Supply Nation.

- By driving understanding that the purchasing power of businesses can be used to deliver positive social outcomes;
- By facilitating connections between indigenous businesses and our members' procurement departments; and
- Through our world-leading 5-step verification (registration, certification, and audit) process.

Overview: The Australian government has been a long time in recognizing the rights of its indigenous people and their connection to the land—a relationship that existed prior to colonization that still exists today. The first recognition came in 1992 with the Mabo decision. In 2008, the Australian House of Representatives Standing Committee made the recommendation to form the Australian Indigenous Minority Supplier Council, or AIMSC. After a three-year pilot phase, it was rebranded to become Supply Nation. Supply Nation has taken their strategy from NMSDC and remains an affiliate for them and other organizations in the U.S.

Blind Spot: In Australia, supplier diversity is still often seen as a social approach rather than a business strategy. That will hold it back until the business strategy overtakes the social significance. That said, they continue to move forward and the success stories on the website continue to grow.

USBC (United States Black Chambers, Inc.)[56]

Established: 2009

Mission: The U.S. Black Chambers, Inc. (USBC) provides committed, visionary leadership and advocacy in the realization of economic empowerment. Through the creation of resources and initiatives, we support African American Chambers of Commerce and business organizations in their work of developing and growing Black enterprises.

---

[56] USBC.

Overview: The Chamber is built on the foundation of their Five Pillars of Service:

1. Advocacy
2. Access to Capital
3. Contracting
4. Entrepreneur Training
5. Chamber Development

There are just over 100 Chambers nationwide across five region offices. There are a number of initiatives on their website for helping Black-owned companies with everything from gaining access to capital to meeting other Black-owned business. The Chamber was founded and is headed by Ron Busby, an entrepreneur himself who honed his skills at a few companies you may have heard of like Exxon, Xerox, IBM, and Coca-Cola.

Blind Spot: There are a lot of broken links on their website and even more places where you would expect to find links and just don't, so it's hard to get the full sense of what is available to Black-owned businesses and how the USBC can help them. But you can't go wrong with 100+ Chambers around the country and Ron is a powerful brand himself.

USHCC (United States Hispanic Chamber of Commerce)[57]
Established: 1979

Mission: To foster Hispanic economic development and to create sustainable prosperity for the benefit of American society.

Overview: With over 200 local chambers across the U.S., USHCC has a powerful network of Hispanic Business Enterprises. They have annual events like their National Convention and

---

[57] USHCC.

Legislative Summit in Washington, D.C. The Summit advocates for a number of issues such as:

- Access to capital
- International Trade and Commerce
- Education and Workforce Development
- Immigration
- Infrastructure

Blind Spot: Try as I might, I could find no listing on their website of the 200-plus local chambers or a way to locate them.

USPAACC (United States Pan Asian American Chamber of Commerce)[58]

Established: 1984

Mission: Their mission is to be the gateway to corporate and government contracts, Pan Asian American (includes East, South, and Southeast Asian and Pacific Islander) suppliers, provide information about Asian American and the Asia-Pacific and Indian Subcontinent markets.

Overview: The Chamber's mission is supported with six items:

1. Promote and Propel Economic Growth
2. Represent a Very Diverse Ethnic Group
3. Support Contracting Relationships
4. Advocate for Asian American and Other Minorities
5. Invest in the Future
6. Embrace Diversity

Headed up by Susan Au Allen, a super-smart and passionate woman who came to the U.S. from Hong Kong via White House

---

[58] USPAACC.

invitation in recognition for her volunteer work for people with disabilities. The organization is based in Washington, D.C, and has a strong legislative advocacy program along with events and educational opportunities for business owner members including innovation and international business.

Blind Spot: Unlike many of the chamber organizations, USPAACC offers certification. This puts them in direct competition with NMSDC. Many corporate programs recognize both certifications, but if they choose one over the other, it is typically NMSDC. That's not to say one is more thorough than the other, it's more that the ethnicity coverage is greater with NMSDC. This puts USPAACC membership as one you look at buying after securing your NMSDC membership. It's too bad, because USPAACC has excellent quality education opportunities and connection network.

WBE-Canada (Women Business Enterprise of Canada)[59]
Established: 2009

Mission: To advance economic growth across Canada through certification, promotion, and development of woman-owned businesses.

Overview: Started by Mary Anderson and currently run by President Silvia Pencak, WBE Canada is a certifying body for woman-owned businesses in Canada. They have a strong board of directors, chaired as of this writing by Catherine Grosz from BMO Financial Group, and Directors like Michelle Albanese of TD Bank Group, Kiruba Sankar of Royal Bank of Canada, and Michael Bourne of IBM Canada. They have several events throughout the year and Silvia is a member of SDAC along with her peers from CAMSC and CGLCC.

Blind Spot: Supplier diversity as a business strategy has not caught on as strongly in Canada as in the U.S. Part of that is because

---

[59] WBE Canada.

Canada doesn't have the government requirements that kicked off many of the strategies in the U.S. Another is Canada doesn't have the history the U.S. has in racism and exclusion. As a result, not all companies see the need, so the corporate support tends to be the automotive and banking industries with some consulting and financial houses and a few others. The result can be that it feels like you are meeting the same folks in the same meeting environment. While WBE Canada has sought to shake things up a bit, time will tell if they can draw the kind of diversity they need in corporate industries and WBE providers to show a strong growth line. That said, I adore the group and their events and always leave feeling like I'm going to go home and do something great. That's hard to put a price on, especially if you are a weary corporate or an overworked business owner.

WBENC (Woman Business Enterprise National Council) (Wee Bank)[60]

Established: 1997

Mission: The mission is to fuel economic growth globally by identifying, certifying, and facilitating the development of woman-owned businesses.

Overview: WBENC is the gold standard for certification of woman-owned businesses. They have 14 strong Regional Partner Organizations (RPOs) or chapters across the U.S. WBENC has two signature events each year that occur in different cities across the country. Summit & Salute, typically held in March, and WBENC National Fair and Business Conference held in June. The business conference includes a trade fair with the first or second largest grouping of companies on a trade show floor for the purposes of supplier diversity. Summit & Salute has some of the best educational content for business owners. They take a deep dive into topics like marketing, financing, brand management, and others that go well

---

[60] WBENC.

beyond the 30-minute overview you often get on such topics. President and CEO Pamela Prince-Eason has joined efforts with corporate members to step up the education game and it shows well. Both events include matchmaking, something they perfected with their software a few years ago, that as a corporate took me from hoping I met someone I could do business with to being excited about each of the meetings I had a hand in selecting and setting up.

Blind Spot: WBENC got a little carried away a few years ago and started having the same issues as some of their peer groups favoring big company sponsors versus everyone else, but they appear to have stepped back from the brink. Now, if they would just fix their silent auction fundraiser. It used to be the coolest in the industry where I could do some Christmas shopping, pick up something for myself, and contribute to a great cause all at the same time. Unfortunately, extreme overpricing of items has knocked the fun out of it. C'mon, WBENC, give a gal a bargain every now and then. They are poised where they could become the largest supplier diversity event in the country. As a WBE, I can't deny I like that.

WEConnect International[61]

Established: 2009

Mission: WEConnect International helps woman-owned businesses succeed in global value chains.

Overview: WEConnect is a Canadian-based organization for woman-owned business. Headed by CEO and Cofounder Elizabeth Vazquez, WEConnect has an impressive board of directors and a truly global reach. They are a certifying body for woman-owned businesses in Canada. Their WEConnect Academy covers a business owner's needs from financing to growing and scaling. Their sweet spot is expertise in trade missions, a Canadian term for groups that go to other countries and meet with the right people there to set up

---

[61] WEConnect International.

business connections and networks. The Canadian government may not have a mandated supplier diversity strategy of its own, but it does support trade missions that open up trade with countries around the world. WEConnect is very good at this.

Blind Spot: Canada is a big country, it's true, but do they really need two organizations to certify their WBEs? It's too soon to tell. In the interim, WEConnect has built a following in their global expertise and that has allowed them to bring some pretty big corporate members in who do business in a lot of the countries those trade missions are visiting.

GOVERNMENT AND PUBLIC POLICY OUTREACH

For purposes of this discussion, we are going to concentrate on the United States government. Each country has their own groups and processes to work with small business owners, so if your interest is in the United Kingdom or European Union or Africa, don't despair. Why? Because universally, it is small business that keeps any country moving and, for the most part, countries get that.

SBA

In the U.S., we have the Small Business Administration, or SBA. It was "… created in 1953 as an independent agency of the federal government to aid, counsel, assist and protect the interests of small business concerns, to preserve free competitive enterprise and to maintain and strengthen the overall economy of our nation."[62] There are a number of laws, policies, and regulations over which the SBA has authority including the Small Business Act of July 30, 1953 that started the group, the Small Business Investment Act that provides ways to invest in small business, and the Code of Federal

---

[62] U.S. Small Business Administration, "Organization."

Regulations (eCFR) among others. How do I spend that you might wonder? The SBA provides assistance for putting a business plan together, launching a business, marketing a business, managing a business, growing a business. They provide free business counseling and they provide SBA-guaranteed business loans. They also provide home and business disaster loans and help in participating in federal government contracting.

The SBA has ten region offices located in:

Glendale, California
Denver, Colorado
Atlanta, Georgia
Chicago, Illinois
Boston, Massachusetts
Kansas City, Missouri
New York, New York
King of Prussia, Pennsylvania
Fort Worth, Texas
Seattle, Washington

Each of the region offices has their own website that provides information on what is available and how to get help whether you are local to the region or not.

For example, my region office is Region IV out of Atlanta. They serve Alabama, Florida, Georgia, Kentucky, Mississippi, North Carolina, South Carolina, and Tennessee.

Each region has District Offices. Region IV has 110 of them, so regardless of where you are, you should have one within 100 miles of where you live. I live in the northeast corner of Georgia, about as far away from city living as you can get, and mine is about 80 miles away. Is that too far for you? No problem, they come to you. I've had SBA people in my little town of Blairsville, Georgia, on more than one occasion. They usually try and set up several appointments but, if not, they will still come. I have met mine in a conference room at the Chamber of Commerce and had coffee at a local coffee house. Whatever works. They will help with everything from logo design to business plans to sales strategies. The region offices also have a number of events and webinars over the course of the year. Get on the mailing list or bookmark their calendar of events and check back often. If you travel a lot like I do, check the calendars for the cities you are in. I've met some great SBA folks by dropping in on a reception in Phoenix before my dinner meeting or hearing a breakfast speaker in Trenton before my client's workshop. No event scheduled? Call and see if you can have coffee with someone in their office. They love comparing notes and they are a great source of sales prospects in the government and out.

Another resource is Procurement Technical Assistance Centers (PTAC). Many people think they are part of SBA and, while some are affiliated or operate out of SBA offices, they are separate entities. The Procurement Technical Assistance Program (PTAP) was authorized by Congress in 1985. Their objective is to expand the number of businesses capable of participating in the government marketplace. Yes, their purpose of existence is to help you do business with the U.S. government. There are 94 PTACs throughout the nation and over 300 local offices. This network is one of the best kept secrets in our government, and I'm not being sarcastic at all when I say that. Each location has counselors from diverse backgrounds from government acquisitions to military attaches to companies that have successfully done business with the government. These counselors receive ongoing training on what is changing in government acquisitions and they network with each other like crazy. The program is designed so they can access their colleagues for specific expertise. If you have ANY interest in doing business with the government, make friends with as many of these folks as possible. There is a bonus here in that most of these folks are really smart, so you see a lot of them move into their own businesses or they are people who have retired from successful businesses and want to give back. Many are affiliated with local universities. The PTAC close to me is in Albany, Georgia, and is housed at Georgia Tech. I can also go to the one at Western Carolina University in Asheville, North Carolina. if I prefer, or University of Tennessee at Chattanooga. They also provide a lot of support via phone, e-mail, and web call, so distance is no excuse.

PUBLIC POLICY ADVOCATES

NSBA (National Small Business Association)[63]
Established: 1937

Mission: NSBA is a staunchly nonpartisan organization with 65,000 members in every state and every industry in the U.S. NSBA represents the small business community before the U.S. Congress, White House, and federal agencies, advocating for the interests of their customers, their companies, and their communities to help ensure the continued viability of their small business way of life.

Overview: NSBA is a group that has been around more than 80 years representing small business owners. They are fiercely non-partisan, are based in D.C. and work with all political parties for the betterment of small business. They are partnered with the SBTC (Small Business Technology Council) and SBEA (Small Business Exporters Association of the United States) and work with a number of affiliates such as the Arizona Small Business Association, Denver Metro Chamber of Commerce, Small Business Advocacy Council, and others. I have served on their board of trustees since November 2017 and it has been a master class in how things get done in Washington. Their staff is based in D.C. and are well connected and knowledgeable.

Since becoming involved, I have attended briefings at the White House and on Capitol Hill, met with staffers from both my federal

---

[63] NSBA.

state senators and my House Representative, met with the head of the SBA committees from the House and Senate. A number of board members have testified before Congress on small business issues. If you want to know what's happening (and there really is some stuff actually happening), get involved with NSBA.

Blind Spot: An 80-year old organization is going to have some things going on that are not leading-edge technology. NSBA has missed the opportunity to get their message out via social media and a strong digital presence. That is changing, albeit slower, than some would like. I'm not saying they should govern by Twitter, but as new business owners get ever younger, the expectation is to be able to interact and conduct business via the latest technology.

SBEA (Small Business Exporters Association of the United States)[64]

Mission: As the nation's oldest and largest nonprofit association representing small business exporters, SBEA works to influence pro-small business policies that will help expand the availability of exporting resources and make exporting a viable option for all small businesses.

Overview: SBEA serves as the international trade arm of the NSBA. They lobby for legislation that will help businesses that want to export their products and represent those small businesses.

SBTC (Small Business Technology Council)[65]

Mission: The Small Business Technology Council is a nonpartisan, nonprofit industry association of companies dedicated to promoting the creation and growth of research-intensive, technology-based U.S. small business. SBTC is a Council of NSBA.

---

[64] SBEA.
[65] SBTC.

Overview: You may look at this and think it's just a committee on NSBA, but it's more than that. It has its own Executive Director, Jere Glover, and there are several programs just for the technology sector of small business including funding for new technologies through its Small Business Innovation Research Program (SBIR) and advocacy work with both the House Committee on Small Business and the Senate Committee on Small Business & Entrepreneurship.

WIPP (Women Impacting Public Policy)[66]

Established: 2001

Mission: WIPP is a national nonpartisan organization advocating on behalf of women entrepreneurs—strengthening their impact on our nation's public policy, creating economic opportunities, and forging alliances with other business organizations.

Overview: I had been aware of WIPP for a number of years because they were at WBENC events. I got much more curious about them after I got involved with NSBA. Candace Waterman, former VP and Chief of Staff for WBENC and dynamo in the diversity arena, heads up the organization. While the name and the mission imply it is a woman-only advocacy, their "Understanding How Policy Works in WIPP" states, "Its focus is exclusively on the economic issues that affect women and minority business owners."

They do a great job of lobbying on behalf of woman-owned business and educating those of us who want to know more.

These are just a few of the organizations that can help you make informed choices in the political arena. They also help provide me with hope for our political system and that, at some point, needed work will get done, despite the best efforts of leadership of both of the major political parties in our nation.

---

[66] WIPP.

STUNT DOUBLES—DATA

We all love to watch stunt doubles at work. They make the things our heroes and sheroes do look easy and graceful. That doesn't happen without a bunch of folks behind the curtain planning out every last detail and bringing in the experts to put it all together.

And so it goes for a successful supplier diversity business strategy. Pretty much any topic that I attend an educational session about these days starts with some sort of data analytics. We have reached a point in technology where the ability to slice and dice data related to our business is getting easier all the time. No longer are the biggest complaints from departments about not having data, more likely are complaints that there is too much data or they aren't sure what to do with all of their data. Of course, some data is still a mess, which means you can mine bad data much faster than you ever could before.

Regardless, there are a plethora of organizations that are happy to help you find, mine, and better understand your data. That has turned into a field unto itself called data analytics.

There are all sorts of consulting houses with tons of data related to supply chain and a few with some information on supplier diversity itself. But where does one go to get such data that isn't part of their very own supply chain? I'm glad you asked.

Supply chain organizations use data from the big consulting firms like McKinsey, EY, PwC, Accenture, and Deloitte. They get more specific data from companies like Gartner that specialize in technology data on everything from what is happening with Artificial Intelligence to who has the best software for running your accounts payable. Some specialize in supply chain data across the board like ISM and CIPS, who we have already met. Companies like Spend Matters also keep track of what's going on in the supply chain industry and related research.

As supplier diversity goes, there are two main players in the third-party reporting space: ConnXus and CVM Solutions.

These are the companies that other companies go to in order to have third-party, arms-length, diversity reporting done. Companies send them their vendor master and/or payables file for a given quarter and ConnXus and CVM bump it up against their data base and tell you which companies are certified and what designation(s) they have. From that, a company can report on their dollar spend by designation and select the type of certifications they accept. Companies also use this data to provide tier 2 reporting (see Chapter 13) to their customers who want it. So, what's the deal on these two companies?

ConnXus[67]

Established: 2010

Mission: The mission of ConnXus is to be the go-to connector between corporate buyers and suppliers. ConnXus makes it simple and easy for them to do business with one another. ConnXus supplier management software solutions simplify the complexities of global supply chains and allow buyers to achieve their goals of responsible and sustainable sourcing.

Overview: Born out of founder and CEO Rod Robinson's frustration with incomplete databases, fragmented resources, and expensive software, Rod set out to create a more complete, convenient, and cost-effective solution to see the needs of both buyers and suppliers. Could this be my much longed-for single point of registration? We will see. I for one hope so. In the meantime, ConnXus provides procurement solutions, risk solutions, the myConnXion platform, supplier diversity solutions, supplier services, the myConnXion Business Center, and, most recently announced, their own certification process for small business. Oh and, by the way, they are an MBE.

Blind Spot: Another certification process, this one dedicated to small business. So, no ethnicities, gender, or orientation issues to

---

[67] ConnXus.

worry about, but when they become successful and are no longer a small business, the company would be outside ConnXus scope. Like any competing certification, it will depend upon who accepts it and who doesn't. If the U.S. government does, that would go a long way. There is no specific verbiage on their website about it being U.S.-only, so it could also be a portal to global registration and that would be a game changer. Their certification was literally announced as the book manuscript was going to the publisher, so we will have to wait and see what happens. I will tell you this, it is a smart, customer-centric group in ConnXus and you know how much I like customer centric. If they can make my one portal dreams come true, all the better, where do I sign?

CVM Solutions[68]

Established: 2002

Mission: Working as an innovative leader in the supplier diversity community, CVM's mission is to support every program by providing strategic and superior end-to-end supplier diversity data and technology solutions. Equipped with unparalleled data intelligence, superior technology, and expert guidance, businesses can effectively establish and advance their supplier diversity initiatives. CVM partners with corporate supplier diversity programs in every stage of their evolution, from those that are just getting started to the most advanced, world-class programs.

Overview: CVM began life as an MBE that provided third-party supplier diversity reporting, something that hadn't been available before and quickly became the gold standard for 1 and tier 2 reporting. The company lost its MBE status when it was acquired in 2011 by Kroll, a risk solutions provider. For a time, it was up in the air whether the diversity reporting would continue. Fast forward two more acquisitions, and today they are owned by supplier.io,

---

[68] CVM.

a company already in the supplier diversity space and they appear to have returned to their roots. In addition to the reporting solutions, CVM has made the news with their annual State of Supplier Diversity report, a survey that in 2019 boasted more than 450 respondents from both the supply chain and supplier diversity side of the business.

Blind Spot: While they were busy going through acquisition after acquisition, ConnXus was hard at work and now there are viable choices for supplier diversity professionals. It remains to be seen how this plays out. With ConnXus now offering certifications of their own and CVM back doing what they have done best it's anybody's market.

Like any market, once customers start looking for a solution, more solutions will pop up to meet the need. Here are a couple to watch:

Quantum SDS[69]

Quantum is a procurement and supplier management software provider. What makes them different? They look to incorporate supplier diversity into the procurement enterprise resource planning (ERP) solution, so it is as much a part of the procurement process as creating a purchase order. If this takes off, it's going to give the reporting houses a run for their money.

SupplierGATEWAY[70]

The company produces procurement apps for buyers and suppliers. That includes SaaS solutions for procurement, vendor management, and corporate responsibility. They also provide vendor portal solutions, which I will rant on in the next chapter on reporting. They boast some pretty high-powered customers on their website,

---

[69] Quantum.
[70] SupplierGATEWAY.

although you can't know if that is in the supplier diversity space. Although the supplier diversity reporting does not seem front and center, they are worth keeping an eye on.

REGISTERING ON THE COMPANY PORTAL

Before we move away from data and reporting, I must say a word or seven about the registration portals. At some point in every conversation a DBO has with an SDP, the DBO will be asked to register on the company portal. The company needs to register information about the company so they can find the company when they have a need. Sounds perfectly reasonable, right? Here's the thing, portals are a huge time suck and, if a DBO hears from 5% of the registrations they complete, it's a chatty kind of day. Yet, every company has one. Here's another thing, they all want almost the exact same information. Name, address, certifications, upload your certificate, what kind of services do you provide, what is the url for your website, what is the contact information, blah, blah, blah. There are third-party companies out there that do reporting, dashboards, data mining, white papers, and all kinds of advice. Why in all that is right with our world is there not a way to point companies to one or two registration points where they can get the information instead of the diverse businesses having to assign the better portion of an FTE to do this for everyone they meet?

As a corporate, I hated managing the portal. It would have been great to be able to get a link from a DBO where I could pull in their information if I needed it in my ERP or just use the third-party database.

As a DBO, it's insane trying to work my way through each of these portals, especially when I get home from an event. I've just been out of the office for a few days, which is difficult enough, now I need two days to fill out a bunch of forms asking for basically the same information, but each one in a little bit different format. For some, I receive the obligatory automatic welcome message. And for most, that's the last I ever hear. There is never any way to confirm my information went through okay; no way to know where, if anywhere the information goes. Honestly, I feel I have a better chance of buying a winning lottery ticket than I do getting a call from a company that found me on their portal and picked up the phone to call. And yet, the saga of the portals plods along.

Somebody create an app or a bot or a something that takes care of this! I'm not talking about inventing yet another place to register, I'm talking about one that replaces all of the others. Gah!

STUNT DOUBLES—MEDIA

Like any industry or business process, supplier diversity has media that reports on and supports their endeavors. If you are going to be in the know on what has happened, what is going to happen, and who is making it happen, the media in the supplier diversity space is going to play a role in your life. If you are managing a business strategy from a corporate chair, you may want to select one or several to advertise in and perhaps to support in other ways. If you are a DBO, you want to know what potential companies and your peers are doing. Regardless of your role, media publications and websites offer you a way to stay in touch with what is happening. There are quite a few out there. Like the organizations, I'm sure I will leave some out and that is not a statement of any kind other than I'm clearly not reading enough.

We will begin with my top four picks in alphabetical order:

Business Equality Magazine (BEQ)[71]
Mission: The Business Equality Network (BEQ) is a group of strategic media, consulting, research and business accelerators

---

[71] *Business Equality Magazine.*

committed to reaching and empowering LGBTQ, women, minority, and other underrepresented, underserved, and underutilized business communities. BEQ leverages its dedicated communication platforms to facilitate an increase in cross-sector (public, private, civil society) engagement of diverse professionals, business owners, and entrepreneurs.

One thing I love about my top four picks is they are more than just a magazine, and BEQ certainly has that covered. Run by dynamo and media whiz Robin Dillard, BEQ brings together all types of print, social media, online news, and information that you want to know. The stories are fresh and give you a peek inside more than who started what and here's what they did with it. Even people who I consider I know well give me a surprise when Robin does a story on them. BEQ has an active website with enough updates to keep you coming back for more. For information on how to advertise with BEQ: https://businessequalitymagazine.com/advertising/

DiversityPlus[72]

Mission: The mission at DiversityPlus is two-fold:

- They help companies better understand how to do business with outstanding women and minority companies.
- They provide women and minority companies with critical insights about how they can bring value to world-class corporations.

DiversityPlus is a fantastic publication and the closest thing to true journalism (not talking heads telling you how to feel journalism, I'm talking Cronkite journalism) for the supplier diversity space as you can get. That's not to say it is all strait-laced or stoic, rather that the publication delves into topics that impact diversity directly

---

[72] *DiversityPlus Magazine.*

and indirectly. Topics like blockchain, succession, and e-procurement. Paul Lachhu, Editor in Chief of not one, not two, but three diversity publications—DiversityPlus, DiversityGlobal, and DiversityCanada, covers all aspects of diversity and does it well. His websites, like the others in my top four, offer more than just a copy of the latest publication. They read like your other news feeds and are just as compelling. Fair warning, I can pop out to one of the websites to look at something and find myself still there reading an hour later. Discipline is necessary. To advertise with them, go to:

DiversityPlus: https://www.diversityplus.com/AdvertiseWithUs. aspx

DiversityGlobal: https://diversityglobal.com/Mediakit.aspx

DiversityCanada: https://www.diversitycan.com/AdvertiseWith Us.aspx

Diversity Professional[73]

Mission: Diversity Professional's mission is to advance economic inclusion for underrepresented groups by focusing on issues that impact employment, entrepreneurship, and business. They engage, inspire, celebrate, educate, and connect diverse professionals and entrepreneurs to opportunities that elevate their careers and businesses.

Diversity Professional (DP). Full disclosure, I have all kinds of conflict here, as I am a contributing writer and on their advisory board. That should tell you how much I love this publication, online, and live community.

DP is elegant, fresh, and looks at all aspects of the professional (employee or business owner) who has a career in supplier diversity, and/or is diverse, and/or is interested in inclusion as a foundation of whatever career they may be in. Yes, there are sections you would expect to find in such a publication like "Diversity," "Leadership,"

---

[73] *Diversity Professional.*

and "Business." But there are also sections on "Lifestyle," "Career," and "How To." DP publishes four times per year. Two issues in print and digital, and two issues in digital alone. President and CEO Melissa Simmons worked for a number of publications before going out on her own.

She had a clear vision of what she wanted, a magazine *and* a community. In addition to the magazine, DP hosts events like:

- Webinars on a variety of topics from how to do business with large companies to a before and after pair of sessions for DBOs on preparing for a conference and then debriefing *after* the event.
- Diversity Professionals Connect (DPC), an invitation-only retreat and think tank for people in the supplier diversity and diverse-owned business space.
- Women of Excellence Awards Brunch that recognizes extraordinary women of diversity who operate at the highest level of excellence in their businesses, careers, communities, and organizations.

To advertise with Diversity Professional, go to: http://diversity-professional.com/request-media/

Minority Business Entrepreneur (MBE) Magazine[74]
Mission: MBE serves as a nationwide forum for minority and women business owners, corporations, and government agencies concerned with minority and women business enterprise development.

MBE Magazine is the original. Founded in 1984, the magazine hired Barbara Oliver in 1989. In 2011, she became the publisher. There is supplier diversity before Publisher Barbara Oliver and there is supplier diversity after. MBE was the first magazine I ever saw

---

[74] MBE.

that mentioned supplier diversity and I remember trying to clear my calendar for the afternoon when it arrived so that I could read it from cover to cover. If you have spent more than 12 minutes in supplier diversity, you have sat and learned at the feet of Barbara in some form or fashion. When I had crazy corporate travel that some months took me from an event in Canada to one in LA to one in Miami, Barbara was at all three. She has semi-retired (does that mean you've cut back to a 40-hour work week Barbara?) but the magazine lives on. To advertise with MBE Magazine: https://www.mbemag.com/index.php/advertising/request-a-media-kit

There are a number of other publications and they are all great in their space. The four above have special meaning for me personally. Here are some additional publications for your consideration.

Affinity[75]

Affinity Inc's mission is to support and promote the business case for LGBT Business Equality in the workforce, supply chain, and marketplace of America's leading corporations.

Biz Journals[76]

Biz Journals are not exclusive to supplier diversity or inclusion. There are 43 publications that are specific to a U.S. city or metropolitan area. They cover everything from business real estate deals to local politics to business leaders in the area. They also devote a lot of ink to diversity topics. Known for publishing "The List" on everything from wealthiest zip codes to woman-owned firms, they also have events that celebrate list items. If you have a vested interest in a particular city, Biz Journals are worth the investment. I have also found them valuable when going into a new area that I am not familiar with.

---

[75] *Affinity Inc Magazine.*
[76] Biz Journals.

Color[77]

Color Magazine is an online and print all-inclusive publication focused on highlighting topics of interest for Corporate America and its diverse professionals. They also host four signature events:

- The Women of Color Leadership and Empowerment Conference (WOC)
- The Men of Color Leadership Conference (MOC)
- The Chief Diversity Officer Summit (CDO)
- The All-Inclusive Awards (AIA)

DiversityComm, Inc. (DCI)[78]

DCI publishes six magazines, each with a different take on diversity, they are:

- *Black EOE Journal*
- *DIVERSEability Magazine*
- *Diversity in STEAM* (science, technology, engineering, art, and math) *Magazine*
- *HISPANIC Network Magazine*
- *Professional WOMAN's Magazine*
- *U.S. Veterans Magazine*

Indian Country Today[79]

Indian Country Today is a newspaper and online community that keeps up with all things related to the Indian tribes and communities.

---

[77] *Color Magazine.*
[78] DiverstiyComm.
[79] Indian Country Today.

MBNUSA (Minority Business News)[80]

Their mission is to support and promote MBE suppliers as well as celebrate the leading corporations and diversity champions who advance the cause of supplier diversity. They have a digital and print version of the magazine.

Supply Professional[81]

The magazine has had a few names (*Modern Purchasing*, *PurchasingB2B*) over the years, but has remained steadfast in publishing information for Canada's supply chain community. They have been great about also covering supplier diversity in Canada in the magazine as well as their online news daily SupplyPro.ca and their weekly newsletter.

Women's Enterprise magazine (WE USA)[82]

Their mission is to support and promote WBE suppliers as well as celebrate the leading corporations and diversity champions who advance the cause of supplier diversity.

 The C-Suite: You don't see many C-suite individuals at outreach events. Over the years, I got a couple of CPOs and COOs, one CFO, and a head of Sales. None of them ever thought it was a waste of time. You could do a lot worse with your day than spending a few hours in a room full of your customers and potential customers who will be impressed that you are there. Oh, and did I mention the people from companies you do business with are likely people who manage your contract? Who weigh in on your supplier metrics? Who will have a hand in the bid when it goes back out? How often do you get a room full of those people who are

---

[80] MBNUSA.
[81] Supply Professional.
[82] WE USA.

happy to see you? When you get the report from your SDP on upcoming events and their locations (and you will as soon as they read the chapter on reporting), pass it to someone on your team who can compare it to your calendar and see if there are any matches.

 The Supplier Diversity Professional (SDP): Contrary to popular belief, events are not the primary activity of the SDP. And to anyone who even hints that the events are a boondoggle has clearly never worked one. That said, SDPs do attend a dozen or more regional and national events every year. It can be easy to turn on the autopilot and that would be a shame. Early in my career, I had the opportunity to do a benchmark exercise with Disney. One of the things they addressed was each family that visited one of their parks had likely saved up to be there. They were using their time off from work. Their children were looking forward to an amazing event. Disney could not afford to let those families be disappointed. That meant that their employees could never be on autopilot. They had to be committed to making everyone's experience everything they had dreamed of and more.

Every event you attend, you are meeting DBOs who have saved their money to attend, who have taken time out of running their business to be there. Do you see where I'm going with this? It's tempting to catch up with your peers from other companies and you should totally do that, but not at the expense of meeting someone new. You are there for DBOs and that should always be the focus.

 The Supply Chain Professional (SCP): They say that the best way to support pretty much anything is to show up. That is certainly true when it comes to supplier diversity events. If you are in supply chain with a company that has a supplier diversity business strategy and you haven't been to an event, it's like doing a bid without doing any spend analytics. You may come away with a good contract, but you are definitely leaving money and time on the table doing it. Almost every supply chain professional (SCP) I've talked to thinks they know exactly what goes on at one of these events. Almost every SCP I've talked to has been misinformed. Sign up and then show up.

Once you are there, engage! By engage, I mean forget about the script where you give the DBO a list of things you buy, the business card of your SDP and remind them to register on your portal. Have a conversation. Attend an educational session or two. Strike up a conversation with a stranger sitting next to you at lunch.

The Diverse Business Owner (DBO): These events, whether about outreach, public policy, or something else, are really here for you. SDPs are looking for you. SCPs who attend are curious about you. Without you, the DBO, there wouldn't be a need to meet. You need to arrive prepared (more on that in the next chapter), rested, and ready to work hard the entire time you are there. It's true that even a blind squirrel finds a nut now and then, but these events are not inexpensive to attend. Don't cast the fate of your business to the wind, be ready to succeed.

The End User: I know if you are the internal client, going to a supplier diversity event seems a little like Six Degrees of Kevin Bacon, but hear me out. If your business unit spends a fair amount (with or without supply chain), you need to see what is going on here. If you have any responsibility for your company's customers (I dare you to say no to that) you should see if any of them are at this event. Or any of your suppliers. Or any who have something you are interested in finding out about. While all of that is going on, you will see exactly what your company's supplier diversity business strategy is about. You don't have to do the whole thing. Walk the trade show floor and call it a day if you must. But it will be worth it for the people you meet and what you learn about the capabilities and opportunities that your SDP has for you. Ask your SDP to send you an event calendar that includes dates and locations and see if any of them match up with trips you already have planned. You won't regret it and I have yet to hear anyone tell me it was a waste of time.

CHAPTER 12

NAVIGATING EVENTS

OUTREACH COMPASS

Throughout the year, there will be a number of events that take place in support of supplier diversity. A company may attend them, have a booth in the event's trade show, sponsor various activities happening at the event, participate in matchmaking sessions, and so on. These events are not inexpensive to attend. Yet time and again, I see companies that get only a paltry surface amount of benefit from them due to poor planning and poorer execution. In fact, I maintain that on average an attendee, whether diverse business owner (DBO), supplier diversity professional (SDP), or otherwise, only captures about 50% of the available opportunities at an event.

Like any other business, it takes money to put together events where corporate members and DBOs can come together and possibly do some business. As the head of supplier diversity for a company that did not have a huge budget, I was often frustrated by the repetition at these events. Each one is an expensive undertaking and, when it feels like you meet the same companies each year or multiple times in the same year, it starts to feel a bit like a treadmill.

As you have probably recognized by now, you could spend an almost unlimited amount of money joining all of the organizations that might have an effect on your business, so how do you make an informed choice as to where the biggest bang for your particular buck is?

The first step is in understanding your business, your budget, what each of these organizations provide, and how those resources will contribute to your business strategy. Many will tell you there are certain organizations that you just have to be a member of regardless of the value you get from them. I would argue that if the organization can't provide a value proposition for your membership, your money may be better spent elsewhere. At any rate, here are a few items to consider when calculating your ROEI (Return on Event Investment).

Regardless of which cast member hat you might be wearing at a given event, you should have set objectives for attending. As an SDP, it might be to meet a minimum of ten new potential suppliers across three spend categories. For example, an SDP could be looking for suppliers in the areas of bulk fuel, IT cloud security, and new employee and driver drug testing. A DBO, on the other hand, might have an objective to identify 30 new business prospects for their business of online curriculum development and delivery.

Either way, there is a defined objective to be met. There will likely be other objectives as well. It might be to learn more about working with the SBA or finding out how the last privacy laws passed are impacting small businesses. Whatever they are, capture them in a format that allows you to track success or failure.

Next, understand what it costs for you to travel. I don't mean just an airline ticket and hotel room, although that is certainly part of it. I also mean time away from your business or office. Add that to the registration for the event, food, and other transportation and you have your investment to attend said event. If you are planning on a booth or other members of your company also attending, add that in.

If there is a trade show at the event you are considering, the biggest dollar impact may be on whether or not you should have a booth. A booth seems like a good idea but bear in mind the only thing worse than having no booth is having an empty booth. If you can bring a couple of people from your company to work the booth while you walk the event, it may make sense. If not, then you will be held captive waiting for the right people to come to you. If you don't have staff, my vote would be no booth.

There are plenty of other things you can spend your money on. If you have advertising dollars and it ties with your business, it may be worth the expense. For example, Kellogg has long been sponsoring breakfast meetings called *Breakfast with the Brands*, where SDPs and DBOs could meet over breakfast and potentially do some business. It is an ingenious way to foster the Kellogg brand, show their commitment to their supplier diversity business strategy, meet companies they may want to do business with, and share the wealth with other corporate members of an organization all at the same time. If you can make a tie-in that will benefit your company, go for it. Otherwise let's move to the next step.

Once you have identified the cost of the investment, you know what you have to recoup in business or suppliers to break even and to come out ahead. Now, you need to determine if you can do that with the event you are considering.

Most events are made up of a mix of the following:

- Educational/information sessions
- Trade show
- Matchmaking sessions
- Various keynotes, usually over meals that are part of the event
- Receptions
- Silent auction or other fundraising events
- Gala and/or awards

Every last one of these is an opportunity, regardless of your role at the event. Your mission is to leverage it to the absolute nth degree. That doesn't even remotely happen by accident or by winging it.

While there is plenty of business to be done at an event, there are other things you can gain as well. One thing I do is to carefully review the educational sessions taking place to see where I can benefit most. For example, at WBENC Summit & Salute in 2018, they had a day-long technology track with excellent sessions on 5G. It wasn't the SDP from Verizon talking about it. It was the person at Verizon who is managing the 5G rollout. It was technology that I needed to understand for my business and for clients' businesses. This was a gold mine and paid for the entire trip just in what I learned and the contacts that I made. I'm still getting white papers from IBM and newsletters from Ericsson based upon those sessions. Don't be myopic about where the returns on your investment might come from.

Next, carefully review the list of exhibitors, speakers, attendees, whatever is provided. Most events have apps now that allow you to connect and message other attendees over the course of the event. I look for businesses that I haven't seen before and am always on the lookout for businesses in nontraditional areas. I look for people I have met before but want to connect with face-to-face while I am there. We may not be doing business right away, but this is part of the relationship building. If I had been impressed with them last year but felt maybe they weren't quite ready for me, I want to check in and see how the year has been for them. I will make note of who has a booth that I want to stop at, message those who may be tough to meet up with. I tend to do a lot of "coffee stops" with folks throughout the conference. Quicker than a meal, it still allows some one-on-one time over a cup of coffee, drink, ice cream, or cocktail, depending upon the time of day. Set up as much as you can in advance but leave some slots open for happy accidents. Also understand these events can get crazy for all of the participants.

Be gracious and understanding if people need to move or cancel. Just be sure to follow up to have the conversation later.

SIX RULES FOR WORKING AN EVENT

I have a few rules for anyone working an event on my dime, and that includes for myself.

1. I did not pay to fly anyone to an event so they could catch up on e-mail or work in their hotel room (that includes the pool at the hotel, too). Once in attendance, you should be present when you are outside the hotel room and you should be outside of the hotel room *a lot.*

2. When outside the hotel room and especially when representing the company at a booth or table, I don't expect to see you on your #$%&@ phone or tablet or laptop or anything else that takes you away from what is happening in front of you. Nothing steams me more than seeing people sitting at a booth with their head in their phone trying not to make eye contact with anyone. What a waste of money! The head should be held high looking around with a smile on the face. The purpose of the trip is to meet potential companies, customers, potential customers, mentors, best practice people and all of their friends. You never know where the best contact of the event will come from. If you need to make a call, step away from your booth, table, or counter and make it brief.

3. Over the course of the event, you will spend a fair amount of time in elevators, on escalators, in coffee lines, at restaurants waiting to be seated, buffet lines, and so on standing next to people with badges on that tell you they have the same interests as you. Strike up a conversation. It makes the wait go faster and I've met some of my best contacts that way. So, just in case you thought that was the time to take your phone out, uh, no. If you

are in the elevator and someone has a first-time ribbon on their badge, welcome them and ask how it's going for them. If you like someone's shoes or tie or lanyard, tell them. It's called an elevator pitch for a reason.

4. Most days of the event there will be a breakfast and lunch served with speakers. It's tempting to step out from the meals and keynotes but try to resist. This is not where you spend some quality time bonding with your coworkers. I expect my team to go to each of these events and sit at a table where they don't know anyone. It's a chance to meet seven to ten new people at every meal and get 20–30 minutes with them. It also saves on the cost of meals because they are provided in the registration cost. Woe be unto team members who expensed the cost of breakfast with each other when one of these events was available. The speakers are usually worth the time as well. Whether a paid keynote or a panel from sponsor companies, you can learn new skills or best practices while you make new friends and eat a free meal.

5. With multiple people working a show comes a diversity of thought and perceptions. Be sure each of your folks has the opportunity to spend some time walking the trade show themselves or attending some educational sessions. Each will bring their own observations, impressions, ideas, and contacts.

6. Unless there is something specific going on, let them go off on their own for dinner. I tried to take everyone out for a fun night, but they also needed time without me. Whether they went to dinner together, went to a different part of town, ordered room service or GrubHub so they can watch a movie or FaceTime with the family. As one of my bosses used to say, "It's hard being both pleasant and attentive for long periods of time." Make sure people aren't burning out. That goes for yourself too.

THE ROADMAP TO TRADE SHOWS

Regardless of which cast member hat I'm wearing, I typically spend a good two to three hours going over the list of exhibitors for the larger shows. I want to identify any customers (current or not so current), potential customers, contacts who may not be potential customers but are good to know, companies I may want to do business with myself, and companies that may have something new that I'd like to see.

If your event has an app with the trade show layout, that helps a lot. This is especially true if you can have the companies appear both alphabetically and by booth number. That way, you make one trip up and down each aisle. You can save thousands of steps doing that versus a hit or miss approach. Your dogs will thank you at the end of the day and you will accomplish more.

Be at the trade show at ribbon cutting and go directly to the back of the trade show hall. While everyone else stands in line to talk to the big sponsors up front, you can talk to a whole bunch of companies that don't have a line yet because the masses have not made their way to the back yet. Start at the back and work your way to the front.

Whatever method of note taking works best for you, be sure to take good notes. I know it doesn't seem like you could possibly forget what the guy from Target said to you, but it will all run together before day's end. Whether you step away and jot a few notes or talk into the recorder on your phone (yes, there are apps for that), make notes for each stop.

When you follow up, you want that person to recall the connect, so if there is anything said that would foster that, put it in your notes. Then, instead of the generic "it was great to meet you at …", you instead can say, "It was great to meet you. I'm still envious of your trip to Vail that you told me about. Who would think you could find that quality of micro distiller there? I'd still love the link when you have a minute." Now think about being able to do that with 50 people you met. Fifty who may actually remember meeting you instead of looking at an e-mail or your business card and wondering which in the hoard of people they met was you.

THE C-SUITE AT TRADE SHOWS

Over the years, I got a couple of CPOs and COOs, one CFO, and a head of Sales to attend an event. It's not easy, but if you are a SDP or supply chain professional (SCP), that should not keep you from trying. I kept an eye out for events that were close to corporate facilities or a frequent visit site. One COO was in love with the training facility the company had built for all incoming technicians. I was able to land a visit when it was in the same city as his favorite facility.

Most C-suite visits will be for part of a day and I was fine with that. If you can get them in the night before, set up a breakfast with one or more large customers of the company. Let them hear the benefit their customers see in the business strategy, receiving, reporting, or whatever else has been done with them. It reinforces how the strategy supports the revenue and customer retention. Then take them to the trade show.

The C-suite has done more than their share of trade shows. However, they still tend to be impressed by the size of something like the NMSDC or WBENC trade show floor. It demonstrates how much their customers, peer companies, potential customers, etc. are willing to invest in this. It also shows them there is serious business to be done at one of these events. Have a set path planned to visit the show but be ready to freestyle and follow your C-suite individual. I've had them get excited and go up and down each aisle to see who is there. I've had them center in on one company and spend a lot of time there. I had one who was car shopping and spent most of the time in the auto section looking at the cars that suppliers had brought in (eye roll), so you never know which way the wind might blow. Usually, they said something like, "Lead the way." That meant it was up to me to show what I thought mattered. In those cases, I had three or four aisles selected that had customers and maybe a potential customer or two in them. For the customers, I had already let them know I was coming by with a VIP. I usually ended in the aisle that had our company booth so they could see the team at work. Don't start with your own booth unless you can guarantee a large turnout right at ribbon cutting.

On this tour, I liked for them to see the different-size booths that companies purchased and how they were staffed. I wanted to get a list of the exhibitors in their hands in case they had any requests. Anyone I ran into during the walk, I introduced them to. If possible, introduce them to someone involved in the organization hosting the event, or at least a region chapter the company has a membership in. Just be sure that person from the organization is going to acknowledge them as a valued customer. I introduced a COO to an organization head once who proceeded to go on and on about how much another company had spent with the organization for the event. It came across as really crass (probably because it *was* crass?) and I got to spend the next two years listening to my COO tell the story every time I was in a meeting where supplier diversity came up. It takes enough of a miracle to get a C-suite person to the event. Don't let some third-rate "this is my chance to make a sale" person turn it into a bad thing. My point is this: an attorney once told me the first thing they teach you in trial law is to never ask a witness a question you don't already know the answer to. Be sure you know what a person is going to say before you make a point of introducing them.

MATCHMAKING

If you are certified by the organization that is hosting the event you are attending, then you will likely be invited to participate in matchmaking. If so, the answer is *always* yes. The best organizations have software that allows DBOs to request meetings with companies that will be attending and allows SDPs to say yes or no to that meeting. All of this should happen weeks before the actual event.

Matchmaking provides a 10- to 20-minute one-on-one meeting between a DBO and a corporate (SDP and/or SCP). There are typically as many of these as can fit into a day with a five-minute gap between each meeting. Corporate members will sit at assigned tables, usually in alphabetical order by company name, and the DBOs will move from table to table.

Tips for DBOs: First, only ask to meet companies you think you can really help. This is not where you find out what a company does or if they have an active HR group. This should be for the solid leads.

Second, learn everything you can about the company, how they use your product/service, who will be there, anyone you know who knows anyone who knows someone from this company. This is where you flex those networking muscles. I have a whole workshop about getting ready for matchmaking sessions but suffice to say plenty can be learned ahead of time to provide the best opportunity for a good "match."

Tips for SDPs: Don't say yes to the first dozen that send you an invite and call it good. If you don't think it is a good match, hold out for a good prospect. That said, if you say no, don't just say no. Give some insight like "we don't use this service" or "we won't look at this until 2025, come back to me in 2023" or "you had 11 misspelled words in your invite."

OTHER HAPPENINGS AT EVENTS

There are all sorts of other things happening at these events. If there is a silent auction—go! If there is a reception hosted by a corporate—go! There may be a gala dinner where awards are handed out to people you may or may not know—go! Everyone who registered for this event did so expecting to meet people. Be one of those people.

POST EVENT

Follow-up, follow-up, follow-up. Opinions are all over the place as to how soon this should happen from before you leave the event to three weeks after so there is time to get back to the office and get back into the e-mail game.

I'm a huge LinkedIn fan, so I tend to send the first note out from the plane on the way home asking to connect on LinkedIn. Once connected there, no need to send a note through there each time. Be sure you send a note with the request, not the automated request. This is the first place you want to use that note you made to yourself on how you connected with the person. You can mention the yellow jacket they had on that you told them was divine or the daughter's birthday party they missed to attend. Whatever will make them remember you.

If the event ended on Thursday or Friday, I would begin sending out the follow-up the following Thursday and have them all done by Monday the week following your return. No message, no matter how tailored, has a nice ring to it when we met in June and you're following up in August.

Finally, invest in the extra hotel night to leave the day after everything is over. I had a boss who suggested this to me years ago and it was such good advice. While everyone else is trying to pack up their hotel room the last morning and get their bags stashed, you can go to the breakfast and meet some more prospects. While people have to leave before the best session is over because they have a plane to catch, you can stay, go meet the speaker, and ask questions. Last day sessions are not as crowded and you have a better chance of actually getting to talk to folks. If there is someone from the event group you would like to meet, none of those people leave the last day, so they will be around. And finally, when the event is over, go back to your room, put your feet up, order room service, and start your follow-ups or binge watch something on Netflix. Either way, you will get a good night's sleep and arrive the next day rested instead of exhausted.

PUBLIC POLICY COMPASS

The 1968 Election

My parents were not particularly political. They didn't spend a lot of time discussing the political activities of the day. The big rule at home was that everyone was treated the same and no one was better than anyone else. As I have mentioned, we lived in Michigan, but home was always Georgia.

In 1968, I was in the third grade and it was an election year. The candidates were Republican Richard Nixon, Democrat Hubert Humphrey, and Independent George Wallace. My teacher announced that we would be studying the election and the following day we were to draw a poster for the candidate we wanted to win the election. The next morning, I did what most of the kids likely did, I asked Mama and Daddy who they were voting for. After some hemming and hawing, Daddy finally mumbled, "I dunno, maybe Wallace." I believe this was because Wallace was from the South more than any knowledge or acceptance of what Wallace stood for, but the damage was done.

I went to school that day and carefully created my Wallace poster. At the end of the hour, the teacher asked how many were for Nixon and a fair number of hands went up. Humphrey was running a close second, so when the teacher asked about him the count of hands was very close. Then she asked about Wallace and one other kid and me raised our hands. He was not someone I hung out with, I didn't think he was particularly nice and, in my 8-year old brain, a caution flag went up. What was going on here? A few minutes later, we were released for recess and I forgot about it and ran outside to play with my friends.

One of the boys came up and gave me a little push and said, "You want Wallace to win, he doesn't think Black people are as good as white people, you're a racist." I was instantly livid. I didn't know what a racist was, but it didn't sound like anything I would be interested in. How dare he! "You're wrong!" I said. I knew that Mama and Daddy would never vote for someone who felt that way. We began to tussle a bit and the teacher came over to break it up. She demanded to know what was going on. "He told a lie!" I exclaimed pointing to him and repeating what he had said. My teacher pulled me over to the side and gently told me a little about George Wallace. I was horrified! I told her I didn't want to support him and she told me I could do another poster over the weekend if I wanted.

The next day was Saturday and, when Mama and Daddy came down for breakfast, I was waiting for them. I told them what had happened at school the previous day. I told them what I had learned about George Wallace and wanted to know if they knew any of that. They admitted that they did. I then proceeded to read my parents the riot act for teaching me that everyone should be treated the same and then supporting someone who clearly did not. I asked them point blank if they were racist. I let them know that I was making a second poster over that weekend because I wanted no part of it. Mama sat down and told me that they were wrong and they hadn't really thought it through when they answered me. She assured me that they did believe everyone should be treated the same. She also said that I could support whoever I wanted to, that was what voting was all about. It wasn't a great recovery, but it helped a little bit. I liked that I got to decide who I would vote for on my own. After all, I couldn't trust them to come up with the right answer.

Years later, I asked Daddy if he remembered this. "Are you kidding me? Of course I remember it," he responded. He then went on to tell me that shortly after becoming a parent he had made peace with the fact that he would screw up occasionally and that would be okay. "I was okay making mistakes, but that was the only time I ever felt like I let you down as a human being. I was trying to move to the next topic and didn't consider the consequences of what I was doing. I never gave you an answer again without giving it thought and consideration." And to my knowledge, he did just that. In fact, I remember a few times when he would ask me to give him a day or two to consider something before we talked about it.

GETTING INVOLVED

So why is the story of the 1968 election pertinent to supplier diversity and navigating their events? Whether you do business with the government, whether you support Republicans, La Gauche Moderne, the New Democratic Party (NDP), Democratic Labour, the Idle Toad (yep, that is an actual party), or something else entirely, if you are reading this book you have an interest in something that is impacted by what your government does. One of my favorite quotes from Dr. Martin Luther King Jr. is, "He who passively accepts evil is as much involved in it as he who helps to perpetrate it. He who accepts evil without protesting against it is really cooperating with it." I still remember the first time I read that. It hit me especially hard because I knew a lot of people I looked up to who did nothing. They looked away. Some of these were the same people who had taught me that it wasn't just my right to vote, it was my responsibility, that a lot of people had died so that I could cast my vote. Now they stood by silently shuffling their feet while a lot of people were denied that right because it was uncomfortable, or inconvenient, or difficult for them to take a stand, to do the right thing.

The events that you attend are put together by a group of dedicated folks who want to make a difference. Whether you get involved in public policy topics or put your efforts towards a better matchmaking event, you are involved in a group of people and businesses that were created from a desire to make a difference and improve business. Don't just be a bystander who shows up, improves your company's supply chain or business opportunities and then ducks out until the next one.

Look, no one abhors the political climate more than I. If I could erase all aspects of news channels, social media, and talk radio from my life, I would pony up for that fee in a heartbeat. But I still have to make informed choices. I read a lot of transcripts, I try to get as much as possible from the origin versus someone who gives me a piece of it and tells me how I should feel about it. I read a lot of the bills in Congress so I know what they say, all that they say. I certainly haven't mastered the art, but I keep trying. Don't ever stop trying. And, don't ever stop holding your representatives accountable. There is an app called Countable. You load it, put your address in, and you receive a direct line to your representatives in the House and Senate. You also see everything they vote on. Give it a try.

To take more responsibility for making an effort, I have become personally involved in a couple of organizations and made friends with another one. One thing I have learned is that the difference between the people trying to actually do work in Washington, D.C., and those you see on television is vast, regardless of whether you are red or blue. The same holds true in the mostly volunteer organizations that certify and/or provide opportunities, training, and much, much more.

The people doing the work know and work alongside their peers on the other side of the aisle. They know what it takes to make change happen. I'm just saying, don't give up. I am as cynical as they come when it comes to the political process and I am more optimistic having spent time in the Capitol meeting with staff members of Congress and the White House.

If you are in a corporate position, take the time to understand any policies your company has about political activities. Yes, it is often there, hidden in the pages of the employee manual. There are some good reasons for this. Companies do not want their workplace to become a stomping ground for everyone's political debates. As someone who cannot even stand to listen to talk radio on the topic, I appreciate it not being in every meeting and conference call I have to attend. I'm not saying you can't have an opinion, just respect when you are representing yourself and when you are representing your company. Make sure your company respects that, too. I remember the first time my employer mailed me a brochure at home on a PAC the company supported that suggested donation amounts by title. Uh, no thank you.

If you are the owner of a small business, understand that you are often most impacted by the legislation from your government lawmakers and the decisions by the boards of your favorite advocacy organizations. If you don't take the time to get involved, don't be surprised if your thinking isn't represented.

At the end of the day, we are responsible for making our own informed choices. And for standing up and speaking out when it needs to be done.

C-Suite: If you have the opportunity to support your SDPs and SCPs by attending one of these events, even if it's only for an hour or two, do it. It can be a great differentiator to have your picture on your company website with your team at a supplier diversity event. It can also keep your team going when they are tired or wondering if anyone cares what they are working on. Do not underestimate the power of your support.

SDP: There is a fair amount of preparation required for an event. In addition to the registration process, due dates for shipping your booth and materials in without it costing you a kidney, and making sure everyone is coming in and going out when they need to, there are the logistics of the event itself. As for the events I just covered, it doesn't sound like much on paper, but it can be a real time suck. Depending on the company I was at, we either had someone who took care of all of this for us or we took turns doing it for a given event. Funding is hard enough to get without squandering it on overnight shipping or last-minute registration prices. At one company, we all agreed to stay at a hotel that was about a mile away from the action. We determined if we did that, we could gain almost a dozen more hotel nights over a years' time. That could mean a couple of extra events a year or something else we could use that money for. I would also note, there is something to be said for getting on an elevator at the end of the day that isn't filled with people trying to meet you. The downside is that once you leave your room in the morning, you likely won't be seeing it again until bedtime.

 SCP: If you are attending a supplier diversity event, you should know there is a lot that you can benefit from other than checking the box that you supported the business strategy. Check out the educational sessions and see if anything appeals to you. If you are new to supplier diversity or it has been some time since you worked in it, this is a great way to get up to speed or a refresher on what's new in the area. Yes, there are new things.

The matchmaking is nonnegotiable. You won't be happy about that because it will almost certainly mean staying an extra day. Do it anyway. Matchmaking is where DBOs have ten minutes or so to meet and talk about their company one-on-one with your company. There are methodologies to select who you meet with, so spend some time with your SDP before you go to the conference to select some that are of interest to you. This is where you should see that just giving a list of what you are bidding this year to your SDP and calling it good is just silly and expensive. There are great sourcing opportunities here. Leverage them.

DBO: Matchmaking is another part of the event that should be prepared in advance by the time you get on the plane to go. Yes, there will be last-minute changes, but for the meetings you schedule ahead of time, they should be researched, prepared, and ready before you leave. This is not an event where you are going to get a lot of work done and you certainly won't have time to do the preparation in your hotel room that you should have done at home. Have your message ready for each of your meetings. Have your materials neatly organized and then go get 'em. Things happen, people have to cancel. Understand if your event host has a place for DBOs to gather at matchmaking if you don't have a slot scheduled or your scheduled appointment had to cancel. Often, they will match you with a company who also has an open slot. It's a roll of the dice, but even if the company isn't a great fit, these people know people. It's better than just waiting for the next meeting.

It's the same for receptions, silent auctions, and galas. You may want to go upstairs, put your feet up, and order room service but that's for the last night. Go, mix, walk up to people and introduce yourself. This is no time to be a wallflower. Other DBOs are in the same shoes you are in. The big corporates? Well, they have paid big money to be there to meet as many DBOs as possible. Be one of them, whether you think you will do business with them or not. Is there really a downside to meeting the head of diversity for a Fortune 50 company?

End User: It's likely you won't be attending one of these events, but that doesn't mean you can't contribute to what is done at one. If you have particular services you are looking for, have a discussion with your SDP or SCP and see what can be found at the events that will help you. And, if one is taking place in a city near you, you could do worse than spending an afternoon attending one and finding out more about the business strategy for your company and maybe the next great supplier for you.

CHAPTER 13

REPORTING

A TALE OF THREE TIERS

If I had a dollar for every hour I've spent explaining what tier 1, tier 2 direct, and tier 2 indirect are, you wouldn't be reading this book. I'd be sitting on a sandy beach somewhere sipping something with a little umbrella in it and I wouldn't have written this. Why? Because it's confusing, that's why. The people who do this for a living can barely keep it straight and then we expect our clients to understand it. Gah!

Here we go, the lowdown on the three tiers. First, we need to clarify the cast of characters in this mini production:

1. **Wendy Weebee:** Wendy is a female, LGBT, Hispanic business owner of Weebee's R Us (no relation to the defunct toy retailer or the hamburger chain). She is certified through the Women Business Enterprise National Council (WBENC), the National Gay and Lesbian Chamber of Commerce (NGLCC), and the National Minority Supplier Development Council (NMSDC).

2. **Great Big Corp. or GBC:** This is a Fortune 50 company that has an award-winning supplier diversity business strategy. George runs their procurement organization.

3. **Minnow Manufacturing:** Minnow is a Fortune 1000 company that does a lot of business with the Great Big Corp. Millie is Minnow's head of supplier diversity.

Wendy wants to do business with George at Great Big Corp, too. She has met him at several diversity and matchmaking events. But George at GBC has told Wendy her company isn't going to get more than a small dollar contract with them. George suggests she talk to Millie over at Minnow. Minnow is one of GBC's prime suppliers and can help Wendy get her foot in the door. Got the stage set in your mind's eye?

Tier 1 are dollars spent directly with a diverse business owner (DBO). When GBC does business with Wendy, she sends them an invoice and GBC writes her a check. Those dollars are spent directly by GBC to Wendy so Wendy is a tier 1 supplier to GBC. When GBC reports out that they have done $X of spend with DBOs, the money they spent with Wendy counts as part of that number. So far, so good?

Since Wendy has three different certifications, GBC gets to choose which of the three categories they are reporting spend with Wendy in. They can count it as women (WBE), LGBTQ, or minority (MBE) dollars. They cannot count it in all three. GBC can't write Wendy a check for $1,000 and report $3,000 in spend. Makes sense, right?

Except in certain government circumstances. Yeah, leave it to the government to take something mildly complicated and make it into a web that Spider Man couldn't unwind.

Some government reporting allows you to count the dollars in all of the categories that they track. Only in the U.S. government can you take $3,000 of credit for $1,000. That would be if they tracked LGBTQ. Currently they don't. Write your congresspeople. So, you can take $2,000 of credit for $1,000. No one else on the planet, to my knowledge, allows this.

There are two types of tier 2, direct and indirect. Minnow is a prime supplier to GBC.

GBC wants to be sure that Minnow is supporting the supplier diversity business strategy, so they require quarterly reporting from all of their prime suppliers like Minnow.

Minnow did one project for GBC last quarter that they brought Wendy in on. Everything Wendy invoiced Minnow for ($2,500) on that project was for work expressly for GBC.

Minnow also used Wendy for several other projects that had nothing to do with work for GBC. Everything Wendy invoiced Minnow for ($5,500) on those projects was for work unrelated to GBC.

Minnow has $8,000 in total spend with WeeBee. Minnow reports $2,500 in tier 2 direct spend to GBC, because those dollars can be tied specifically to GBC work. Minnow reports $5,500 in tier 2 indirect spend to GBC because, while the dollars are not specific to GBC, they are spent with a DBO and therefore support the business strategy indirectly. It doesn't matter what type of business Wendy has, it can be tier 2, indirect. So, if Minnow has a DBO doing the roofing work on their new location, shoveling snow in their parking lot in Minneapolis, or providing uniforms for their employees, it all counts.

A Tale of Three Tiers

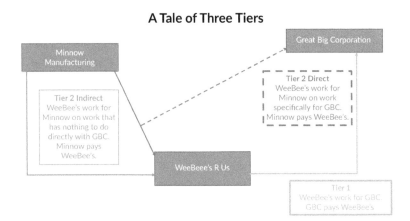

You may also hear supplier diversity professionals (SDPs) talking about tier 3-level spend. Tier 3 involves George from GBC getting not just Millie's spend at Minnow, but the spend reports that Millie gets from her suppliers. Before you threaten George at GBC with physical damage for starting another level of reporting, understand what George is trying to accomplish. He wants to ensure that his supplier diversity business strategy is trickling down to Millie's supply chain. There are a lot of companies out there who provide reporting to their customers, but don't ask their own suppliers to do the same.

George also wants to be sure that Wendy is implementing a supplier diversity strategy For some reason I cannot fathom, I remain amazed that when I ask diverse-owned companies about their strategy, they clarify for me that they are diverse owned. Yeah, so?

Now that we know what types of spend dollars there are, let's find out what we need to do to report them correctly and in a way that services our many clients:

We have talked a lot about accountability and using data and business processes to gain funding and acceptance of our business strategy for supplier diversity. It is now time to talk about reporting. That might seem like a pretty straightforward topic, but where there is data, there is mud in the water and supplier diversity reporting is no exception. Fair warning, I have definite opinions about reporting.

Credibility: You are reporting to your C-suite, your internal clients, the government, and to external companies that include customers and potential customers. If your numbers are called into question, you might as well be pulling them out of a tequila-soaked hat at the end of each quarter. Your numbers must be credible with all of the folks who are looking at them.

Dollars spent: One of the data points you need to know is how much was actually spent with DBOs in the last period (quarter, month, year) and how that compares to past periods. Most reporting happens on a quarterly basis, so we will work with that for purposes of our discussion here. Your spend numbers need to be validated by a third party. Lucky for you, there are companies out there that do just that. ConnXus (https://connxus.com) and CVM Solutions (https://www.cvmsolutions.com) are two of my favorites. Each quarter, you send them your accounts payable file(s) and your credit card spend file(s). They take those files and match them against their database of all of the suppliers all of their customers are using and the companies that have registered with their sites. They are responsible for keeping track of diversity certifications to ensure they are current and accurate. They will also research companies you have in your data that they don't have information about. In return, they provide back to you a reporting tool where you can slice and dice your spend results. Need to know how many woman-owned companies you have in the state of Nebraska? No problem! Want to know how many veteran-owned companies are also minority owned? Got it! You can also select what type of certifications you accept and how they are counted. Remember, everyone has their own yardstick about what counts and what doesn't. This allows you to tailor tier 2 reporting to whatever the customer wants.

The third-party solutions aren't cheap, so I want to address a question that I get a lot: Can we not do this ourselves? No, no you can't. Two reasons. First, you can't possibly research and maintain certificates on all of the companies in your payables file unless there are only a dozen companies you do business with. Second, credibility. You need that third party saying these are the numbers. These are numbers that should be able to stand up to rigorous audit.

As data becomes cheaper to store, smaller companies are now in the data business. This may create a situation where you have companies that can do reporting for you for a lot less than who you have talked to. I would never say never. I would also say some things, like LASIK surgery and diversity reporting, shouldn't automatically go to the least expensive provider. At the least, you should be able to get a trial run on a subset of your data. If they aren't willing to do that, pass. If they are, give them a nice smorgasbord of your data. Then review it carefully. I did this with a *very* well-known risk mitigation company a few years ago and they provided a report that listed the United States Postal Service as a minority-owned company.

Percentage of Spend: This is a simple calculation of the dollars you spent with DBOs divided by everything you spent through Accounts Payable and your credit, travel, or purchasing card (p-card) programs. Note that doesn't include payroll because the supplier is, well, the company itself.

Addressable Spend: I need to take a moment to discuss something that is all the rage in supplier diversity reporting. It's called addressable spend. Addressable spend works like this: Companies spend lots of money each quarter on things that can never be spent with a DBO. Things like their utility bill, or jet fuel for an airline, or taxes, etc. A few years ago, companies started removing those dollars from their total spend dollars. Instead of reporting their total spend, they reported *addressable* spend, those dollars that *could* be spent with a DBO. As a result, their percentage spent with DBOs went up (dividing the same number by a smaller number will do that for you). Now, instead of announcing they had spent 6% with DBOs they could announce 20% or 30%. That worked so well, some companies decided to take out any dollars that were currently under contract, even if DBOs existed that provided that product or service. The argument was that they wouldn't unwind a five-year agreement, so it couldn't be addressed for five years. Now they were reporting 50% and 60%.

The reason that Winston Churchill talked about lies, damn lies and statistics and not data points is because no one was calling it data points in the 1940s.

I don't like addressable spend and here is why. Remember those multiple clients? The ones you need for funding and support to make your strategy dreams come true? Ask your C-suite if they can go to Wall Street and tell them that EBITDA is up 40% over last quarter because they counted *addressable* earnings, so that includes the work they did for contracts they haven't landed yet. See if the accounting firm signs off when they validate the books and how that presentation goes.

Now go talk to your colleagues in procurement who get paid on savings dollars they generate. Ask them if they are allowed to report savings calculated only on the contracts and categories they were able to *address* in the last quarter. Maybe they can deduct that $40 million fuel contract because they didn't get to that RFP yet, so it wasn't *addressable*. Spoiler alert! A lot of procurement organizations only allow savings to be reported for the first 12 months of a contract, even if it's a five-year agreement. I didn't care much for that strategy either and usually threatened 5% per year instead of 25% from the first year, but I wouldn't recommend that as a strategy. My point is that you won't find a sympathetic ear in supply chain about your addressable spend trials.

Now go have the same conversation with the sales organization and see if they can get paid on the customers they called on, not the total revenue potential in their region because they didn't *address* it all.

Now go re-read the paragraph above on credibility. Here's the thing. Puffing up that percentage didn't put an extra nickel in the pocket of a DBO anywhere. When it comes to reporting, there is no room for the spin doctor.

If you are going to report based on addressable spend, at least have the decency (and the guts) to show your math. Tell the total spend and the addressable spend. Supplier diversity reporting should be like algebra was in high school, you have to show the math to get the credit.

Okay, now that we've covered the basics on reporting, let's talk about what else we should be reporting on.

The spend numbers are important. They have been validated by a third party and you have shown the math needed to understand how you did last quarter. You should also compare to at least the past 12 months. Hopefully, this will create a little chart with a line or arrow going up and to the right (executives love those).

What else? Well, I like to show how the strategy is aligned with the business. If you are in a B2C business, your marketing group will have demographics on your customer base. How does your spend align with those demographics? Do women make up 60% of your customer base? What is your percentage of spend with WBE companies? Is it 40% LGBTQ? How do those numbers compare to your spend? Remember, studies show that people like doing business with people like them. Don't worry if your spend numbers look paltry. This shows that no matter how well the business strategy is working, there is still work to be done.

How about a B2B business? I like to look at total revenue and how much of it is represented by customers who demand tier 2 reporting. For example, if you are providing tier 2 reports to 15 customers, what is the percentage of revenue those 15 customers represent (total revenue, not addressable revenue)? Report the number of customers, the amount of revenue, and the percentage of total. Going in with a dashboard item like: "Last quarter we provided reporting by 15 customers who represent $20.2 million in revenue or 14% of our total revenue" is pretty impressive. It ties you to revenue and customer retention. And by the way, when you attend your next diversity trade show, look at the list and see which customers are there, which customers who are there that are NOT getting tier 2 reporting, and which potential customers are there. Go to the booth and thank existing customers for their business. If they aren't currently getting tier 2 reporting, ask them if they'd like to have it. Much of the time, you'll find they were told your company didn't do

that or couldn't get it. Finally, introduce yourself to potential customers. One of my best sales techniques was to ask them if they did
business with my company. If they said no, I asked them what they
thought of my competitor's booth there at the event. They would
usually say something like they hadn't seen it and I would respond
that was because they weren't there. I may not have been working for
a DBO at the time, but I did work for a company that supported it.
It was not unusual for my company to get another look.

Another data point are metrics on meetings you had over the
last quarter. At least half of the executives seeing your dashboard live
in or touch the sales organization where everything is broken down
by number of prospects, calls made, and sales generated. Want to
get them over thinking you were in Miami last month running on
the beach like you were in a light beer commercial? Show them some
stats. Meetings can be broken down into event meetings, match-
maker meetings, and everything else. If you have the tools, track
first, second, or more number of meetings with a prospect. I also use
this data when I'm looking at the return I receive for the investment
in a given event or organization, but we will talk about that more in
the chapter on outreach.

Also, let them know what is coming up. I like a small box with
the date, event, and location. Remember, you are always trying to
find that spot where a C-suite member is in the area you are going to
be in. Invite them and often and take a couple of hours, a stop on the
way to the airport, whatever they can offer enthusiastically. Trust
me, you probably don't want to try and get work done and entertain
them for longer than that anyway. In the end, here are a couple of
sample dashboards for your consideration:

Sample 1:

The report above is for a mature strategy, so you beginners can
breathe a sigh of relief. Most companies have a template for their
presentations. If you don't have it, reach out to that relationship

The Richwell Group
Supplier Diversity – Q4, 2019

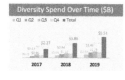

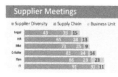

2019 Metrics

- 30% spend increase YOY.
- 35% Diverse Spend
- Almost 50% of customers receiving diversity reporting

Outreach Events

Calendar	Date	Location	Type
NVBDC	Jan 23	San Diego	SD/VBE
S&S	Mar 16-18	Nashville	WBE
RES2020	Mar 25-29	Las Vegas	MBE
USPAACC	Apr 17	Houston	MBE

you've built with Public Relations or Sales or Marketing. The last thing you want is a supplier diversity report that looks like it came from a different company. Here's a recap of this slide:

Top left: The last three years of diversity spend by quarter and total. This could be the entire time of the program or a time period that makes sense. What does your company show on financial reports? Two years? Three? Mimic what your C-suite is reporting unless you don't have that much data or there is another reason why you shouldn't show that much history.

Top center: This shows the tier 2 reporting to revenue. This company was B2B and had a lot of national accounts (translation: lots of large companies that have their own supplier diversity business strategy). Almost half of their revenue received some sort of diversity reporting. That is a strong metric, but even if it's 5%, it's a strong statement and should be tracked.

Top right: This shows the percentage in each of the categories the company tracked. They combined veteran and disabled veteran categories together. Some companies only show the diverse categories and don't include nondiverse. I disagree. I think it's good for the C-suite to see how much is NOT being spent with diverse-owned companies. One company I worked with was B2C and did an overlay of the demographic of their customer base to show how it aligned (or didn't). It was a strong picture.

Bottom left: I really like this one. This company had a strategy that had plateaued (translation: we've been at the same *&$# percentage for the past four years). They wanted to involve those end users along with supply chain in the vetting process so they used their company's salesforce.com tool for tracking supplier prospect meetings. The first number was what supplier diversity held and included everything except matchmaking. They didn't think those were enough time to vet and found their internal clients thought it was a quick way to inflate their numbers. The second band are the number of meetings supply chain did based upon recommendations from supplier diversity. The third was the number of meetings the internal client participated in. That could be due to bid projects or some other reason. For example, marketing didn't think anyone could vet a supplier for them except marketing, so the expectation was they would meet with more potential suppliers.

There was another benefit from this. They were able to see which events were generating the best contacts with potential suppliers who were vetted through each step of the process to success. They used this information when they evaluated investment in various events and organizational memberships.

Bottom center: This is a quick recap of the numbers, the top three or four things you want that C-suite individual to see who won't look at all of the charts.

Bottom right: This shows upcoming outreach events, the dates, locations, and focus of the event. You want the C-suite to be able to look at it and say "Hey! I'm going to be in Houston on the 17th." It also lets them know there is a focus to these different events. You may want to break out the MBE category further for their knowledge. For example, here, the RES2020 is for the MBE category of Native American business owners. The USPAACC is for Asian American and Asia and Indian Subcontinent owned businesses.

Sample 2:

The Richwell Group

Supplier Diversity Q4, 2019

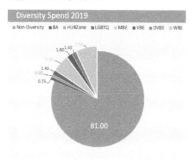

If you are intimidated by the first slide, fret not. The idea of reporting is that you report on the data that you have. And you must report! Don't wait until you have tons of things to report or great numbers. When you begin to implement your strategy, you begin reporting. In this example, we have three areas.

Left: This is the percentage of spend in each of the areas being tracked. This company is probably doing business with the U.S. government because they are tracking 8a and HUBZone. But they could be doing business with companies that have GSA contracts. And while the government doesn't care about tier 2 spend (I know, it's weird, right? Write your congresspeople), customers may still want you to demonstrate you support the concept by reporting it to them. Don't worry about the amount of non-diversity spend you have when you begin. Whatever you have, it's going to get better.

Upper right: Since this is a new program that has shown improvement, we are tracking each quarter since the start 21 months ago. Use a unit of measure that shows some difference across the time periods. This could be thousands, millions, whatever makes sense. No one ever got support for a chart that was flat all the way across because you started with billions and only have

$6 million in spend. You can always change it in a year or so when the numbers get bigger.

Lower right: Don't be afraid to toot your own horn a bit, or that of your team. When you begin a new strategy, there are a lot of thankless jobs that need to be completed to lay the foundation for success. You needn't write down every item on your to-do list, but let management know that things are happening. Implementing third-party reporting can be a nightmare, especially if you are taking data from, say, three payables systems and p-card spend from three different banks. You could also use this space to identify challenges or upcoming items to do, but the C-suite likes things to talk about results and that means things that have actually happened. Besides, you don't want to be that person who has the same to-do on their list for the past three quarters even if you have a great reason why it hasn't been done yet.

At the end of your company's fiscal year, publish a report that talks about the results and successes you had in the past 12 months. Public companies publish an annual report that has the financials and all of the great, cool stuff they accomplished in the previous year. A lot of companies also publish reports on sustainability, climate change management, etc. You don't need to publish a 30-page book, but you should have something every year that comes out reasonably soon after your company publishes their annual report.

Your audience for this document is, well, diverse. At diversity events, it provides information to DBOs who are thinking of trying to do business with you or other companies that are looking for best practices. Your sales team can include it in RFP responses from potential customers who have supplier diversity as part of their vetting. It's one thing to write a response that says your company is committed to it. It's an entirely different level to include last year's annual report on the topic.

You can also put it on your website so it can be downloaded. If you do that, track how many download requests you have. If people on your website are taking the time to download the document, they are probably interested in suppliers who are committed to a business strategy.

The C-suite: Whatever reporting you receive from supplier diversity, it should speak to the overall business strategy, success, and what is left to be done. Just as one figure doesn't give the financial overview of the company, so a list of spend percentages doesn't provide a true look at the supplier diversity business strategy.

The Supplier Diversity Professional (SDP): Business strategies have good reporting metrics that are kept up to date. Understand where your strategy is at and have the numbers to back them up. And show your work that supports your math.

The Supply Chain Professional (SCP): You contribute to the business strategy metrics, so understand how you can impact them—and then do that.

The Diverse Business Owner (DBO): Get familiar with the reporting that your various corporate customers provide. This is at least as important as studying their financials and press releases.

The End User: Do you know what your company reports for supplier diversity? No? Why not?

CHAPTER 14

POLICIES AND GOALS

O pinions vary as to how critical it is to have a supplier diversity policy document, or defined goals and objectives. In the end, I think it depends upon what your company does about its other business strategies. Consistency is key. If your company doesn't create policy documents on how to conduct the day-to-day business, there isn't much sense in demanding it for supplier diversity. On the other hand, if your company has a policy manual that is used, then this strategy should be in there along with all the others. The critical factor is that this strategy gets everything the other strategies receive. Equality: see what I did there?

Often, supplier diversity policies are made part of the supply chain policies since that is where the requirements come into play. I like having them as part of those policies. However, remember that not everything is typically purchased through supply chain. You don't want to give an out to everyone who doesn't utilize the supply chain process. Some of the areas that supply chain struggles to gain admission to, Human Resources, marketing, technology, legal, etc., have some of the greatest possibilities of diversity inclusion. For that reason, my preference is a supplier diversity policy that can be referenced in the supply chain and any other related polices like p-card spend, or nontraditional procurement. This approach also means that you own the policy versus having to engage supply chain each time you want to make an update because it's under their ownership.

As with other policy writing, the policy itself should show the intent and leave the changing numbers, such as percent or spend goals, to a non-policy document. This keeps required updates to a minimum. You want your policy to stay meaningful and you don't want to have to engage in a lengthy review process every time a percentage point changes. You can do this by having the policy state, as an example, that annual percentage goals will be established, announced, whatever you do with yours.

The policy should also address how results are measured and how often they are updated. This comes in handy if you have to engage other departments to assist with this. Having it in the company policy at one company, for example, ensured that the technology group had to address it if they changed any systems. You don't want to get down to the end of the year and find that your data source disappeared last February when a new system was put into place and no one considered that you were using it. Year over year results are important, so make sure you continue to receive those. If you change measurements for any reason, carry over as much data as you can to show year over year. There is nothing worse than trying to cobble together results with questionable data. It puts the credibility of your entire strategy at risk.

Even if you are putting the data together yourself, I recommend having your own log-in versus having someone else provide the information to you. At one company, the data I needed came out of the BI (business intelligence) software. For the first few months, one of the technology folks was sending it to me. I thought that would be handy but I found myself chasing him down when I was on deadline and I didn't know when changes were being made. Once I got my own log-in, I was able to get the data when I needed it. I was also able to see what other data was available and began using that as well. Sometimes, it can be a trial to get your own log-in because, if the company pays a license fee by user there is a cost associated with it. The technology group also often purchases those licenses in blocks and, if there are only a couple of licenses left, it can be like pulling hens teeth to get one. But if you can swing it, it is worth the cost. I have also pitched technology (with varying levels of success) to make one of the licenses one of their contributions to the supplier diversity strategy. If you do that, be sure to give them credit. Just beware when their budget gets cut that your license may go with it. Paying your own way and being a full-blown internal client is always best if you can do it.

ESTABLISHING A SOLID BASELINE

One thing that is sometimes overlooked when companies look at goals and reporting is a solid baseline. Even if your company has never done anything for supplier diversity, you will almost always have diverse spend already in your supply chain. Understanding where you start from is important, so don't skimp on getting that information. If you contract with a third party for your reporting, make sure your initial year includes a good baseline. Most will work with you to get that for the same cost as the subsequent years, as long as the data can be ported over to them in a reasonable fashion. You want a good solid number to start from and report that first year's work.

Opinions also vary as to what the goals of supplier diversity should be. Most have some sort of spend or percentage goal, but there are others worth considering. Some companies publish those while others do not. Let's tackle this one head on.

Spend goals are usually done by diversity designation and look something like this:

Supplier Diversity Strategy Spend Goals +		
Certification Designation	**Percentage Goal**	**Spend Goal**
Disabled	4.25%	$55,250,000.00
LGBTQ	9.75%	$126,750,000.00
Minority	12.50%	$162,500,000.00
Service-Disabled Veteran	3.75%	$48,750,000.00
Veteran	5.75%	$74,750,000.00
Woman	12.50%	$162,500,000.00
Total	**48.50%**	**$630,500,000.00**

+Based upon a spend of $1.3 billion

The supplier diversity professionals (SDPs) should have these numbers further broken down to show female veterans or Hispanic LGBTQ, but for our purposes here we will keep it basic.

If you are serious about the goals, your credibility, and being accountable, you will have both the percentage and the dollar spend. If your goals are based upon addressable spend (see my rant in Chapter 13 on the concept of addressable spend) you should include the make-up of that as well. How much is addressable and how much is the total? In short, treat it like algebra class in high school. If you want full credit, you have to show the work. People who pick and choose the numbers put those of us who deal in numbers in a highly skeptical frame of mind. That includes, by the way, your C-suite, most of supply chain, and a lot of your internal clients.

Goals can be a double-edged sword. There should be some method to the madness, don't pull the percentages out of a hat or base them on what you think you can achieve. I tend to start with the population of small business ownership. That is readily available in the United States from the government website and it's also available from many other countries. I also look at what the make-up of the designation is for the overall population, especially in B2C businesses, where you are selling directly to that population. Your desired percentages should reflect those numbers.

If you are doing business in the U.S., and you are a GSA contract holder, you have directed percentages for your GSA contract. Those tend to be dictated and have little bearing on what you can actually accomplish. As such, I did not mirror those goals to my business goals, which I wanted to be based in some sort of reality.

DEFINING OBJECTIVES THAT ARE EQUITABLE, INCLUSIVE, AND AUTHENTIC

Goals can become polarizing if they are too much of how the SDPs are evaluated. I've heard companies tell diverse business owners (DBOs) they are only looking at *minority* veteran companies, or companies that have more than one designation. Shame, shame on them. When the numbers begin to matter more than the results you achieve for your company and for the diversity community, you have lost your way. By the same token, people pay attention to what you pay them for. If your goals are designed to make them want to play the system to get the best results, then it is back to the drawing board for you.

Goals should also incorporate more than the dollars; they should include the components that make up a successful strategy. To that end, here are a few suggestions for your consideration:

- A specific number of employee touchpoints throughout the year from education and training to attendance at diversity events to activity on the company website.
- A specific number of DBO touchpoints from some meaningful measurement more valid than a business card collected. Consider matchmaking meetings, after meetings, introductions, etc., something that shows DBOs moving through the company

process. The idea, after all, is about getting them as a supplier, not just meeting them once and never again.

- Instead of tracking how many events were attended (a popular measurement), how about the results of the events? This also helps with those ROI meetings and decisions you have to make about where to put your money each year when the membership invoices show up. How many DBOs did you meet for the first time? How many repeats? How many suppliers have made it to a bid invite? The short list? An actual contract?

- If your company does mentoring, follow the progress of the companies you work with and make that part of the measure of success. You obviously can't make them choose wisely or do the right thing, but if you have an influence, there should be some leadership points for that.

- Use of multiple communication channels is a must for keeping team members up to date on what is happening. Do you post on the company websites and submit to the employee resource groups? Do you use Twitter and LinkedIn when you are at events or celebrating a milestone? Do you raise the level of the company brand?

Finally, one of the key elements of keeping all parties aligned on the supplier diversity business strategy is for everyone to have some skin in the game. That works best if it is included in all parties' goals and objectives or whatever term is used for periodic appraisals. This may sound practical enough, yet it can be one of the more difficult things to pull off. It involves Human Resources, senior leadership, and some work on someone's behalf that probably isn't you. All of those things can hurt the chances, but if you can make it happen, the results will be worth the effort. At minimum, it should be SDPs and supply chain professionals (SCPs) but, as we know, all dollars do not flow out of supply chain. Whether it is addressed as an item on its own or through the more ambiguous "abides by company policies and procedures such as …" if you can get it mentioned, you will be doing yourself and the company a favor. It immediately stops the "I didn't know" conversation.

If you're not sure where to begin with this request, think about the last thing that was added to your last review and who monitors it. Then go talk to them. If they weren't involved in setting it up, they probably know who did and maybe even some information on how it happened. If not, talk to your manager or your Human Resources contact if you have one assigned to your business unit.

 The C-Suite: People will do what is rewarded. I worked at one company as an SCP where we had savings targets each year. We negotiated multiple year contracts but could only claim the first 12 months of savings. No credit was given in any form to the savings in subsequent years unless the price changed. I was negotiating a three-year agreement and could have 32% across the life of the contract or 12%, 10%, and 10% for each year of the contract. What do you think I did? I actually went to my CPO and asked him which he wanted. He wanted 32% of course. I then asked him why he incentivized me to do the other option. We did 32% and we changed up the annual review guidelines a bit. People will do what you reward them for.

 The Supplier Diversity Professional (SDP): When you are driving in traffic, stop signs don't stop cars, people who abide by stop signs stop cars. If you find yourself referencing your policy on a regular basis to try and get things done, you need to take a step back. Having a policy doesn't remove the need to sell the business strategy. If the policy is the strongest leg you have to stand on, better order a wheelchair.

When I was interviewing for a supply chain position where we would be centralizing indirect spend for the first time, I asked the COO what type of policies there would be for using supply chain.

He smiled and responded, "If we put together a good strategy that saves the company money and delivers the goods and services needed, there won't be any problem at all. If we put together a poor strategy that only looks at price or doesn't deliver, there is no amount of policy that will be able to enforce using supply chain." Well played, COO. I've seen it mandatory, strongly suggested, and casually mentioned. I had to sell the business proposition in every single case.

 The Supply Chain Professional (SCP): Please be sure that your policies align with and include the supplier diversity business strategy. This can be one of the first areas of conflict if this isn't reviewed up front.

 The Diverse Business Owner (DBO): You usually won't see policy documents. It is, however, a fair ask to understand how the policy works regarding both supplier diversity and supply chain. It's also fair to understand whether or not the goods and services you provide are procured through the supply chain area.

 The End User: You are dealing with the policies of your company already, so this shouldn't be breaking new ground for you. Please be sure you understand the intention of the policy as well as the letter of it and how that translates into success for you as a client and the business.

ACT IV

CHAPTER 15

PULLING IT ALL TOGETHER

So, at this point, you may be saying, "This is all well and good, Jamie, but what do I do with all of the newfound knowledge?" Well, it's time to think about building your supplier diversity business strategy. This works whether you are just starting out or if you've been at it awhile. Where to begin?

I have six steps that are outlined below. These are my steps. For example, I use McKinsey's 7-S model for strategy building. If your company has another model they use, by all means use that. You want the structure and vocabulary to be what your company uses and what your C-suite is accustomed to seeing (and most likely selected) to make it as comfortable as possible. Besides, whether you use 7-S, 5 Pillars, or 6 Unicorns, it's about doing the homework and putting a solid plan together. The rest is just accessorizing.

1. Company Structure Analysis

We begin with a candid look at the how your company is structured. What works and what will be a challenge in relation to your company and your business strategy success?

2. Stakeholder Analysis

Next, we look at your stakeholders, all of them. Who is on board and who isn't, who will help and who won't? Who do you need for success and how do you get them on board?

3. Strategy Model

This is where we take our knowledge from steps 1 and 2 and build out a strategy model for success.

4. Value Proposition

One question I often get is: why we don't begin with the value proposition? We can't know exactly what the proposition looks like until we know what tools we have and don't have. Once we know all of that, then we can articulate the value as it relates to the company in question.

5. Project Plan

Once you have steps 1through 4, then it's just another project to be implemented. You need the same things as other projects.

6. Launch

Whether you are kicking this off for the first time or refreshing a strategy that has plateaued, do something deliberate to mark it. We will look at ways of telling the story in the best way for your situation.

For each of these steps, you need to take a hard, honest look. You may have the document you show others within the organization and the one you work on at home, but have it all somewhere. If you aren't sure of something, note that. Okay, now we have a script, let's get to work!

1. COMPANY STRUCTURE ANALYSIS

A. Actual State Cultural Analysis

Begin with an inventory, an assessment of what you have and do not have. First and foremost, what is driving the interest in supplier diversity? Customers? The C-suite? New government contract? All of the above? This is important, not only to craft a strategy that speaks to the primary drivers, but also in determining who is on board and who isn't.

Take a frank look at your company culture or style. Look at what has been done so far and why it worked or didn't work. Is everyone aware of the company's belief in diversity? Look beyond the halls of headquarters. What is known in the field, at branch locations, or however your company is spread throughout the geographic footprint? If your company is global, do the answers change from country to country? If so, how and where?

Assess how supply chain works within your company. Is it centralized? Decentralized? Hybrid? Remember, supply chain rarely has all of the spend. How much does it have where you are?

When you are through, you should have spent some time thinking about each of the business units that make up your company structure.

B. Strengths and Weaknesses

This is a basic SWOT (strength, weakness, opportunity, and threats) exercise now that you understand your company culture. For the purposes of your strategy, you want to know who will support it, who will the detractors be, what obstacles will you face, etc.

You also need to understand what type of financial support you have. Sometimes, companies decide to do this without realizing the cost associated with the strategy. As you think about the questions below, others will come to mind. Include them. This is just to get things started. Questions and certainly answers will be different from company to company depending upon the existing culture and whether any of this has been done before.

C. Need for Action

In this step, you start to formulate action that needs to be taken based upon what you discovered in steps 1 and 2. Are there certain detractors you need to bring into the fold? What needs to happen with supply chain? What do you need from your supporters? Whether launching for the first time or a relaunch, you could use some help. Think of this in terms of the company overall, not your grocery list of what you need to assemble a trade show booth. That type of detail comes later. This is what you need on a company level. It might be getting technology on board so you can get the data you need. It might be working with supply chain and Human Resources to align goals and objectives.

D. Implementation

Finally, put some thought into how the needs for action in step 3 will be implemented. How will you know when you are done with an action? Have definitive measurements so you will know what success looks like and when you have reached it. Now, it becomes project management. Schedule, act, communicate, repeat.

Ideally, this is done with more than one person. If you are going to be responsible for supplier diversity and you are doing this alone, I worry for you. That's not to say you can't start it alone on the train on a Tuesday, but bring some other perspectives into this before you map out a strategy. Diversity of thought, see what I did there?

COMPANY ABC STRUCTURE ANALYSIS
Supplier Diversity Business Strategy

1 — ACTUAL STATE CULTURE ANALYSIS	2 — STRENGTHS AND WEAKNESSES	3 — NEED FOR ACTION	4 — IMPLEMENTATION
• What is the catalyst for doing this? • What has the company done so far for supplier diversity? • How well known is supplier diversity to the company? • Has the company undertaken any other related strategies? (D&I, ERG, etc.) • How is the company supply chain structured? (central or decentral, ERP, etc.)	• How likely is the company to support the strategy? • What obstacles to success do you anticipate? • Do you have financial support? • Do you have c-suite support? • Where does/will supplier diversity sit in the organization?	• Derive need for action as result of analysis • Who needs to be brought on board and how will you do that? • What needs to be done with supporters? • What needs to be done with detractors?	• Determine concrete measures • Recognize limits and success factors • Create schedule • Communicate results • Repeat

2. STAKEHOLDER ANALYSIS

Now that you have identified the current state, it's time to evaluate your stakeholders. You can do this on a legal pad, the nifty spreadsheet below, or the back of a cocktail napkin, just do it for each of your stakeholders. This is individually, not as a group or business unit. List your stakeholders and then think about what is the behavior you desire from each of them? Try not to make it generic, like "to support the strategy." What would you have them do in an ideal state? Think ideal and specifics. You can always negotiate your expectations downward, it's tough to negotiate up so let's start at the top.

Do you want your CEO to put a video on the company website? How about your CPO? Do you want each of the supply chain professionals (SCPs) you work with to sign on to attend an event each year? Do you want the head of sales to let you have ten minutes on the agenda at the next sales meeting? Remember, you have external stakeholders, too. Who are they and what do you want from them?

Once you have identified what you want from each of these, candidly assess the amount of support you have from them now, not where you want to get them to. Then assess how much influence they have on the overall strategy. I may want nothing more from the head of sales than the ten minutes to let the salesforce know we can provide tier 2 reporting. Their influence on the sales team taking this to heart, getting excited about it, and using this new tool could be a pretty big deal. How much sway a stakeholder has over others and how meaningful that can be to the success of your strategy can have a huge impact on how hard you need to work to get them fully on board.

 Elephant Alert: This sounds like a simple process, but there are a lot of things at play here, not the least of which are the emotions of the assessor. There is a difference between someone being a tool at work and whether or not they support diversity. There is a difference between someone who is crass and whether or not they support diversity. This is about their support for the strategy, not how well you work with them or agree with them or like them. I have had very successful working relationships with people who I would never have cocktails with over the holidays. This is about the strategy, not you personally. That doesn't mean they won't have their own attitude or bias when you want to talk to them, but we will address those challenges later.

STAKEHOLDER ANALYSIS
Supplier Diversity Business Strategy

STAKEHOLDER	SUPPORT OF STRATEGY					INFLUENCE ON THE STRATEGY			DESIRED BEHAVIOR
	++	+	o	-	--	high	moderate	slight	
Stakeholder #1									
Stakeholder #2									
Stakeholder #3									
Stakeholder #4									

STRATEGY MODEL

As I said, I use the McKinsey 7-S model for strategy planning, you should use whatever your company is using. If they don't have anything specific, this should get you going.

The model is based upon seven success factors. The shared values or center of our map below is what everything else revolves around. All of the factors are interrelated, thus the connections between the various factors.

The shared values are, at their essence, what you want to achieve, or your objective behind the strategy.

Structure is about how the company is put together and operates. In addition to just where the authority lies and how it reports within a company, it also takes into account the complexity of the structure with the advent of things like cross-functional teams. There is authority and then there is the power within an organization.

Systems are about how the work gets done, the company processes. They're also about how those processes get updated and changed, if necessary.

Style, or culture of the company, is about the informal rules of how people within a company interact. Part of this is inherently the leadership style of the company as well. Are you "on" 24/7/365? Is it a culture of competition or working together? All of that will dictate how you map your strategy for success in supplier diversity.

Staff are the people, but it goes a bit deeper than that. It's also about the scope of the strength of those people and how the company fills any gaps in the strengths. The diversity of the company is also a component because with that comes broader ideas, more and different approaches to solving problems.

Skills are about the skill sets of the company as well as at an individual level and how those gaps are compensated for. Does your company tend to train or outsource? Years ago, I was working in supply chain and we were installing a new ERP system. The company ended up sending me to programming school at IBM every other week for a week at a time for almost eight months. Today, that would be outsourced and the needed skills brought in. At that time (because I remember when dirt was a youngster), everyone did everything in-house. How does your company make the decision today of train versus hire versus outsource?

Strategy is about the competitive advantage that you seek. It used to be a company would write its mission and vision and it almost never changed. Now the mission may be static or only updated every few years, but the vision has to be adaptable to the changing environment and business climate. Customers are fickle, technology is always changing, and there is always a better mousetrap available around the corner.

If you look at each of these in terms of how your supplier diversity business strategy will improve the competitive landscape for your company, you will have a solid strategy that can be articulated, measured, and appreciated.

7-S MODEL
Supplier Diversity Business Strategy

- Shared Values – what do you want to achieve?
- Structure – the classic organization, the authoritative relationships
- Systems – the processes of the company, how work gets done
- Style – the culture of the company, the informal rules of conduct
- Staff – the people, their intrinsic talent
- Skills – the institutional and individual skills, needed acquisition of skills
- Strategy – the competitive advantage being sought

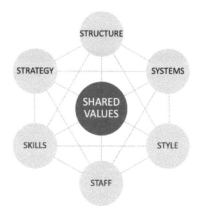

83

To get the conversations and creative juices flowing, the two slides below have always helped me. It can be tough sometimes to bring a group together and say, "Let's build a strategy." To get away from the blank page and the paralysis it can generate, check out the questions below. They are not meant to create a supplier diversity strategy for you, but to get you thinking about each of the success factors on their own. Answer the questions, then talk about them in relation to a supplier diversity strategy. It will help you craft what is (and isn't) relevant in building and selling your strategy. I have also found that this exercise makes it easier for me to tailor my presentation to my audience when I am trying to bring stakeholders to the

---

[83] McKinsey & Company.

7-S MODEL
Supplier Diversity Business Strategy

SHARED VALUES [1]

- What are common values of the company?
- Which company philosophy and what self-image characterize the company?
- Do employees share understanding of these values?
- Is the development of values in a more rigid frame or is it dynamic and adaptable?
- Are values suitable in order to promote the company's culture?

STRUCTURE [2]

- What affects structures of the company?
- Does the necessary complexity or simplicity suit the actual structure?
- Is there a clear organization chart?
- Is the corporate structure helpful or a hindrance for the job?
- Are competencies of the organization areas adequately defined?
- Which structural changes are planned? Who is involved in the change process?

SYSTEMS [3]

- What processes have high importance in the company?
- How is the quality of these processes assessed?
- How are processes organized? Are they transparent enough?
- Which interfaces have frequently caused conflicts?
- What formal and informal processes are in place to implement the overall strategy?
- Where do you see development needs in the processes?

STYLE [4]

- Which rules and standards are enforced with the staff?
- What kind of reward and punishment mechanism exists?
- What effect have collaboration and cooperation on the company?
- How are errors treated?
- How is the relationship among the staff?
- What are the qualities of leadership?
- Does the leadership style concur with the targeted company culture?

STAFF [5]

- Is the actual staffing structure suitable for the formulated guidelines?
- Is the staff vital capital or simply means to an end?
- Are strengths of the staff providing a competitive advantage over the competitors?
- How does the company promote and encourage the employees and what are the development possibilities?
- How high is the fluctuation?
- What areas concerning staff need to be developed?

SKILLS [6]

- Which outstanding abilities does the company have?
- Do any competitive advantages result from these abilities?
- What do you know about the core capabilities in the company? Is it tied to specific people?
- How is knowledge shared within the company? What happens with new knowledge and expertise?
- Are there incentive systems for knowledge processing and distribution of knowledge?
- Which knowledge management systems exist in the company?

STRATEGY [7]

- How are vision and strategy of the company designed?
- How big is the opportunity to implement the desired short-term strategy?
- Are there opposing goals?
- Is the strategy likely to overcome challenges in the future?
- Is the company clearly enough defined?
- Who develops the strategies in the company? Which people and departments are the drivers of development?

table or launch supplier diversity to the company at large. You can begin with this and then tailor to your audience.

Regardless of the tools you use, whether it be chevrons or bullets, PowerPoint or YouTube, having a plan is essential. This also allows you to share it with people who are not fluent in supplier diversity and may be confused or even intimidated by it. Give them something they are accustomed to.

The value proposition is a key piece of both your strategy and your sales technique. Any supplier diversity event you attend, you will hear diverse business owners (DBOs) being asked to define what their value proposition, or value prop, is. It encompasses everything from your elevator pitch to a full-blown presentation. You need to be able to state the value of your business strategy in 1, 3, 5, and 20 minutes. In my experience, if you can do that, you are on your way.

We have all sat through the painful presentation. The person has 30 minutes to speak and brings 60 slides. Fifteen minutes in, they are on slide four. What will they do? They get the ten minutes left sign and don't appear to pick up the pace at all. At five minutes left, they begin to panic. They start talking faster, but somehow the presentation doesn't really speed up. They end up either getting cut off or going dreadfully over their time limit. The next speaker shooting daggers at them from the back of the room. My point is, you actually need to be able to encapsulate what your business strategy is about in 1, 3, 5, and 20 minutes and not by talking really, really fast. Take it down to its essence and then add good stuff.

VALUE PROPOSITION

When people ask what I do for a living or what The Richwell Group does, I start with: "The Richwell Group is a supply chain and supplier diversity consultancy for both large and small companies."

If there is time for more than that, or I'm asked for more information: "We provide everything from overall strategies to specific category or project expertise in supply chain; we provide complete plans for new supplier diversity strategies or update existing plans if it has plateaued or something key in the business has changed. For DBOs, we help them leverage their certification across all of the opportunities that it brings to their business."

The point being, have something clear and concise to start with and then augment that with clear benefits within the timeframe.

The slide below highlights a way of thinking about the value proposition of your business strategy. Once you have all of that, then you edit it down to the shortest possible delivery. Once that is done,

BUSINESS STRATEGY TOOLS

Supplier Diversity Business Strategy

CLARITY OF INFORMATION AND CONTRIBUTIONS TO STRATEGY

VALUE PROPOSITION	ARCHITECTURE OF VALUE CREATION	YIELD AND GROWTH MODEL

• Benefit to customers
• Benefit to stakeholders
  • Supply chain
  • Sales
  • Marketing
  • Human Resources
• Benefit to profitability
• Benefit to community
• Benefit to brand
	• Performance objectives
	• Measures of success
	• Steps of value creation
	• Target group/target market
	• Distribution channel
	• Communication channel
	• Value adding partner / stakeholder
	• Cooperation
		• Price of performance
		• Growth generators
		• Standard creation
		• Substitution demand
		• Increased demand
		• Transformation in new business fields
		• Innovation

then you can add to it depending upon the time and who you are talking to.

GET SET, STRATEGIZE, AND EXECUTE!

The strategy is the plan, and you must have that. But once you have determined what needs to be done, then it's a matter of executing the project. The best-laid plans are no good without an effective means of putting them into practice. Execution happens to be my superpower, so I've got the elements practically running through my veins. For those of you who may not find it as sexy as I do, here are a few things that I don't think you can shortchange to be successful.

RESOURCES

Capacity planning is essential. And do this before you start selling it to someone or answer the question: Just ballpark it. How long will it take? You need to be able to say who has to be involved and how much time will it take each of these supporting cast members. Do you need technology support to get it done? What order do tasks need to be performed in? If you are building a house, there is no point in bringing the cabinet guy out if the kitchen hasn't been framed in yet.

Resources and their order are critical to developing the overall timeline, and this is not something you want to guesstimate. The fact is, you could give an executive the eleven herbs and spices that Colonel Sanders uses and they might forget two or three of them, but they will never, EVER forget the off-the-cuff date you gave them on a project. Use whatever tool works for you, but below is a sample template for capacity planning.

CAPACITY PLANNING – IN WORK DAYS

Project name

NO.	WORK PACKAGE	EA 1	EA 2	EA 3	EA 4	EA 5	...	TOTAL
1.1	<description>	5		1				6
1.2	<description>	2	5			5		12
1.3	<description>					10		10
1.4	<description>				15	6		21
...								0
2.1			2	4		3		9
2.2			7					7
...								0
...								0
TOTAL		7	7	12	15	24	0	65

Employee Initials:
E 1   < name >   E 4   < name >
E 2   < name >   E 5   < name >
E 3   < name >   E 6   < name >

On-Call Updates

Once you get the go-ahead, all parties become a four-year-old in the back seat on a long trip. "Are we there yet? Are we there yet? Are we there yet?" Have some way of reporting out how it's coming. If you have the ability, put that mechanism on the intranet or in a shared Dropbox or something so folks can just go look at it and then update it often. Below is the classic Gantt bar chart, the gold standard in project progress. It provides a quick way for everyone to see what's been done and answers the four-year-old's next question, "How much farther?"

Finally, if your strategy is important to the company (it is) and is going to be taken seriously (it should be), then it's going to show

GANTT CHARTS – GANTT / BAR CHART
Project plan

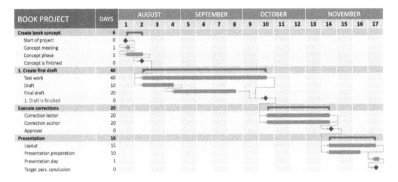

up on a dashboard somewhere, somehow. You might as well have a periodic report that gives an overall snapshot. The template below uses the classic traffic light method. Green for everything is running smoothly, yellow for if something doesn't happen here soon something bad may happen, and red for everyone needs to put their phone down and talk to me.

Do not feel compelled to have all lights green. If I had a dollar for every crisis meeting I've been in where someone said something to the effect of, "Why the $%&*^ wasn't this red on the last status report?" I'd be wintering somewhere with clear turquoise water every year. It's a status, not an advertisement.

OVERALL STATUS (TRAFFIC LIGHTS)
Project name

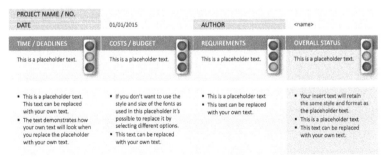

Despite what tools you use and once the strategy has been laid out, execute with precision. It's a business strategy, treat it like one. The person who undersells it the most is often the one responsible for it. If the strategy for your company was for the sales team to get a new piece of software to make the customer experience better, you can bet no one is underselling the need for supply chain to get the contract done, or technology to get the testing completed, or, well, you get the idea. It's a business strategy and business strategies are for things that matter to the company.

THE LAUNCH

Every company launches differently. Whatever your company does, make sure your supplier diversity business strategy is launched that way. It will be easier to do that since it is a business strategy as opposed to that thing that Jamie's been working on about diversity something or the other. Use every tool in the company toolbox.

I still remember one company I worked for and the response I got when I called marketing and told them I needed ad copy in three sizes for a supplier diversity advertisement for the company. In their defense, they hadn't bothered to show up to any of the prep meetings they had been invited to, so they didn't really know what I was talking about. They also hadn't read the project updates I'd been doing. When I told them that this was a dependent item to several others and was soon going from yellow to red on the company dashboard ... they completely got that. Treating this like every other project that gets done in your company will help you expedite tasks like every other task gets expedited. I'm not saying it will put you ahead of whatever they are working on for the CEO, but it does give you a common language and less chance of misunderstanding because it is the same as they have seen a thousand times before. It's just that this time, it's about supplier diversity instead of whatever it was the last time they saw it.

If you work for a large company, the toughest challenge can be making sure everyone knows about supplier diversity. It's uncanny that a business strategy never seems to hit all of the areas it needs to. The VP whose wife trashed his car in the parking garage during their divorce, who everyone knows, including the intern in Manilla who started working this morning. Go figure. Use all of the channels at your disposal. The intranet, the company Twitter feed, the newsletter, a team call, QBRs throughout the company. I've put notices up in the coffee room, on the door of the coat closet, you name it and I've used it as a launch site. And do more than write a memo.

At events, take pictures of the trade show floor from above if possible. Then have pics and a couple of short videos showing the company booth or a sign for your company that sponsored something. Give updates from an event. Show any recognition or accolades the company receives. Introduce the company to diverse-owned companies that are now suppliers. Employees like feeling that their company is doing cool things. Catch the company in the act of doing a cool thing.

The launch is the first step, keep the information flowing. Make sure all of your stakeholders hear about your business strategy all year long, not just when the annual update is done or at budget time.

 The C-Suite: If your company has a set of templates that it uses for business strategies, make them available to your supplier diversity professional (SDP) early on. If your SDP hasn't done a lot of strategy build out, consider giving them that training either through coursework or a mentorship. This shouldn't be something that has a different look and feel to it.

 Supplier Diversity Professional (SDP): First see my suggestion to the C-suite above. It may feel like this is an awful lot of work for something no one has demanded from you, but trust me, it will be well worth your time and effort. You are competing with all sorts of peers and colleagues for support and funding who have a lot less than I am asking you to prepare here. Sometimes, half the battle is showing up with a plan. Invest in your plan.

 The Supply Chain Professional (SCP): A strong supplier diversity business strategy will raise the level of your supply chain, there is no doubt. Don't wait for a consulting group to come into your company and tell your C-suite where their supply chain is falling short. Get out in front of this one.

 The Diverse Business Owner (DBO): If you find a company that has a strong supplier diversity business strategy and you can provide them with whatever your goods and services are, hang on for dear life to that customer. You will get so much more than the check they write you to pay your invoices.

 The End User: If you want to be the best, you want the best options. There is no denying the data that shows that means you need a diverse supply chain providing your solutions. Lucky for you, we have that solution right here.

EPILOGUE

You may debate who you think has been disadvantaged in a given geographic area. You may debate what steps need to be taken in order to successfully and constructively incorporate supplier diversity in or for your organization. But you cannot debate whether or not it is a necessary business strategy any more than you can debate whether or not you can grow your business without a marketing strategy.

Diversity is a business necessity. And if it is necessary for your business, your supply chain must also have it to be of optimal service to your business. We depend upon supply chain partners too much for them to be the weak link in the chain (pun intended).

If you hope to attract and retain the best talent, if you want the best technology, if you want to not just stay up with but surpass your competition, you need supplier diversity for all of that.

Supplier diversity used to be something in a diversity magazine and nowhere else. Now, you read about it in the *Wall Street Journal*. The top consulting firms are asking if you have it. Your customers want to know why there aren't women or people of color on your board, at the executive level, and everywhere else in your company.

One of the places where diversity delivers results the most is in your company supply chain. For there, you have every supplier leveraging the diversity of their company for your company. It is not about a nice thing to do.

It is necessary if your company is going to survive. I hope that you are able to take some of the lessons I've learned and insights I've witnessed and put them to work for your company, for your supplier diversity business strategy.

GLOSSARY

8a—The U.S. Small Business Administration has a program to "help provide a level playing field for small businesses owned by socially and economically disadvantaged peoples or entities. The government limits the competition for certain contracts to businesses that participate in the 8(a) Business Development program.

Disadvantaged businesses in the 8(a) program can:

- Compete for set-aside and sole-source contracts in the program
- Get a Business Opportunity Specialist to help navigate federal contracting
- Form joint ventures with established businesses through the SBA's mentor-protege program
- Receive management and technical assistance, including business training, counseling, marketing assistance, and high-level executive development

The U.S. Federal government has a goal to award at least five percent of all federal contracting dollars to small disadvantaged businesses each year."

Certification in the program can be up to nine years in length. "To qualify, you must:

- Be a small business
- Not have already participated in the program

- Be at least 51% owned and controlled by U.S. Citizens who are economically and socially disadvantaged
- Be owned by someone whose personal net worth is $250,000 or less
- Be owned by someone with $4 million or less in assets
- Have the owner manage day-to-day operations and also make long-term decisions
- Have all its principals demonstrate good character
- Show potential for success and be able to perform successfully on contract"

Affiliates—For the U.S. government, "affiliation with another business is based on the power to control, whether exercised or not. The power to control exists when an external party has 50 percent or more ownership. It may also exist with considerably less than 50 percent ownership by contractual arrangement or when one or more parties own a large share compared to other parties."[84] The receipts and employees of an affiliate are included in the calculation of a small business by the SBA.

Annual Receipts—For the U.S. government, annual receipts "is the 'total income' (or 'gross income') plus the 'cost of goods sold.' These numbers can normally be found on the business' IRS tax return forms. Receipts are averaged over a business' latest three complete fiscal years to determine the average annual receipts. If a business hasn't been in business for three years, multiply its average weekly revenue by 52 to determine its average annual receipts."[85]

Asian-Indian—A U.S. citizen whose origins are from India, Pakistan, or Bangladesh.

Asian-Pacific—A U.S. citizen whose origins are from Japan, China, Indonesia, Malaysia, Taiwan, Korea, Vietnam, Laos, Cambodia,

---

[84] SBA, "Affiliation."
[85] SBA, "Size Standards."

the Philippines, Thailand, Samoa, Guam, the U.S. Trust Territories of the Pacific, or the Northern Marianas.

B2B—Business-to-Business "is a form of transaction between businesses, such as one involving a manufacturer and wholesaler, or a wholesaler and a retailer. Business-to-business refers to business that is conducted between companies, rather than between a company and individual consumer."[86]

B2C—Business-to-Consumer "refers to the process of selling products and services directly between a business and consumers who are the end-users of its products or services."[87]

B2G—Business-to-Government "is the sales and marketing of goods and services to federal, state, or local agencies."[88]

Black—A U.S. citizen who is of African descent.

C-Suite—"C-suite, or C-level, is widely-used vernacular describing a cluster of a corporation's most important senior executives. C-suite gets its name from the titles of top senior executives, which tend to start with the letter C, for "chief," as in chief executive officer (CEO)."[89]

CAMSC—(CamSee) Canadian Aboriginal Minority Supply Council and the certifying body for minority business enterprise (MBE)-owned businesses in Canada.

Capability Statement—"… a capability statement is a promotional or marketing statement about your business and its capabilities and skills that advertises who you are and what you do." They typically have five key areas: core competencies/capabilities; differentiators; past performance; corporate data including industry codes; and contact information.[90]

CEO—the Chief Executive Officer of a company. *See* C-Suite.

---

[86] Chen, "B2B."
[87] Kenton, "B2C."
[88] Kenton, "B2G."
[89] Bloomenthal, "C-Suite."
[90] SAP&DC, "Capability Statement."

CFO—the Chief Financial Officer of a company. *See* C-Suite.

CGLCC—Canadian Gay and Lesbian Chamber of Commerce and the certifying body for LGBTQ2-owned businesses in Canada.

CIO—the Chief Information Officer of a company. *See* C-Suite.

CMO—the Chief Marketing Officer of a company. *See* C-Suite.

Competitive set-aside contracts—"When at least two small businesses could perform the work or provide the products being purchased, the U.S. Government sets aside the contract exclusively for small businesses. With few exceptions, this happens automatically for all government contracts under $150,000."[91]

COO—the Chief Operating Officer of a company. *See* C-Suite.

CPO—the Chief Procurement Officer of a company. *See* C-Suite.

CTO—the Chief Technology Officer of a company. *See* C-Suite.

Diversity Spend—"Diverse supplier spend, often shortened to diverse spend, refers to the procurement dollars spent solely with small and diverse businesses, often expressed in a dollar amount or percentage of total procurement spend."[92]

DBO—Diverse Business Owner

Diverse Business Owner—"Broadly defined, a diverse business … is any enterprise in which 51 percent of the ownership is of a designated diverse background, or even multiple diverse backgrounds. This may include women, minorities, LGBT individuals, veterans, or service-disabled veterans." Many companies also include disabled-owned businesses.[93]

Diversity and Inclusion—"Diversity is the range of human differences, including but not limited to race, ethnicity, gender, gender identity, sexual orientation, age, social class, physical ability or attributes, religious or ethical values system, national origin, and political beliefs.

---

[91] SBA "Set-Aside Procurement."
[92] CVM, "Diverse Supplier Spend."
[93] CVM, "Diverse Supplier, Defined."

Inclusion is involvement and empowerment, where the inherent worth and dignity of all people are recognized. An inclusive university promotes and sustains a sense of belonging; it values and practices respect for the talents, beliefs, backgrounds, and ways of living of its members."[94]

EBITDA—"EBITDA, or earnings before interest, taxes, depreciation, and amortization, is a measure of a company's overall financial performance and is used as an alternative to simple earnings or net income in some circumstances. EBITDA, however, can be misleading because it strips out the cost of capital investments like property, plant, and equipment."[95]

Elevator Pitch—"… a slang term used to describe a brief speech that outlines an idea for a product, service or project. The name comes from the notion that the speech should be delivered in the short time period of an elevator ride, usually 20-60 seconds." In supplier diversity, the speech describes a diverse business owner telling someone about their company.[96]

Employee Calculation—For the U.S. government, "This is the average number of people employed for each pay period over the business' latest 12 calendar months. Any person on the payroll must be included as one employee regardless of hours worked or temporary status. The number of employees of a concern in business less than 12 months is the average for each pay period that it has been in business."[97]

Employee Resource Group—"Employee resource groups (ERGs)—voluntary, employee-led groups made up of individuals who join together based on common interests, backgrounds or demographic factors such as gender, race or ethnicity."[98]

---

[94] Ferris State University, "Diversity and Inclusion Definitions."
[95] Hayes, "EBITDA."
[96] Kenton, "Elevator Pitch."
[97] SBA, "Size Standards."
[98] SHRM, "ERGs."

End User—"the ultimate consumer of a finished product."[99]

EO 11458—"1969: President Nixon signs Executive Order 11458 creating OMBE and the Advisory Council for Minority Business Enterprise. OMBE (Office of Minority Business Enterprise) and the Advisory Council partner with the U.S. Census Bureau to conduct the first Survey of Minority-Owned Business Enterprises."[100]

EO 11625—"1971: President Nixon signs Executive Order 11625 and expands the scope of MBDA and its minority business programs by authorizing grants to public and private organizations to provide technical and management assistance to minority business enterprises (MBEs)."[101]

ERP—"Enterprise resource planning (ERP) is a process used by companies to manage and integrate the important parts of their businesses. ... An ERP software system can also integrate planning, purchasing, inventory, sales, marketing, finance, human resources, and more."[102]

Executive Order—"noun, an order having the force of law issued by the president of the U.S. to the army, navy, or other part of the executive branch of the government."[103]

General Counsel—"The role of a general counsel is—firstly—an on-staff attorney for a company. The attorney provides numerous types of legal services and manages legal actions affecting the company."[104]

General Services Administration—"The General Services Administration manages federal property and provides contracting options for government agencies." A contract is referred to as a

---

[99] Merriam-Webster, "End User."

[100] MBDA, "The History of MBDA."

[101] Ibid.

[102] Labarre, "ERP."

[103] Dictonary.com, "Executive Order."

[104] LawTrades, "General Counsel."

GSA contract and is given a number when executed. In supplier diversity circles you will hear people say they are a GSA contract holder which means they have been vetted and accepted by the government.[105]

GLAAD—Gay & Lesbian Alliance Against Defamation. An American nongovernmental media monitoring organization founded by LGBT people in the media.

GSA—*See* General Services Administration.

Hispanic—"A U.S. citizen of true-born Hispanic heritage, from any of the Spanish-speaking areas of the following regions: Mexico, Central America, South America, and the Caribbean Basin only. Brazilians (Afro-Brazilian, indigenous/Indian only) shall be listed under Hispanic designation for review and certification purposes."[106]

HUBZone—Also part of the U.S. Small Business Administration, the HUBZone program benefits businesses in identified business zones. "The government limits competition for certain contracts to businesses in historically underutilized business zones. It also give preferential consideration to those businesses in full and open competition."[107]

"HUBZone certified businesses also get a 10 percent price evaluation preference in full and open contract competitions."[108] This is in addition to the set-aside contracts.

To qualify the "business must:

- Be a small business
- Be at least 51% owned and controlled by U.S. Citizens, a Community Development Corporation, an agricultural cooperative, a Native Hawaiian organization, or an Indian tribe

---

[105] Usa.gov, "General Services Administration."
[106] NMSDC, "MBE."
[107] SBA, ""HUBZone Program."
[108] Ibid.

- Have its principal office located in a HUBZone
- Have at least 35% of its employees live in a HUBZone"[109]

IFB—*See* RFQ.

Indigenous—By definition, this means "originating in and characteristic of a particular region or country; native (often followed by *to*)."[110] "In Canada, the term Indigenous peoples) or Aboriginal peoples) refers to First Nations, Metis, and Inuit peoples. These are the original inhabitants of the land that is now Canada."[111]

Invitation for Bid—*See* RFQ.

LGBT—Lesbian, Gay, Bisexual, Transgender.

LGBTBE—LGBT Business Enterprise. The term used for a business that has been certified by NGLCC.

LGBTQ—Lesbian, Gay, Bisexual, Transgender, Queer or Questioning. The term "Queer" has increased in use because it's not specific to sexual orientation or to gender identity. It means you are at least one of LGBT, but you could be all of those and not knowing is okay. "Questioning" is someone who is figuring out their gender identity and figuring out how they want to identify their sexual orientation.

LGBTQ2—Primarily used in Canada by some indigenous people, the "2" refers to being two-spirited or a person who identifies as having both a masculine and a feminine spirit. It is a translation of the Anishinaabemowin term *niizh manidoowag*, meaning "two spirits."

Matchmaking—A matchmaking event is held to put DBOs and companies together for a brief face-to-face meeting to discuss business opportunities for the DBO. They are typically set up so that each side can conduct several meetings at the event.

---

[109] Ibid.
[110] Dictionary.com, "indigenous."
[111] Canadian Encyclopedia, "Indigenous."

MBDA—"MBDA is an agency of the U.S. Department of Commerce that promotes the growth of minority-owned businesses through the mobilization and advancement of public and private sector programs, policy, and research."[112]

MBE—(MeBee) Minority Business Enterprise. In the U.S., MBEs are defined as: "United States citizens who are Asian, Black, Hispanic and Native American."[113] The National Minority Supplier Development Council (NMSDC) further defines this as:

"... a minority group member is an individual who is a U.S. citizen with at least one quarter of the following:

Asian-Indian—A U.S. citizen whose origins are from India, Pakistan and Bangladesh.

Asian-Pacific—A U.S. citizen whose origins are from Japan, China, Indonesia, Malaysia, Taiwan, Korea, Vietnam, Laos, Cambodia, the Philippines, Thailand, Samoa, Guam, the U.S. Trust Territories of the Pacific or the Northern Marianas.

Black—A U.S. citizen who is of African descent.

Hispanic—A U.S. citizen of true-born Hispanic heritage, from any of the Spanish-speaking areas of the following regions: Mexico, Central America, South America and the Caribbean Basin only. Brazilians (Afro-Brazilian, indigenous/ Indian only) shall be listed under Hispanic designation for review and certification purposes.

Native American—A person who is an American Indian, Eskimo, Aleut or Native Hawaiian, and regarded as such by the community of which the person claims to be a part. Native Americans must be documented members of a North American tribe, band or otherwise organized group

---

[112] MBDA, "About MBDA."
[113] NMSDC, "MBE."

of native people who are indigenous to the continental United States and proof can be provided through a Native American Blood Degree Certificate (i.e., tribal registry letter, tribal roll register number)."[114]

In Canada, MBEs are defined as: "Aboriginal peoples and/ or visible minorities … for purpose of CAMSC certification, visible minority is based on ethnic origin and not gender."[115]

NAICS Codes—"The North American Industry Classification System (NAICS) is the standard used by Federal statistical agencies in classifying business establishments for the purpose of collecting, analyzing, and publishing statistical data related to the U.S. business economy."[116]

Native American—"A person who is an American Indian, Eskimo, Aleut, or Native Hawaiian, and regarded as such by the community of which the person claims to be a part. Native Americans must be documented members of a North American tribe, band, or an otherwise organized group of native people who are indigenous to the continental United States, and proof can be provided through a Native American Blood Degree Certificate (i.e., tribal registry letter, tribal roll register number)."[117]

NDA—*See* Non-Disclosure Agreement.

NGLCC—National Gay and Lesbian Chamber of Commerce and the certifying body for LGBTQ-owned businesses in the United States.

NMSDC—National Minority Supplier Development Council and the certifying body for minority business enterprise (MBE)-owned businesses in the United States.

---

[114] Ibid.
[115] CAMSC, "Certification."
[116] U.S. Census Bureau, "NAICS."
[117] NMSDC, "MBE."

Non-Disclosure Agreement—"a legal contract in which one or more parties agree to keep information, as a trade secret, confidential and protected for a specific amount of time."[118]

Return on Investment—"Return on Investment (ROI) is a performance measure used to evaluate the efficiency of an investment or compare the efficiency of a number of different investments. ROI tries to directly measure the amount of return on a particular investment, relative to the investment's cost. To calculate ROI, the benefit (or return) of an investment is divided by the cost of the investment. The result is expressed as a percentage or a ratio."[119]

RFI—"A request for information is made typically during the project planning phase where a buyer cannot clearly identify product requirements, specifications, and purchase options. RFIs clearly indicate that award of a contract will not automatically follow."[120]

RFP—"A request for proposal (RFP) is a business document that announces and provides details about a project, as well as solicits bids from contractors who will help complete the project. Most organizations prefer using RFPs and, in many cases, governments only use requests for proposal. A request for proposal for a specific program may require the company to review the bids to examine their feasibility, the health of the bidding company, and the bidder's ability to do what is proposed."[121]

RFQ—"A request for quote (RFQ), also known as an invitation for bid (IFB), is a process in which a company solicits select suppliers and contractors to submit price quotes and bids for the chance to fulfill certain tasks or projects. The RFQ process is

---

[118] Dictonary.com, "nondisclosure agreement."

[119] Chen, "ROI."

[120] Business Dictionary, "RFI."

[121] Kenton, "RFP."

especially important to businesses that need a consistent supply of a specific number of standard products. Companies may send RFQs alone or before a request for proposal (RFP)."[122]

ROI—*See* Return on Investment.

Scope creep—When the agreed upon deliverables of a project start to grow per conversations but not in the contract.

SCP—*See* Supply Chain Professional.

SDP—*See* Supplier Diversity Professional.

Set-aside—"To help provide a level playing field for small businesses, the U.S. Government limits competition for certain contracts to small businesses. Those contracts are called "small business set-asides" and they help small businesses compete for and win federal contracts. There are two kinds of set-aside contracts: competitive set-asides and sole-source set-asides."[123]

Size standards—"Size standards define the largest size a business can be to participate in government contracting programs and compete for contracts reserved or set aside for small businesses. Size standards vary by industry, and are generally based on the number of employees or the amount of annual receipts the business has."[124]

Sole-source set-aside contracts—"Most contracts are competitive, but sometimes there are exceptions to this rule. Sole-source contracts are a kind of contract that can be issued without a competitive bidding process. This usually happens in situations where only a single business can fulfill the requirements of a contract."[125]

Supply Chain—"A supply chain is a network between a company and its suppliers to produce and distribute a specific product to

---

[122] Kenton, "RFQ."

[123] SBA, "Set-asides."

[124] SBA, "Size Standards."

[125] SBA, "Sole-source."

the final buyer. This network includes different activities, people, entities, information, and resources. The supply chain also represents the steps it takes to get the product or service from its original state to the customer."[126]

Supply Chain Professional—A person who works in the profession to manage "the flow of goods and services and includes all processes that transform raw materials into final products ..." and all goods and services in the supply chain.[127]

Supplier Diversity Professional—a person whose profession is to ensure that a company has "a business strategy that ensures a diverse supplier base in the procurement of good and services for any business or organization."[128]

Tier 1 Supplier—"A company that supplies directly to the organization in question. Think of a Tier 1 supplier as the second-to-last link in the supply chain, with the buying organization being the final link."[129]

Tier 2 Spend—"The amount of spend, or procurement dollars, that an organization's suppliers spend with their Tier 1 suppliers. In regards to supplier diversity, Tier 2 diverse spend represents only those dollars spent with diverse suppliers."[130]

Value Proposition—"A value proposition refers to the value a company promises to deliver to customers should they choose to buy their product. A value proposition is also a declaration of intent or a statement that introduces a company's brand to consumers by telling them what the company stands for, how it operates, and why it deserves their business."[131]

WBE—(WeeBee) Women Business Enterprise.

---

[126] Kenton, "Supply Chain."

[127] Hayes, "Supply Chain Management."

[128] CVM, "Supplier Diversity."

[129] CVM, "Tier 1."

[130] CVM, "Tier 2."

[131] Investopedia, "Value Proposition."

WBE Canada—Women Business Enterprise Canada and a certifying body for women business enterprise (WBE) businesses in Canada.

WBENC—Women Business Enterprise National Council and a certifying body for women business enterprise (WBE) businesses in the United States.

BIBLIOGRAPHY

1. Dictionary.com. "diversity." https://www.dictionary.com/browse/diversity?s=t
2. Dictionary.com. "inclusion." https://www.dictionary.com/browse/inclusion?s=t
3. Wikipedia. "Supplier diversity." https://en.wikipedia.org/wiki/Supplier_diversity
4. Richard Nixon Presidential Library and Museum. "President Richard Nixon's Daily Diary March 1, 1969–March 15, 1969." https://www.nixonlibrary.gov/sites/default/files/virtuallibrary/documents/PDD/1969/004%20March%201-15%201969.pdf
5. Minority Business Development Agency—U.S. Department of Commerce. "The History of the MBDA." https://www.mbda.gov/about/history
6. U.S. Small Business Administration (SBA). "8(a) Business Development program." https://www.sba.gov/federal-contracting/contracting-assistance-programs/8a-business-development-program
7. CVM. "Ethnicity definitions." https://www.cvmsolutions.com/glossary/ethnicity-definitions
8. U.S. Small Business Administration (SBA). "Office of the HUBZone Program." https://www.sba.gov/offices/headquarters/ohp
9. Dictionary.com. "indigenous." https://www.dictionary.com/browse/indigenous?s=t

10. Canadian Aboriginal and Minority Supplier Council (CAMSC). "What is Certification and Why is it Important?" https://www.camsc.ca/what-is-certification

11. National Minority Supplier Development Council (NMSDC). "What is a MBE?" https://www.nmsdc.org/mbes/what-is-an-mbe/

12. Office of Small Business Programs—Department of Defense. "Service-Disabled Veteran-Owned Small Business." https://business.defense.gov/Small-Business/SDVOSB/

13. National Veteran Business Development Council (NVBDC). "What is a veteran?" http://nvbdc.org/certification.html

14. National Minority Supplier Development Council (NMSDC). "What is a MBE"? https://www.nmsdc.org/mbes/what-is-an-mbe/

15. Canadian Aboriginal and Minority Supplier Council (CAMSC). "What is Certification and Why is it Important?" https://www.camsc.ca/what-is-certification

16. Institute of Race Relations. "Definitions." http://www.irr.org.uk/research/statistics/definitions/

17. Minority Rights Group International—World Directory of Minorities and Indigenous Peoples. "Japan." https://minorityrights.org/country/japan/

18. American Sociological Association. "Diversity Linked To Increased Sales Revenue And Profits, More Customers." https://www.sciencedaily.com/releases/2009/03/090331091252.htm

19. Ibid.

20. Ibid.

21. Dodgson, Lindsay and Marguerite Ward. "Here are the exact reasons why diverse companies are more profitable, according to neuroscience and leadership expert." Business Insider. https://www.businessinsider.com/benefits-of-diverse-companies-2017-3

22. Lorenzo, Rocio and Martin Reeves. "Diversity Drives Financial Performance." Harvard Business Review. https://hbr.org/2018/01/how-and-where-diversity-drives-financial-performance

23. Ibid.

24. Hunt, Vivian, Dennis Layton, and Sara Prince. "Why diversity matters." McKinsey & Company. https://www.mckinsey.com/business-functions/organization/our-insights/why-diversity-matters

25. Ibid.

26. Ibid.

27. Ibid.

28. Bersin by Deloitte—Deloitte Consulting LLP. "Diversity and Inclusion in Canada." https://www2.deloitte.com/content/dam/Deloitte/ca/Documents/human-capital/ca-en-human-capital-diversity-and-Inclusion-in-canada.pdf

29. Ibid.

30. CVM. "Supplier Diversity." https://www.cvmsolutions.com/glossary/supplier-diversity

31. *Diversity Professional*, Winter 2019. https://mydigitalpublication.com/publication/frame.php?i=647292&p=&pn=&ver=html5

32. Ibid.

33. National Association of Women in Construction (NAWIC). "Join NAWIC." https://www.nawic.org/nawic/default.asp

34. Billion Dollar Roundtable (BDR). https://www.billiondollarroundtable.org

35. National Minority Supplier Development Council (NMSDC) Conference. "The Bigger Discussion V: Future of Supplier Diversity (SS7)." http://www.nmsdcconference.com/portfolio-items/the-bigger-discussion-v-future-of-supplier-diversity/

36. Canadian Aboriginal and Minority Supplier Council (CAMSC). https://www.camsc.ca

37. Canadian Council for Aboriginal Business (CCAB). https://www.ccab.com

38. Centre for Women in Business. https://www.centreforwomeninbusiness.ca/en/home/default.aspx

39. Canadian Gay and Lesbian Chamber of Commerce (CGLCC). https://www.cglcc.ca/about-us-2/about-us/#governance

40. Chartered Institute of Procurement and Supply (CIPS) USA. https://www.cips.org/

41. Disability: IN. https://disabilityin.org/

42. Global Supplier Diversity Alliance (GSDA). https://www.gsda.global

43. Institute for Supply Management (ISM). https://www.instituteforsupplymanagement.org/index.cfm

44. Global Supplier Diversity Alliance (GSDA). https://www.gsda.global/wp-content/uploads/2016/10/MSD-China-InCountry-Business-Case-Infographic.pdf

45. Minority Supplier Development UK (MSDUK). https://www.msduk.org.uk

46. National Veteran-Owned Business Association (NaVOBA). https://navoba.org

47. National Association of Women Business Owners (NAWBO). https://www.nawbo.org

48. The National Center for American Indian Enterprise Development (NCAIED). https://www.ncaied.org/about-ncaied

49. National LGBT Chamber of Commerce (NGLCC). http://www.nglcc.org

50. National Minority Supplier Development Council (NMSDC). https://nmsdc.org

51. National Veteran Business Development Council (NVBDC). http://nvbdc.org
52. OMNIKAL. https://www.omnikal.com
53. South African Supplier Diversity Council (SASDC). https://www.sasdc.org.za/#become-a-corporate-member
54. Supplier Diversity Alliance Canada (SDAC). http://www.supplierdiversityalliance.ca
55. Supply Nation. https://supplynation.org.au
56. U.S. Black Chambers, Inc. USBC. https://usblackchambers.org
57. United States Hispanic Chamber of Commerce (USHCC). https://ushcc.com
58. United States Pan Asian American Chamber of Commerce (USPAACC). https://uspaacc.com
59. Women Business Enterprise (WBE) Canada. https://wbecanada.ca
60. Women Business Enterprise National Council (WBENC). https://www.wbenc.org
61. WEConnect International. https://weconnectinternational.org/en/
62. U.S. Small Business Administration (SBA). "Organization." https://www.sba.gov/about-sba/organization
63. National Small Business Association (NSBA). https://nsba.biz
64. Small Business Exporters Association of the United States (SBEA). https://sbea.org
65. Small Business Technology Council (SBTC). https://sbtc.org
66. Women Impacting Public Policy (WIPP). https://www.wipp.org
67. ConnXus. https://connxus.com
68. CVM. https://www.cvmsolutions.com
69. Quantum. https://www.quantumsds.com
70. SupplierGATEWAY. https://www.suppliergateway.com

71. *Business Equality Magazine.* https://businessequality magazine.com

72. *DiversityPlus Magazine.* https://www.diversityplus.com

73. *Diversity Professional.* http://diversityprofessional.com

74. *Minority Business Magazine.* https://mbemag.com

75. *Affinity Inc Magazine.* https://affinityincmagazine.com

76. Biz Journals. https://www.bizjournals.com

77. *Color Magazine.* https://colormagazine.com

78. DiversityComm. https://www.diversitycomm.net

79. Indian Country Today. https://indiancountrytoday.com

80. Minority Business News (MBNUSA). https://mbnusa.biz

81. Supply Professional. https://www.supplypro.ca

82. Women's Enterprise (WE) USA. https://weusa.biz

83. McKinsey & Company. "Enduring Ideas: The 7-S Framework." https://www.mckinsey.com/business-functions/strategy-and-corporate-finance/our-insights/enduring-ideas-the-7-s-framework

84. U.S. Small Business Administration (SBA). "Affiliation." https://www.sba.gov/sites/default/files/affiliation_discussion.pdf

85. U.S. Small Business Administration (SBA). "Size Standards." https://www.sba.gov/federal-contracting/contracting-guide/size-standards

86. Chen, James. "Business-to-Business (B2B)." Investopedia. https://www.investopedia.com/terms/b/btob.asp

87. Kenton, Will. "Business-to-Consumer (B2C)." Investopedia. https://www.investopedia.com/terms/b/btoc.asp

88. Kenton, Will. "Business-to-Government (B2G)." Investopedia. https://www.investopedia.com/terms/b/business-to-government.asp

89. Bloomenthal, Andrew. "C-Suite." Investopedia. https://www.investopedia.com/terms/c/c-suite.asp

90. SAP&DC. "Creating an Effective Capability Statement."
http://www.sapdc.org/documents/Contracting_Tools-Tool_2_
Creating_an_Effective_Capability_Statement-Tool.pdf

91. U.S. Small Business Administration (SBA).
"Set-aside procurement." https://www.sba.gov/partners/
contracting-officials/small-business-procurement/
set-aside-procurement

92. CVM. "Diverse Supplier Spend." https://www.cvmsolutions.
com/glossary/diverse-supplier-spend

93. CVM. "Diverse Supplier, Defined." https://blog.cvmsolutions.
com/what-makes-certain-suppliers-diverse-suppliers

94. Ferris State University. "Diversity and Inclusion Definitions."
https://www.ferris.edu/HTMLS/administration/president/
DiversityOffice/Definitions.htm

95. Hayes, Adam. "EBITDA." Investopedia.
https://www.investopedia.com/terms/e/ebitda.asp

96. Kenton, Will. "Elevator Pitch." Investopedia.
https://www.investopedia.com/terms/e/elevatorpitch.asp

97. U.S. Small Business Administration (SBA). "Size Standards."
https://www.sba.gov/partners/contracting-officials/
small-business-procurement/small-business-size-standards

98. SHRM. "ERGs." https://www.shrm.org/hr-today/news/
hr-magazine/0916/pages/are-employee-resource-groups-
good-for-business.aspx

99. Merriam-Webster. "End User." https://www.merriam-webster.
com/dictionary/end%20user

100. MBDA. "The History of MBDA."
https://www.mbda.gov/about/history

101. Ibid.

102. Labarre, Olivia. "Enterprise Resource Planning (ERP)."
Investopedia. https://www.investopedia.com/terms/e/erp.asp

103. Dictionary.com. "Executive Order." https://www.dictionary.
com/browse/executive-order?s=t

104. LawTrades. "What Does a General Counsel Do?" https://www.lawtrades.com/answers/what-does-a-general-counsel-do

105. USA.gov. "General Service Administration." https://www.usa.gov/federal-agencies/general-services-administration

106. NMSDC. "MBE." https://nmsdc.org/mbes/what-is-an-mbe/

107. U.S. Small Business Administration (SBA). "HUBZone Program." https://www.sba.gov/federal-contracting/contracting-assistance-programs/hubzone-program

108. Ibid.

109. Ibid.

110. Dictionary.com. "indigenous." https://www.dictionary.com/browse/indigenous?s=t

111. The Canadian Encyclopedia. "Indigenous Peoples in Canada." https://www.thecanadianencyclopedia.ca/en/article/aboriginal-people

112. MBDA. "About MBDA." https://www.mbda.gov/about-mbda

113. NMSDC. "What is an MBE?" https://nmsdc.org/mbes/what-is-an-mbe/

114. Ibid.

115. Canadian Aboriginal and Minority Supplier Council (CAMSC), "What is Certification and Why is it Important?" https://www.camsc.ca/what-is-certification

116. U.S. Census Bureau. "Introduction to NAICS." https://www.census.gov/eos/www/naics/

117. NMSDC. "What is an MBE?" https://nmsdc.org/mbes/what-is-an-mbe/

118. Dictionary.com. "nondisclosure agreement." https://www.dictionary.com/browse/nondisclosure-agreement?s=t

119. Chen, James. "Return on Investment (ROI)." Investopedia. https://www.investopedia.com/terms/r/returnoninvestment.asp

120. Business Dictionary. "request for information (RFI)."
     http://www.businessdictionary.com/definition/request-
     for-information-RFI.html

121. Kenton, Will, "Request for Proposal (RFP)."
     Investopedia. https://www.investopedia.com/
     terms/r/request-for-proposal.asp

122. Kenton, Will. "Request for Quote (RFQ)." Investopedia.
     https://www.investopedia.com/terms/r/request-for-quote.asp

123. U.S. Small Business Administration (SBA). "Set-
     asides." https://www.sba.gov/federal-contracting/
     contracting-assistance-programs

124. U.S Small Business Administration (SBA). "Size Standards."
     https://www.sba.gov/federal-contracting/contracting-guide/
     size-standards

125. U.S. Small Business Administration (SBA). "Sole-source set-
     aside contracts." https://www.sba.gov/federal-contracting/
     contracting-guide/types-contracts

126. Kenton, Will. "Supply Chain." Investopedia.
     https://www.investopedia.com/terms/s/supplychain.asp

127. Hayes, Adam. "Supply Chain Management (SCM)."
     Investopedia. https://www.investopedia.com/terms/s/scm.asp

128. CVM. "What Is Supplier Diversity and Why Is It Important?"
     https://blog.cvmsolutions.com/what-is-supplier-diversity

129. CVM, "Tier 1 Supplier." https://www.cvmsolutions.com/
     glossary/tier-1-supplier

130. CVM, "Tier 2 Spend." https://www.cvmsolutions.com/
     glossary/tier-2-spend

131. Twin, Alexandra. "Value Proposition." Investopedia.
     https://www.investopedia.com/terms/v/valueproposition.asp

ABOUT THE AUTHOR

Jamie Crump has focused her career in strategic sourcing and supplier diversity across a variety of industries including: banking, catastrophic insurance, heavy equipment rental, IT, pharmaceuticals, telecommunications, and welding and medical supply.

A frequent speaker at sourcing and supplier diversity events across the U.S. and Canada, Jamie has also been responsible for strategic sourcing, business services and operations, software development, capacity provisioning, and supplier diversity over the course of her career.

She has also served on a number of boards and in industry/ trade associations. Currently, she is on the Board of Trustees for the National Small Business Association (NSBA), an advisory board member to Diversity Professional, ProcureCon and Spend Matters.

She is a member of Association for Luxury Suite Directors (ALSD), the Chartered Institute of Procurement & Supply (CIPS), Global Business Travel Association (GBTA), Institute for Supply Management (ISM), the International Association for Contract & Commercial Management (IACCM), and the National Association for Women Business Owners (NAWBO).

She lives in Blairsville, Georgia, with her husband Bill Thebert.

Website: http://www.therichwellgroup.com/
E-Mail: info@therichwellgroup.com

ABOUT THE RICHWELL GROUP

The Richwell Group brings you 30+ years of supply chain experience. Across industries. In the U.S.A. and internationally. Under a host of organizational structures. And we live diversity. The Richwell Group is a woman-owned business. The Richwell Group is a member of NAWBO and will seek certification through WBENC at the end of their third year of operation, or 2021.

STRATEGIC SOURCING

Indirect spend, cash not spent on the primary good and services a company sells, can represent 25% to 90% of a firm's accounts payable. Whether you need a full strategy, category expertise, or help with an RFx, The Richwell Group provides the expertise and negotiation skills to make the most of each dollar spent.

SUPPLIER DIVERSITY

Supplier diversity allows a company to leverage the full power of its supply chain. Consider that 83 of the 2017 Fortune 100 companies have a commitment to supplier diversity on their company websites. Understand how to expand your customer base, target new business opportunities, and even improve your standing with potential investors. The Richwell Group has experience in all aspects of the supplier diversity business strategy.

Website: http://www.therichwellgroup.com/
E-Mail: info@therichwellgroup.com

RICHTALK: JAMIE CRUMP SPEAKING

Would you like to have Jamie Crump speak at your next event or meeting? She speaks and conducts workshops on a number of topics and can tailor messages to your company or organization. Here are a few of her topics:

BACKSTAGE PASS

Book Keynote
Cast Members
Chapter Workshops

SUPPLY CHAIN

A Seat at the Table
Negotiations That Last
Should Cost

SUPPLIER DIVERSITY

Supplier Diversity's Customers
The Missing Business Strategy
Success by the Numbers

SMALL BUSINESS

Growing Pains
Doing Business with Friends and Family
Nothing Like an Idea Whose Time Has Come

LEADERSHIP

Found Money
The Pebble in Your Shoe
C-Suite Translator

Website: http://www.therichwellgroup.com/
E-Mail: info@therichwellgroup.com

CONFERENCE COMPASS—
COMING IN 2021

Stay tuned for more information on Conference Compass, a collection of learning and preparation tools and services to get the most from your conference and matchmaking experience.

For more information check us out here:

Website: http://www.therichwellgroup.com/
E-Mail: info@therichwellgroup.com

Lightning Source UK Ltd.
Milton Keynes UK
UKHW021410171222
413968UK00011B/240